The American Exploration and Travel Series

The Discoverie of the Large, Rich, and Bewtiful Empyre of Guiana

The Discoverie of the Large, Rich, and Bewtiful Empyre of Guiana

by Sir Walter Ralegh

Transcribed, annotated and introduced by

Neil L. Whitehead

UNIVERSITY OF OKLAHOMA PRESS : NORMAN

The Discoverie of the Large, Rich, and Bewtiful Empyre of Guiana
is Volume 77 in The American Exploration and Travel Series

University of Oklahoma Press edition published by special arrangement with
Manchester University Press, Oxford Road, Manchester M13 9NR, UK.
 First printing.

ISBN 0 8061 3019 9 cloth
0 8061 3020 2 paperback

1 2 3 4 5 6 7 8 9 10

Printed in Great Britain by
Biddles Ltd, Guildford and King's Lynn

Contents

Illustrations

Preface and acknowledgements

The text of the *Discoverie,* which has been newly transcribed and annotated for this work, is taken from the first edition (sixty-four leaves) of 1596. There were three editions printed in 1596 which may be distinguished by their typographical variants. One on page 21 and another on the title-page have been considered sufficient to differentiate the three 1596 editions. In the first edition (used here), the end of line 14 on page 21 reads *Nuevo reygno de granada.* In the second edition, first issue, line 6 of the title-page ends *City*; in the second edition, second issue, line 6 of the title-page ends *Citie.* In both issues of this edition the end of line 14 on page 21 reads *Nuevo reygno de Granada.* In the third edition, the end of line 14 on page 21 reads *Nuevo reyno de Granada,* and there are further variants in this edition.

The aim of the transcription has been to alter as little as possible; however, changing fonts and typographical conventions have made necessary the following practices; ſ changes to *s*, *vv* to *w*, *ō* to *on/om*, *ē* to *en/em.* I have modernised *u/v* and *i/j.* However, all typographical inconsistencies and errors have been preserved, as with 'which' for 'with' [15], 'marveylons' for 'marveylous' [16], 'Tuuja' for 'Tunja' [24] and 'calley' for 'galley' [44]. Letters that have been omitted are supplied without comment. Page numbers in square brackets refer to the original pagination of the first edition, which has been preserved in this text, as have the original paragraph breaks. Words which were hyphenated in the original text because they spanned page breaks have been assimilated to the text of the page on which the word begins. The abbreviations 'n.' and 'fn.' indicate the endnotes to the introductory essay and the footnotes to the text of the *Discoverie* respectively. All other spellings, italics, capitals and forms of punctuation have been retained as in the original. A brief Glossary of obscure or archaic works (indicated * in the text) appears at the end. Italics in the introductory text are used for non-English words or phrases.

This work was effectively begun some ten years ago and so the debt to my colleagues is extensive indeed. Moreover, the interdisciplinary nature of this project means that my debt is not to anthropologists alone. Among literary scholars I would like to thank, in particular, Peter Hulme, Tim Youngs and Sara Mills for their informed and patient interest, as well as the participants in the 1992 University of Essex Symposium 'Writing Travels' who encouraged my first attempts to confront the textual issues raised by the *Discoverie.* In a similar way presentations made at the Institute for Research in the Humanities while a resident Fellow in 1993-4, to the Latin American & Iberian Studies Program, and to the Department of Classics, all at the University of Wisconsin-Madison, as well as to Center for Latino and Latin American Studies (University of Northern Illinois) proved invaluable. In addition, numerous conversations, particularly with my colleagues in Madison, Susan Friedman, Paul Boyer, Heather Dubrouw, Denis Feeney, Robert Kingdon, Emiko Ohnuki-Tierney, Thomas Spear and Jan Vansina were both an encouragement and stimulus.

More widely I wish to thank Peter Rivière, whose own work on Richard Schomburgk is a model of patient historiography, and Malcolm Deas for providing me with the very first opportunity to reflect on the nature of Ralegh's text. Jonathan Hill and Brian Ferguson provided critical feedback on many of my wilder notions. Nelly Arvelo provided the opportunity for my first visit to *el gran rio Orinoco* and to her, and to all my friends and colleagues at IVIC (Caracas), my heartfelt thanks. Denis Williams and Jenny Wisehart of the Walter Roth Museum have generously supported both my field work in Guyana and offered numerous valuable observations on the archaeology and history of the region. Anna Benjamin kindly took an interest in my historiographical efforts, while George Simon tutored me in the pragmatics of ethnography and field archaeology. Matteson Williams permitted me to survive the rigours of the *asanda* in the Pakaraimas while hunting *kanaimas*, Roger Harry and Clarence Alfred also led me to the enigma of 'Ralegh's Door'. To all these individuals I am very grateful for many things.

Various bodies have provided funding for my research over the last decade but special thanks are due to the Graduate School at the University of Wisconsin-Madison for the funding to bring various threads of investigation together and the written work to a final fruition. I would also like to thank the H. F. Guggenheim Foundation and the Wenner-Gren Foundation for their support in the earlier phases of research. The staff of the Archivo General de Indias (Sevilla), Algemeen Rijksarchief (Den Haag), Koninklijk Instituut voor Taal-, Land-, en Volkenkunde (Leiden), Archive Nationale (Paris), British Library, Public Record Office, Bodleian Library, Rhodes House (Oxford) and the Memorial Library (Madison) are due special thanks for patiently assisting my search and retrieval of materials. Matthew Frost, Editor, Gemma Marren, Rachel Armstrong, Stephanie Sloan and John Banks at Manchester University Press, as well as John Drayton, Editor-in-chief at the University of Oklahoma Press, are due thanks for their professionalism in bringing this work to press. My family has quietly endured the consequences of all this scholarly obsession, which is, I trust, finally assuaged by the text that follows.

Neil L. Whitehead

Part 1

Introduction

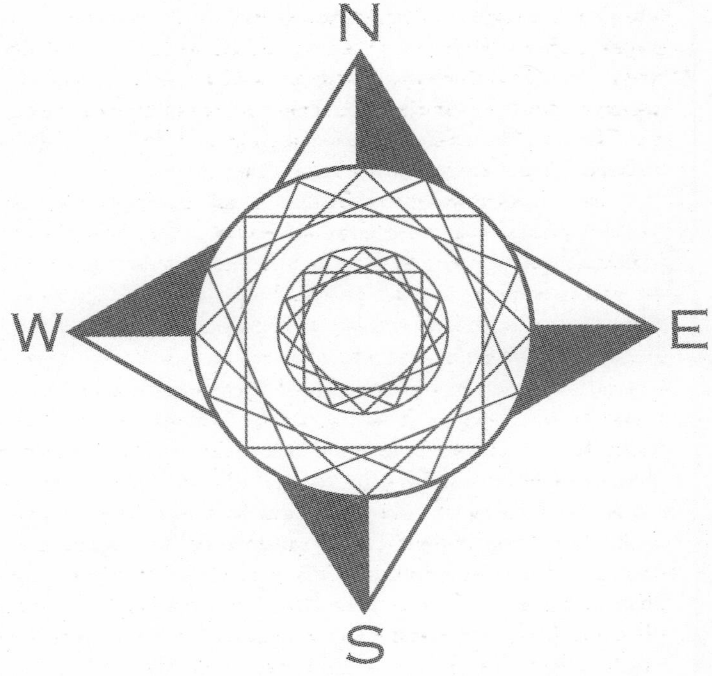

The *Discoverie* is a fundamental source for the historical anthropology of the Americas, but how Ralegh garnered the information it contains, and the interpretation of that information, remain basic issues in reading the *Discoverie.* It is the purpose of this edition to consider both these questions, as well as how the literary qualities of the text mark the *Discoverie* off from earlier works with ethnological and historical pretension. Anthropological theory has been much concerned of late to better understand the interactions between literary form and ethnographic representation, as well as how historical dimensions may be added to such representation (see Chapter 1 (iii)). As such the *Discoverie* offers a sustained opportunity for the critical application of current theory. This will involve an evaluation of the ethnographic basis of Ralegh's text as well as placing the text itself in the context of other contemporary 'discoveries'. This exercise is particularly significant since it avoids treating the *Discoverie* as merely a representative form of western colonial ideology. Even though the *Discoverie* may be examined in this aspect, the text also has very firm connections with the particular circumstances of such discovery in the Orinoco at the end of the sixteenth century. Accordingly, both the published accounts of contemporary voyages to northern South America and the Caribbean, as well as the routine correspondence of colonial authorities with their metropolitan masters, will be considered as bearing on the interpretation of Ralegh's writing (see Chapter 1 (iv)). As we shall see, the theme of first encounter and discovery is dominant in Ralegh's text, but, given a century of prior European activity in this region, this was anachronistic. This is not to suggest that native societies in the Orinoco basin in 1595 were already despoiled, but rather should remind us that Ralegh's 'Indians' were sophisticated actors having had plenty of prior experience of Europeans and their political and economic stratagems.

Almost all the recent introductions to the life or works of that quintessential Elizabethan, Walter Ralegh, have begun with a paragraph or two that first confesses to an enchantment with the legend that is 'Sir Walter Ralegh'. Indeed a half-garbled version of his name, 'Guatteral', even emerged in both Spanish and native accounts, serving to add a mythic-like quality to his existence – which no doubt would have pleased him well. This strange fascination is true not only of his many biographers but also of historians, geographers and literary scholars – all seem to some extent confounded by the man. The specific forms of those enchantments and how they have influenced the various evaluations of Ralegh's Guiana voyage and the text of the *Discoverie* will be discussed below in Chapter 1. Chapter 2 then asks the critical question as to whether the *Discoverie* is merely a florid fantasy of English colonial possession, or whether its ethnological reportage offers substantive insight into past native cultural practices. For now we should note that despite the certain accomplishments of Ralegh, as in the siege of Cadiz or the initiation of the Virginia colony, this persistent perplexity in regard of the 'curious impermanence' (Latham 1951: xiv) of his achievements is unavoidable; for it is the manner of Ralegh's failures, and the means by which he sought to turn those practical disasters into textual triumphs, that continues to fascinate and challenge interpretation.

This introduction is no exception to these tendencies, and as for Robert Schomburgk, the editor of the 1848 edition, part of the power of Ralegh's enchantment of the present editor stems from personal experience of the places and practices he describes. My own traverse of the lower Orinoco took place in 1989, in the company of the Venezuelan anthropologists Nelly Arvelo and Horacio Biord-Castillo. We were charged with delivering copies of a history of the Karinya (Caribs) to their settlements along the south bank of the Orinoco. Travelling from Caracas along the northern coast of Venezuela, we stopped at Piritú, site of the great fortified missions of the Franciscans who conquered the Karinya during the eighteenth century, and then moved on to Barcelona and Cumaná, where Ralegh made a parting assault on the Spanish garrison. From here we turned due south across the great *llanos* (plains) of the Orinoco which stretch for hundreds of miles to the west. This region was dubbed the 'Plains of Sayma' by Ralegh, for the Chayma nation that was once here. The area is now bisected by the *Carretera Negra*, so called for the oil pipeline that runs the length of the road. As a massive thunderstorm paralleled our journey down the 'Black Track', flashes of lightning briefly illumined the glistening waters of the great serpent Orinoco in the failing light. Our night's stop was in Ciudad Bolívar, the old Spanish colonial capital of the Guayana province, and then next day we travelled on to the 'experimental' city of Ciudad Guayana. The Harvard urban planners who assisted this project, itself born from the discovery of black gold in the 1960s, situated their 'great and Golden Citie' at the confluence of Caroni and Orinoco, right on the site of Topiawari's port where he held conference with Ralegh four centuries ago. A few miles further east, the recently renovated old Spanish fort of Los Castillos still commands the approach from the delta of Orinoco, and from its battlements one can look west into the valley of Orinoco, south to the Sierra Imataca and east towards the sea. It has been suggested that Ralegh's reportage of the landscapes of Orinoco was so strongly influenced by his desire to make it seem a favourable place for settlement, and to make the exotic acceptably familiar, that he was led into projecting an English landscape on to an American wilderness. While this certainly calls necessary attention to the way in which description is never neutral, it should not blind us to the possibility that such analogies were also apt, that is they made accessible the encounter with the unfamiliar. Ralegh [92 *sic* 82] wrote of this view to the south as 'fayre grounde, and as beawtifull fieldes, as any man hath ever seene, with divers copses scattered heere and there by the rivers side, and all as full of deare, as any forrest or parke in England' and to those familiar with both English and Orinocan landscapes the analogy would seem appropriate, even as it licenses a colonial possession.

Ralegh's description was not simply a fantastic projection of the colonial mind but also a reasonably good attempt to depict the landscape of this region. The lower Orinoco was heavily settled by native people and their own active management of landscape which, anthropology is only just beginning to appreciate, would have been reflected in the practices of maintaining coppices, burning off savanna grasses and a husbandry of fauna, especially deer (see [48], fn. 70). Such native activity has been denied or ignored, in both colonial and anthropological rhetoric, through the ideas of 'wilderness' and the 'natural' landscape, which erase signs of human intervention and so render such regions fit for colonial possession and development (Denevan 1992). It is notable that Ralegh [96] himself suggests that Guiana has not lost her 'maydenhead' and that 'the face of the earth hath not beene torne, nor the vertue and salt of the soyle spent by manurance' and here colonial rhetoric certainly overwhelms description. However, that the lower Orinoco plains do indeed conform to an pastoral aesthetic, as Ralegh suggests, is also ironically confirmed by the way in which the amenities of the new colonising city of Ciudad Guayana have been developed. The land around the lower Caroni Falls is now a recreational park for picnics and family outings and the great 'overfals' themselves, for which Ralegh used the odd metaphor of church towers, are now also a part of this municipal garden – sometimes the exotic wears an appropriately familiar mask.

From Ciudad Guayana we travelled west along the Banda del Sur, visiting with Karinya communities that have been here for at least three hundred years. We stopped at Moitaco, site of the eighteenth-century fortified Franciscan headquarters, and on to Maripa, a community of blacks that was founded by black slaves fleeing from Surinam in the eighteenth century. They were led to freedom by a woman who was justly known as *La Pantera Negra*, and who is still strongly present in the folk memories of Maripa. Here we crossed the Caura river, home to Ralegh's *Ewaipanoma*, 'whose heades appeare not aboue their shoulders' and who have been conflated with the *Acephali* (headless-men, men-with-heads-in-their-chests) of Classical legend, as Ralegh notes [70]. The people of the Caura are still wild and threatening to those from outside, for at the head of this river are the Ye'cuana. Like the Karinya, they were one of the native groups that successfully resisted the Spanish, as they now continue to negotiate cautiously the encroachment of modern Venezuela. Finally we re-crossed the Orinoco at Cabruta, a deeply significant site since it is here that the Orinoco swings south as its western tributaries drain the high cordillera on which Santa Fe de Bogotá sits. Cabruta therefore controls both east–west and north–south movement and so was chosen to demarcate the Franciscan and Capuchin evangelical territories from those of the Jesuits. It was from Bogotá to the west that Antonio de Berrio, Ralegh's rival for the prize of 'Guiana', began his three journeys in search of *El Dorado*, but whose entrance he only finally found at the Caroni confluence with Orinoco.

Like Robert Schomburgk in his travels to delineate the border between Brazil and the then British Guiana, I also have walked parts of the Pakaraima Mountains, fabled location of *El Dorado*. It would be less than honest were I to suggest that, as we traversed the now empty landscapes of mountain and wide savanna valleys, I did not hope to espy some anomalous landform that might, just as lost Mayan temples emerged from the Central American rainforest, indicate the forgotten presence of Ralegh's *Epuremei*. Modern anthropology has seen this region as a marginal place because of its poor agricultural soils away from the forest floor, but that marginality has been as much a product of the course of colonial conquest in this region as it has of the supposed ecological adversity. In the more distant past, as is strongly evident from the oral history of the Patamona (Whitehead 1996d), these mountains provided many routes for communication between the Amazon, Orinoco and Essequibo river basins and so were a crossroads in a continental system of interaction. It is with this observation that a proper context for understanding Ralegh's 'discoverie' of the 'Empyre of Guiana' begins to emerge. Thus, it should not be forgotten that at this moment the Pakaraima Mountains are full of individual gold and diamond miners, as well as large commercial dredging operations, and it is as a result of their activities, in the absence of professional archaeology, that finds of complex artefacts have been made, including gold work. The Patamona also know of 'Ralegh's Door', a large slab of fashioned rock that appears to close off a passage in the side of a mountain. Behind this door lies a great treasure, but the police will not allow any informal attempts to blow it open and so such 'discoverie' as there is to be had must wait upon some other discoverer.

It is precisely this kind of personal engagement that is the ground for Ralegh's enchantments. However, by the idea of an 'enchantment' of his commentators I do not mean to imply a suspension of their critical faculties with regard to his texts and actions, but rather the way in which any contemplation of Ralegh's works requires complex judgments and involves intellectual risks – there is little middle ground of interpretation, nor was there even in his own day. So we are faced with claims both marvellous and fantastical, which are apparently borne out in the words and deeds of others, but yet in ways that do not quite leave us secure in the probity of Ralegh's own texts or the certain meaning of his actions. As a result initial presumptions count for much in subsequent interpretation and unless we grant Ralegh some benefit of the doubt it becomes quite impossible to make any interpretation at all, other than as to the fabricated nature of his writing; but this is hardly insightful or novel. Clearly it is the way in which Ralegh's credibility has been variously constructed from his acts that is key to the interpretation of his texts, both then and now. This is especially the case for Ralegh's *Discoverie,* where the issues of performance and practice in Ralegh's life come together with particular forcefulness – sufficient indeed to result in his execution following his final return from South America in 1618.

Accordingly, Ralegh can be said to have matched intellectual risk with physical consequence in the most dramatic way, and the words of Malcolm, on the death of Cawdor in Shakespeare's *Macbeth*, seem strangely apt, and even prophetic, for the fate of Ralegh:

> Nothing in his life
> Became him like the leaving of it: he died
> As one that had been studied in his death
> To throw away the dearest thing he ow'd
> As 'twere a careless trifle.
> (Act I, Scene IV)

Perhaps nothing has so much troubled our interpretation of that life as Ralegh's return from Guiana to face certain judicial execution. The death of his son Wat and the immediately subsequent suicide of his lifelong companion, Lawrence Keymis, were obviously relevant events in the formulation of his final course of action, but the fact of his return created a new presumption as to the credibility of the man. As he himself wrote on the night before his death, 'Cowards fear to Die, but courage stout, Rather than live in Snuff, will be put out' (*Remains of Sir Walter Raleigh* 1651: 138, BL Add. MS 18044, f.156). So it was that he extinguished his own bright flame.

1 • The *Discoverie* as enchanted text

(i) The *Discoverie* as geography and history

The first edited and annotated edition of the *Discoverie* was issued in 1848 by the Hakluyt Society. The editor, Robert Schomburgk, grounded Ralegh's credibility in the geographical and ethnological accuracy of his description, as had Richard Hakluyt by his inclusion of the *Discoverie* in the first edition of *The Principal Navigations* (1600). To a large degree then the geography of the *Discoverie* is accurate as regards the places which Ralegh personally visited (Skelton 1963, Lorimer 1982), and this was copiously demonstrated by Schomburgk himself, whose specific identifications, unless otherwise indicated,[1] are generally accepted here – see Map I. It is, of course, in the matter of that less certain 'discovery' of an 'Empyre of Guiana' that opinion divides. Given the nature of this debate it is the purpose of this and subsequent chapters to assess those opinions from an anthropological viewpoint, but, as we shall see, part of the narrative force, the magic, of the *Discoverie* stems precisely from this apparent blending of the factual and fictitious.

Schomburgk (1848: vii) boldly confesses his own enchantment by the *Discoverie* in the opening paragraphs of his edition: 'every page, nay almost every sentence, awakened past recollections, and I felt in imagination transported once more into the midst of the stupendous scenery of the tropics. As Her Majesty's Commissioner to survey the boundaries of British Guiana, I explored in 1841 that wondrous delta of the Orinoco.'

With such credentials (see Rivière 1995) Schomburgk intended 'to prove, from circumstances which fell within my own experience, the general correctness of Ralegh's descriptions, and to exculpate him from ungenerous reproaches'. In addition the publication of two contemporary manuscripts, connected with or authored by Ralegh, provided a historiographical justification for the occasion of this positive evaluation. Schomburgk summarises his interpretative strategy thus: 'I do not deny that I am strongly biased in favour of Ralegh, but this partiality has not blinded me to his numerous failings' (1848: x).

Such failings, in the eyes of both Schomburgk and subsequent commentators, originate in his being 'not a man of achievement, but a man of promise' (Latham 1951: xiv). Nevertheless, for Schomburgk, as for such historians as David Quinn and Vincent Harlow, Ralegh is the precursor of British Empire, for he attempted settlement in Virginia while others, such as Francis Drake and John Hawkins, practised only trade and plunder. Schomburgk (1848: xxvi–xxvii) sees this as one compelling reason why the *Discoverie* is so concerned with issues of gold and the location of *El Dorado*. However, Schomburgk is perhaps too easily content to suggest that 'gold-fever' sufficiently explains European motivations in this matter, not least since Ralegh patiently explains the political and strategic importance of 'Indian Golde' in European dynastic politics at the turn of the seventeenth century, which 'disturbeth all the nations of Europe, it purchaseth intelligence, creepeth into Councels, and setteth bound loyalty at libertie, in the greatest Monarchies of Europe', noting that 'Those princes which abound in treasure have greate advantages over the rest, if they once constraine them to a defensiue warre' [*To the Reader* 3–4].

Such was the form of argument that Ralegh was to use later as he vainly attempted to persuade James I of England (VI of Scotland) to allow him to return to Guiana in order to seize gold mines on the Caroni river. Schomburgk further suggests that the failure of the earlier Virginia colony, which Ralegh had financed to the tune of some £40,000, meant that a more glittering lure would be needed to induce participation in the Guiana enterprise.

I *How Sir Walter Ralegh conquers a city and captures the Spanish governor*

The immediate relevance of the *Discoverie* to the embryonic empires of Europe in America is amply attested to by the importance given to the account by his contemporaries, a brief examination of which will also provide the opportunity to iterate the various editions of the *Discoverie* which preceded Schomburgk's 1848 annotation. This should also serve to remind us that the *Discoverie* was treated at the time as a source of practical knowledge from the pen of one who had already experience in the colonisation of America, even if aspects of the *Discoverie* were also seen as quite possibly fanciful or even entirely invented.

Most significantly, the Elizabethan doyen of travel literatures, Richard Hakluyt, explicitly acknowledges Walter Ralegh in the preface to *The Principal Navigations,* as the person from whom he had received 'his chief light into the western navigations'. It is not surprising then that the manuscript account of René Laudonnière's expedition to Florida, which was personally sent by Hakluyt to Martin Bassanière of Paris, contained a dedication to Ralegh on its publication in 1586. Ralegh in turn aided financially in the publication of the sketches and descriptions of Jacque Morgue, who had accompanied Laudonnière to Florida. When Hakluyt came to publish an English version of Laudonnière's reconnaissance it was likewise dedicated to Ralegh, and afterwards inserted in the third volume of *The Principal Navigations.*

At least four different editions of the *Discoverie* appeared in 1596, the first year of publication, according to Penzer's (in Harlow 1928: vi) analysis of the four extant copies, three in the British Library, one at Harvard.[2] It was reprinted for inclusion in Hakluyt's *The Principal Navigations* (1600: vol. iii), in Thomas Birch's *The Works of Sir Walter Ralegh* (1751: vol. ii), Arthur Cayley's *The Life of Sir Walter Raley* (1805) and by the Clarendon Press in *The Works of Sir Walter Raleigh* (1829). More significant to an assessment of the general impact of the work on Ralegh's contemporaries was the publication of an abridged Latin version, *Brevis et admiranda descriptio regni Guianae, auri abundantissimi, in America . . . ,* and a German version, *Kurtze wunderbare Beschreibung des Goldreichen Königreichs Guiana in America . . . ,* in Nuremburg in 1599, both by the geographer Levinius Hondius. Ralegh's text was also published by Theodore de Bry in the eighth part of his massive *Collectiones Peregrinationium in Indias Orientales et Occidentales* (Frankfurt, 1590), which eventually appeared also in French and German.[3]

By 1602 three more German editions had appeared, as had a Dutch version in 1598 which was reprinted in 1605, 1617, 1707, 1727 and 1747. The Dutch reprints of the early eighteenth century coincided with a renewed commercial interest in the exploitation of gold mines in Guiana by the West India Company (see Chapter 1 (iv) and Chapter 2 (ii)). A French translation, *Relation de la Guiane, du Lac de parima et des provinces d'Emeria, d'Arromaia et d'Amapaia* . . . appeared in 1722 in the second volume of François Coreal's compendium, *Voyages à l'Amérique.*

The historians Vincent Harlow (1928) and David Quinn (1947) both configure Ralegh in accordance with the unfolding of British, or specifically an English, imperial ambition, though not with its realisation. Ralegh is seen as an inspirational figure in the awakening of that imperial ambition, and he overtly remarks [*Epistle* A3] that it was not his purpose to 'goe journeys of picorie' (i.e. 'pillage', after the Spanish *picaro*). None the less Quinn and Harlow both see Ralegh as having fallen short of real colonial achievement in both Virginia and Guiana. His faults are those of an inept practitioner, led on by dangerous vision. He is compared unfavourably to Francis Drake, Thomas Frobisher and even Richard Hawkins, whose own slave-trading and piracy, if hardly the stuff of imperial destiny, were actually more financially remunerative than Ralegh's diplomatic dance with the indigenes of Orinoco. So, in turn, the historian A. L. Rowse (1966: 4) characterises Ralegh as an intellectual man of action with the caution that for such men 'their ideas were apt to become *idées fixes*', as in the matter of *El Dorado.*

In contrast then to Schomburgk's elegiac annotation, Vincent Harlow inaugurates a modern tradition of disdain for Ralegh's intellectualism or romanticism, and praise for the pragmatism and effectiveness of other of his less lettered contemporaries. However, as Ralegh's military service in Ireland shows (see Chapter 1, n. 7), he was hardly uninitiated in the arts of war and colonial conquest. None the less, Harlow sustains a severe questioning of Ralegh's actual achievements, leaving only his intellectuality, artistry and literacy as positive aspects of his character. This judgment has been effectively carried over uncritically by subsequent literary commentators and practitioners, such as Stephen Greenblatt and V. S. Naipaul, allowing them to suggest, without making the argument, that such an evaluation of Ralegh is historiographically unquestionable (see discussion below).

Despite this, Harlow (1928: xvi) too succumbs in part to Ralegh's enchantment:

> The age of Elizabeth is environed with the golden haze of romance, that only by considerable effort can the men and women of that time be discerned in their true proportions . . . Life [. . .] was also fraught with cunning and brutality. The 'paladins of the Virgin Queen' . . . were steeped in faction and intrigue . . . Sordid meanness and calculating treachery are to be found cheek by jowl with sublime devotion to duty and quixotic knight-errantry . . . In

> the personality of Walter Ralegh are concentrated in intensified form almost all the virtues and failings characteristic of his generation. He is not therefore a typical Elizabethan; indeed all but a few of his contemporaries failed to understand him. *He is an epitome.* [my emphasis]

However, Harlow will not succumb to the enchantments of the age, or be bewitched by the dazzling creative imagination of Ralegh. In his introduction Harlow therefore sets himself three tasks – first, to assess Ralegh's 'title to fame', second, to provide a narrative and analysis of prior Spanish expeditions in search of *El Dorado*, and, third, to set the *Discoverie* in the context of the years until Ralegh's final return to Guiana in 1617-18. There can be little doubt that in choosing this editorial strategy Harlow is thereby distancing himself from the 'geographer's elegy' that Robert Schomburgk produced. The rise of professional scholarship after the First World War had necessarily to detach itself from its Victorian predecessors, and, whatever may have been Schomburgk's talents in the assessment of Ralegh's geographical and ethnological observation, he was not a professional historiographer. As a result Harlow's trawl of the archival materials provides him with sufficient opportunity to return to that view of Ralegh's *Discoverie*, best exemplified by Hume in his *History of England*, and noted as such by Schomburgk, which sees it as being 'full of the grossest and most palpable lies' (Schomburgk 1848: xlviii). Harlow (1928: xvii) lays out the transformations of the Ralegh legend thus:

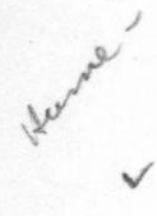

> The seventeenth century, smarting under Stuart misgovernment, idealised the great days of Elizabeth, and revered the name of Ralegh (himself the victim of a Stuart) as the champion and martyr of a national liberty. The legend . . . continued to flourish as a pleasing contrast to the régime of the Hanoverians. Later . . . opinion became divided. The omniscient Hume, happening upon Ralegh's description of Guiana dismissed him for a liar and a cheat: on the other hand, brilliant and enthusiastic biographers tripped lightly over the dark places or turned to argue them laboriously away. *But the legendary Sir Walter dies hard.* [my emphasis]

Some of the reasons as to why there is a persistent lack of resolution as to the meaning of Ralegh's actions and writings have already been discussed, but Harlow is undoubtedly correct in also stressing the kinds of ideological use to which Ralegh has been put (and see further discussion below). Against this ideological background almost all interpretations of the *Discoverie* treat the text as a source of exemplary material for bolstering a critique of Ralegh that relies on a demonstration of his artifice in using clever words to recast the meaning of his actions, or making bold promise in the face of small achievement. But this is precisely to evaluate the *Discoverie* only from the point of view of the Elizabethan court, or of the political career of Ralegh, whereas, just as Schomburgk intuited, the *Discoverie* can stand on its own as a competent and informative account of the lower Orinoco at the end of the sixteenth century. It is in this aspect of the text of the *Discoverie* that this edition is principally interested.

By implication of course, any positive anthropological re-evaluation of the text of the *Discoverie* is of significance for the biographers and historians of Ralegh as well, not least because, apart from the efforts of Robert Schomburgk, no anthropological assessment of the *Discoverie* has yet been made. If Ralegh can be shown to have had a substantive understanding and impact on native political life at the end of the sixteenth century, and if it can be shown that the political legacy of that moment was discernible in native consciousness, not just when Ralegh returned in 1617-18 but over the subsequent decades as well, then the limitations to a purely historiographical approach to the interpretation of the *Discoverie* will have been sufficiently demonstrated. Furthermore, since previous commentators are largely silent on the native context, a specific re-examination of the claims of the *Discoverie*, and some re-assessment of the achievements of Ralegh himself, seem also in order. Although this edition is principally concerned with the first of these two exercises, it is necessary to make some evaluation of Harlow's findings with regard to the latter, because of the way in which, as has been suggested, these two issues interact in the reading of Ralegh's life and works.

Harlow first takes on the 'misconception' that Ralegh was a 'first-rate seaman', as evidenced by his supposed role in the naval attack on Cadiz in 1596. Referencing Corbett's *The Successors of Drake* (1900), the suggestion is made that Ralegh's 'ardour cooled' in the face of engagement, just as he was 'found wanting' in facing off bad weather in the English Channel on two subsequent occasions. Harlow concludes that 'He was no coward . . . He was simply not a sailor' (1928: xviii–xix). This lack of pragmatic resolution is then immediately and, suspiciously, contrasted with Ralegh's custom of taking to sea a trunk full of books in his cabin – 'an outward and visible sign of his character'. In fact Ralegh himself explicitly rejects this judgment that he was 'too easeful and sensuall to undertake a jorney of so great travel' [*Epistle* A3], but Harlow persists in suggesting that these personality components produced a man of such complexity that 'all but a few of his contemporaries were startled into fear and disgust', not least since 'To gain his ends he would crush all opponents, would lie unblushingly, would grovel and whine despicably' (1928: xix). These contrasting tendencies are seen as stultifying his character and he is judged too much the armchair intellectual to be a successful man of the world.

Quaint though this pseudo-psychology may now appear, a lack of appreciation for the cultural distance of Ralegh from the modern commentator is all too evident from Harlow's critique. Yet it remains important for the way in which it has made possible a modern tradition of viewing the *Discoverie* as a work that most perfectly exemplifies these flaws in Ralegh's character – brilliance, complexity, beauty, fabricated from desire, ambition and deception. As Harlow notes, Thomas Scott (Bodleian MSS, 14520 – Rawl. Poet. 26, f.6) versified a similar evaluation of Ralegh's *History of the World*:

> In greatness thou art lost, as in a wood;
> Treadinge the paths of flattery, falshood, blood,
> The way to Heaven neglected, thou didst stray
> As others now doe in thy Politick way.
> But now thou'st found thyselfe; and we have found
> That sicknes taught thee Art to make men sound.
> For hadst thou never fall'ne'th hadst nevr writt.
> Nor hadst thou cleer'd, but clouded us with witt.
> But now thy falshood hath the truth so showne
> That a true World from a false World is known.

Harlow therefore limits Ralegh's achievement to that of intellect rather than action. In this sphere Harlow sees Ralegh as comparable to the philosophers Montaigne or Berkeley, and his personal contacts with the poet Christopher Marlowe are emphasised in order to substantiate this analysis (1928: xxxii–xxxv).

In the century after his death Ralegh's image was transformed against the background of growing opposition to the Stuart dynasty. The regicide of Charles I and the establishment of the Protectorate of Oliver Cromwell thus saw Ralegh's image in the ascendant as the new Republic took over the expansionist and anti-Spanish policies of the Elizabethans. Both the Virginia and Guiana enterprises were seen as models for the work of empire in the Americas since they stressed settlement and exploitation of *local* resources rather than viewing such establishments as staging posts for access to the Indies and Cathay.

In his consideration of the *Discoverie* itself Harlow sidesteps issues of the veracity of Ralegh's ethnological reportage and fixes on the issue of whether he can be said to have 'discovered' anything at all. Indeed Ralegh confesses that he had stopped 'fower daies' [75] short of *El Dorado* and, 'being a very ill footeman' [67], goes on to cite a whole breviary of logistical and military reasons for not pressing on at that point. For Harlow this is a perfect expression of those qualities of intellectual vacillation and lack of pragmatic resolve which he had already diagnosed. Of course this is to have a very restricted understanding of 'discovery', and Ralegh may well have been able to claim that he had brought the opportunities for imperial ambition on the Lower Orinoco and Guiana coast to the attention of his peers, even if geographical delineation had not been so well achieved. Indeed, we should remember that Schomburgk thought this aspect of the *Discoverie* to be a certain achievement, even drawing our attention to precise latitudinal and longitudinal information published to accompany the Latin edition of Helsius.[4] Harlow also reviews the Spanish materials on the search for *El Dorado* at some length (1928: xlv–xcv), which perhaps should have suggested to him another way of viewing the nature of 'discovery' in the *Discoverie.* These materials and the meaning of *El Dorado* in both native and colonial understandings are extensively discussed below (Chapter 1 (iv) and Chapter 2 (ii)).

For all the negative criticism, Harlow none the less credits Ralegh for his more statesmanlike approach to colonisation, in contrast to Spanish 'jorneys of picorie'. The origins of the Guiana project itself are directly linked to issues of how Ralegh stood as courtier to Elizabeth I, especially his disgrace following marriage to Elizabeth Throckmorton. The 'wonders' that are recorded in Ralegh's text are of limited relevance to its interpretation since, in Harlow's view, they are mentioned as a matter more of entertainment than of testament. For the rest of his introduction Harlow concentrates on the fate of Ralegh after his return from Guiana in 1596 – his committal to the Tower under sentence of death in 1603, his attempts to win reprieve through a series of petitions over the years 1607-16, then freedom via a return to Guiana in 1617-18, and the promise of gold for James I. The personal tragedies of the death of his son, Wat Ralegh, and his own friend, Lawrence Keymis, during this voyage are only a prelude then to Ralegh's execution, on 19 October 1618, for his failure to fulfil the impossible conditions of his release.

David Quinn, styled as Ralegh's 'Boswell' by H. Jones (1987), developed a more complex – and forgiving – historiography of Ralegh through his close professional attention to the early colonisation of North America. The Virginia enterprise thus stands in complementary opposition to that in Guiana. Virgin Queens loom large as inspirational icons of both endeavours but Ralegh's substantive commitment in financial and political terms was to the earlier Virginia project, with the Guiana episode appearing as a hastily conceived attempt to re-run the Virginia enterprise. A crucial difference was the attitude taken to the native population, for the Virginia experience had firmly implanted the lesson that colonisation could rarely succeed in the face of indigenous opposition. Lawrence Keymis in his *A Relation of the*

Second Voyage to Guiana (1596) specifically calls attention to this in his discussion on the prospects for settlement in Guiana, and John Scott (BL Sloane 3662, f.37b–42b), in his later seventeenth-century catalogue of European attempts to settle Guiana, suggests this as a crucial element in explaining the rapid turnover of colonial enclaves in the Guiana coastal zone between 1600 and 1680. As with Harlow's introduction, there is little attempt by Quinn (1947) to grapple with the ethnological substance of the *Discoverie* other than to review the progress of Spanish explorations of the Orinoco basin, culminating with the successive attempts of Antonio de Berrio, whom Ralegh captured at Trinidad, prior to his own reconnaissance of the lower Orinoco and Caroni river. Quinn also reminds us of the previous English and French expeditions to this region whose participants were either questioned by Ralegh or had financial and political connections with him, particularly Jacob Whiddon and George Popham; the former being despatched by Ralegh in 1594 to survey Spanish positions on Trinidad, the latter capturing Spanish documents that related directly to the situation on Orinoco which came to form an addendum to Ralegh's own text. The Guiana enterprise is then situated as Ralegh's response to his brief imprisonment and disgrace by Elizabeth I, stemming from her outrage at his marriage to Elizabeth Throckmorton, one of the Queen's courtiers. Given, in the eyes of Quinn and Harlow, that Ralegh was 'no hardened explorer' (Quinn 1947: 149) the rash and unlikely formulation of the Guiana expedition can only then be explained by reference to this need to regain the favour of a Queen unhinged by a jealousy of the carnal nature of relationships among her courtiers.

The text of the *Discoverie* is analysed by Quinn (1947: 148-59) also for its political content, and he rightly emphasises the degree to which Ralegh was careful to act with a diplomatic circumspection towards the native population, fully communicating his understanding of native political life via a detailed rendering of his conversations with native leaders, particularly Topiawari. Quinn (1947: 159) concludes that 'The *Discoverie* aroused much interest in, though little support for, a project for which he had overstated his case, *but that was all*' [my emphasis].

So we appear to have come full circle from the suggestion that Ralegh's *bewtiful empyre* had some real referents (Schomburgk), through the notion that the *bewtiful empyre* was a token of Ralegh's own enchantment of others and bewitchment of himself (Harlow), to the suggestion that the *bewtiful empyre* was a rhetorical flourish on the quotidian business of colonial establishment. But of course it was all of these things.

Under the weight of this hermeneutic complexity Quinn prefers to situate the *Discoverie* alongside other contemporary English texts, particularly

Keymis's *A Relation of the Second Voyage to Guiana* (1596), and so gives a different context for its interpretation than the endgame of 1618, selected by Harlow. A similar contextualisation is presented below, where the writings of Keymis and other of Ralegh's contemporaries are examined extensively in order to evaluate the way in which the *Discoverie* relies on information available to and used by others. This critical exercise displaces Ralegh as an ethnographic hero, but enhances the credibility of the information on native people he relays. It is for this reason that the *Discoverie* is separately evaluated as ethnology (Chapter 2), as well as literature (Chapter 1).

Modern Spanish and Venezuelan historiography focuses also on the imperial dimensions of Ralegh's Orinocan adventure, but from an opposed perspective, as legatees of *Nueva Andalucia* and rivals in the conquest of Guiana. However, as Pablo Ojer in his *La formacion del oriente venezolano* (1966) rightly reminds us, Vincent Harlow himself inherited the historiographical problematic, if not the opinions, of Schomburgk. Harlow worked exclusively from the materials held in the British Library and in other United Kingdom repositories. The British Library material includes an extensive series of notarised transcripts taken from the *Archivo General de Indias* by the British government to use in support of its case before the United States Commission on the arbitration of the boundaries between Venezuela and British Guiana; in whose delineation, as already mentioned, Robert Schomburgk played a critical role. None the less, they hardly represent a complete or thorough selection of material relevant to Ralegh's sojourn in Orinoco. Ojer therefore suggests that both Harlow and Schomburgk necessarily underplay the significance of the early expeditions of the Spanish *doradistas* in the formulation of Ralegh's ideas about *El Dorado*, as well as in his reportage of the local conditions on the lower Orinoco. This is not because Schomburgk and Harlow fail to recognise that Ralegh acknowledged his place as a successor to the prior Spanish *conquistadores*, but because the idea that Guiana was the location for *El Dorado* was *not* a matter of published record. Rather, the ethnological details that make Ralegh's *Discoverie* so unique in its account of *El Dorado* were part of a local tradition of the Spanish colonists in Margarita or a specific outcome of the recent explorations of Antonio de Berrio, on whom Ralegh *did* rely for the much of his geographical and ethnological information. Similarly, Ojer argues (1966: 496-7) that the contacts between Ralegh and the Spanish at Margarita and Cumaná, despite the abortive attack on Cumaná that occurred at the end of Ralegh's 1595 voyage, and the many English losses suffered, were the source for Ralegh's theory of 'Incan invasion' by the *Epuremei* who founded the city of *Manoa*. More specifically, Ojer notes that Berrio himself, despite extensive journeys across the western plains of the

Orinoco and his initial certainty as to the location of *El Dorado* in the *cordilleras* of the *Sierra Parima*, eventually concurs with the Margaritan tradition that the Caroni river is the gateway to *El Dorado*. This firm local tradition as expressed through Berrio then also accounts for the prominence given to the Caroni river in Ralegh's text and the certainty with which Keymis independently alludes to the mine, and continued to seek it, on the fatal voyage of 1617-18.[5] Thus Ojer (1966: 521) plausibly suggests that the identification of the lake on which the golden city of *Manoa* stood, with the flooding of the Rupununi savannas in the vicinity of Lake Amuku, and identified by Ralegh [69] as *Cassipa*, as well as appearing in the map of Guiana attributed to him (British Library Add MS 17940 A – see discussion Chapter 2 (iv)), was an identification already made by the Magariteños. This cartography of *Manoa* and the sea of *Parima* or *Roponowini* (Keymis 1596: 8) was subsequently expressed in the maps, overtly derived from Ralegh, by de Bry (1599), Hondius (1599) and Blaew (1629). Moreover, the enthusiasm that later commentators have shown for Ralegh's claims to have pulled off a diplomatic coup with the leaders of the lower Orinoco has to be set in the context of the explicit declarations of allegiance to the Spanish that were given by the *caciques* ('chiefs', 'lords') Carapana and Morequito in 1593, as well as the formal acts of possession that were carried out by Berrio and his Campmaster, Domingo de Vera y Ibargüen, on various large native settlements in the region of the Caroni river.[6] The Spanish were even permitted by Carapana to build a small fort opposite Tórtola island.

More broadly Ojer (1966: 543-53) sees Ralegh through the lens of Harlow's historiography, as a man of minimal achievement but lasting influence. The attack at the Spanish outpost of San José de Oruña on Ralegh's arrival in Trinidad is represented as an episode in English treachery, a 'crime' involving the butchery of most of the inhabitants, not unlike the episode in Ireland in 1580.[7] None the less, the capture of the 'Governor of El Dorado and Guyana', Antonio de Berrio, served Ralegh well, since it gave the opportunity for a sustained interrogation of Berrio, as well as his lieutenant Alvaro Jorge (see Plate I). Berrio, in his despatches to the Spanish authorities, certainly tries to downplay the extent to which he gave critical information to Ralegh, suggesting that the *cacique* Topiawari, in Morequito's province, was actually Ralegh's principal source and that Ralegh anyway had the benefit of seeing much at first hand. Moreover, Ralegh's [28] own suggestion that Berrio was unskilled in matters of geographical and ethnological observation was convenient for them both, and the suggestion that Ralegh was given his information by native informants is therefore also affirmed by Berrio (AGI *SD* 180, Carta de Don Pedro de Salazaar, 12 June 1595). In this light Ralegh's exploration seems very amateurish, especially when Spanish sources suggest that Ralegh took over thirty-one days to traverse a route through the Orinoco delta that the Spanish sailed even at night, so well did they know it (AGI *SD* 180, La Relación de Liaño, 8 May 1595). In sum Ojer (1966: 547) judges that 'his Guiana expedition, to territory well travelled by Spanish boats, has little interest for our history'. However, Ojer does grant that the revelation of the Caroni mine to Ralegh, and the exchange of persons with Topiawari, represented a meaningful alliance at that time, but not that hostility to the Spanish was so general and so widespread among the native population of Trinidad and Orinoco that it might have been a basis for an English occupation and expulsion of the Spanish.[8] Perhaps the reality of the Spaniards' confident possession of Orinoco, confident enough that it was a matter of intra-Spanish rivalry, which fact in itself bore strongly on Ralegh's success as interloper, is best demonstrated by the way in which the Lieutenant Governor of Cumaná, Lucas Fajardo, could entertain Ralegh, Berrio and Jorge just a few days after the abortive attack by the English on Cumaná and deliberate the terms for the release of Berrio and Jorge.

Demetrio Ramos-Perez (1973) has made a voluminous study of the *doradistas* that sees Ralegh as a final flourish at the end of a sixteenth-century tradition of the search for *El Dorado*. Despite this the text of the *Discoverie* is seen, somewhat surprisingly, as the 'most typical' (1973: 479) of all the *doradistas*; a judgment reminiscent of Harlow's notion of Ralegh as epitome, rather than stereotype, of Elizabethan public character. Indeed, Ramos-Perez, noting Schomburgk's own familiarity with the lower Orinoco, suggests that his 1848 edition of the *Discoverie* is more a work of hagiography than the 'serious' historiography of Harlow, which, as we have seen, does much to undermine the probity of Ralegh and veracity of his text. Ramos-Perez also notes the earlier Spanish edition of the *Discoverie*, *En pos del dorado* (1947), edited by Luis Oramas, and the identification that Oramas makes with Ralegh as a man 'with inflamed Quixotic passions' (1947: 79), despite the difficulties this creates for his own *venezolanidad* (Venezuelanness). The silent implication becomes that, as with Harlow's historiographical advance on the hagiography of Schomburgk, so Ramos-Perez will improve on the passion of Oramas. Echoing the ideas of A. L. Rowse (see above) as to the role of *idées fixes* in the deeds of Ralegh, Ramos-Perez (1973: 480-5) also uses this notion to analyse Ralegh, with the significant difference that it is no longer *El Dorado* that is the obsession but 'the Spanish'. Indeed the thesis continues that such was the power of this obsession that it actually 'hispanised' (*españolizarse*) Ralegh, since the *Discoverie* attests to his own identification of himself as a Columbus, Cortéz or Pizarro. Ralegh's extensive reading and research in the documents of conquest thus destabilized his judgment, inducing that quixoticism which Oramas identifies. The model for Ralegh's prior Virginia enterprise is seen as an extrapolation of Spanish methods of colonisation, even down to imitation of the *quinto real* and the *Requerimiento.*[9] Although similar rituals of possession were used by the English, Ralegh suggests [103] that such ceremonies as the *Requerimiento* were not understood by the native population and sardonically adds that the killing of Berrio's men in Caroni (see Plate V) gave them that 'full and complete possession' which their ceremonies had failed to achieve.

Ramos-Perez also notes that the activities of the French in coastal Brazil, and the publication of André Thevet's *Les Singularités de la France antartique* (Paris, 1558) and *La Cosmographie universelle* (Paris, 1575) may well have influenced Ralegh in his ethnological theories. However, in literary terms the work of Thevet's Protestant rival, Jean de Léry, in his *Historie d'un voyage fait en la terre du Brésil, autrement dite Amérique* (La Rochelle, 1585) may have had a greater impact on the style and form of the *Discoverie.*

A more significant feature of the *Discoverie*'s literary production, emphasised by Ramos-Perez, are the manuscript sources Ralegh reprints. By locating the Spanish originals of the letters that Ralegh reprints in the *Discoverie* as 'captured at sea' by Popham, Ramos-Perez is able to show how Ralegh manipulated the Spanish material to make his claims as to *El Dorado* all the more convincing. This matter is discussed in detail in this chapter (section iv) since the significance of this manipulation is complicated by the fact that Ralegh would have been using transcripts of letters that were in very poor condition. But it can be noted briefly here that, according to Ramos-Perez (1973: 492-3), the key textual differences between Ralegh's transcription and the Spanish originals result in an exaggeration of Spanish difficulties in the face of native hostility, and an exaggerated depiction of the native population as *deslumbrantes* ('dazzlingly exotic'). Ramos-Perez sees such wanton manipulations as evidence of Ralegh's 'fanatical doradism'.

However, Ramos-Perez undermines this careful historiography by adopting inadequate editorial and translating procedures for the presentation of Ralegh's text itself. In particular attempts to 'modernise' orthography have led to precisely those outcomes that this present edition has striven to avoid; a failure to appreciate the significance of Ralegh's observation due to the resulting homogenisation of native terms and the subtle transformation of meaning in the text through the hispanisation of geographical terms. So, for example, 'Guiana' becomes the *Guayana* of Spanish historiography and, of perhaps greater significance, the 'Guianians' become *Guayaneses* or *Guayanos,* anthropological inferences which have to be argued for, not slipped in under the guise of editorial decision. Moreover, the way in which

Ramos-Perez (1973: 633) handles the native term *salvaios* [3, 93], by reducing it to the conqueror's notion of *salvajes* (savages), suppresses one of the more interesting implicit observations of Ralegh, as to an apparently ordered relation between ethnic groups. Such infelicities require justification and are not merely issues of editorial choice of style for they may affect our appreciation of the complexities of native practice registered in that text. In the case of the term 'Guianians' since Ralegh's own usage is inconsistent in its reference, the term should not be given a uniform referent, since that inconsistency points to ethnic and political distinctions that are very relevant to interpreting the text. Even the inconsistency in Ralegh's spellings of English terms and names seems relevant to a reading of the work, for we might wonder how carefully or intently the *Discoverie* was fabricated, if such small inconsistencies are so frequent. Likewise, the editor's redesign of the text into sections with 'explanatory' titles seems only to pre-empt our own interpretation of its fluency, or lack of it.

None the less, even if Ralegh was a kind of plagiarist on the ideas and discoveries of those Spanish heroes of epic conquest, Ramos-Perez has considerably amplified our appreciation of Ralegh's textual manipulations and the dependency of Ralegh on the information given by those such as Antonio de Berrio. Even if such information is ultimately unquantifiable it must certainly have been significant. The *Discoverie* would have been a very different document had Ralegh not intercepted Berrio on Trinidad and this consideration is critical for assessing how truly 'ethnographic' his reportage is, as opposed to 'ethnological' – that is whether Ralegh merely synthesises the ethnography of others, or whether he actually gathered that reportage first hand. Accordingly an assessment will be made below of how directly (or not) Ralegh may have culled his information from native sources, not least because Ralegh himself suggests that 'Many yeares since, I had knowledge by relation, of that mighty, rich, and beawtifull Empire of Guiana' [*Epistle* A3 verso]; which may imply he had access to both oral and textual sources.

This close historiographical questioning of the relative contributions from Ralegh's own reconnaissance and from extant Spanish intelligence on the native polities of the Orinoco basin relates also to the pattern of colonial occupation of this region, as well as the continuing political disputes as a result of the colonial boundaries thereby formed. In short, evaluation of the extent of English, and Dutch, influence and alliance with the native groups of the Orinoco mouth played an important role in the nineteenth-century arbitration of the boundary between Venezuela and Guyana. In this context Robert Schomburgk's evaluation of Ralegh's claims to influence over the Orinoco groups, his documentation of Spanish policy and action, and geographical knowledge of the lower Orinoco, were, and still are, seen as suspect, since

Schomburgk also carried out a survey for the purposes of political delineation of the contested Guyana–Venezuela boundary on behalf of the British Government.

The Venezuelan historian Angelina Lemmo (1977: 74-85, 1986) has looked closely at the English historiography of Venezuela, particularly as expressed through the writings of Ralegh and his contemporaries in the Guiana enterprise, Lawrence Keymis, Robert Harcourt and Francis Sparry. She stresses that, whatever the various intellectual engagements that these authors may have had with the ideas of *El Dorado* or other medieval wonders, the grim business of colonisation was the dominant force in action. Colonisation was laid out in their writings as a business of penetration – expansion – establishment. The lure of *Manoa* thus becomes a factor facilitating English attempts to settle Guiana, but not its prime motive. The earlier attempts by Ralegh to establish a colony in Virginia are then adduced as proof positive of the concrete colonial intents of the English in Guiana. Moreover, whatever the strategic significance of gold discoveries in Guiana, or the political implications of Ralegh's attempts to control them, it was the trade in tobacco, with both the native population and the *vecinos* of Trinidad, that actually was the substance of English colonial activity in the period between the first and final expeditions of Ralegh.[10]

Lemmo argues (1986: 26-7) that Ralegh's *Discoverie,* along with the texts of the above-mentioned of his contemporaries, constitutes a class of literature that has specific characteristics that also sets it apart from earlier Spanish writings – i.e. they have a minimally systematic content, a biographical-descriptive quality, a tendency to generalise without analysis and 'monothematic' ideas (as in the matter of native gold). This contrasts with the evangelical, even millennial, motivations that activate Spanish 'discoveries' with all the epic-romantic overtones that they embodied. As we shall see, the literary scholars, particularly Mary Campbell, have focused on the liminal aspect of the *Discoverie,* as a text that announces exotic encounters in the modern genre of travel writing, but with backward glances to the medieval forms of 'discovery', which encountered cosmological and biblical analogy in the marvels at the peripheries of the civilised world. However, in Lemmo's argument, the new form and motivation in English colonialism is based on a commercial rather than spiritual interest in America, and is derived from the anti-Spanish stance of the Elizabethan throne. These pragmatic priorities then require the formulation of policies towards the native population, for which the ethnographic and ethnological aspects of such texts as the *Discoverie* supply the necessary local information. However, there is necessarily distortion as well since the ethnological agenda is driven by this colonial interest, not an ethnographic programme of data collection.

For example, in 1597 the oracular fire-spirit *Wattopa* spoke to a 'captain' of *caribes* who was about to be hanged by the Spanish and he prophesied 'deliverance through the Dutch and English'. But what the nature of *Wattopa* was, or the forms of prophecy were, are not told to us. This is therefore a very good example of how colonial texts, driven though they may be by policy and interest that is inimical to the survival of indigenous society and culture, yet register curiously intimate details from the past practice of native peoples. The complex chain of inference derived from other materials that is required to situate such an observation as that concerning the prophecy of *Wattopa* is also indicative of why our histories are always incomplete and often impossible to construct (see Chapter 2 (i) and n. 4, 5). Historians often solve this dilemma by historicising only from extant or near complete series of documents and records, which is why we may know much about the domestic workings of a royal household, but very little about a personage such as William Shakespeare – and of course even less about the spirit *Wattopa*.

As a result this 'promotional literature' (Lemmo 1986: 44) for English colonialism in Spanish America, lacking an evangelical dimension, has a purely pragmatic view of the indigenous population, although one often derived directly from the Spanish chroniclers and particularly the writings of Las Casas.[11] English promotional literature, including the *Discoverie*, is thus characterised as merely the collation of 'derived observations' (Lemmo 1986: 45). Even were this an adequate judgment we shall see that issues of 'derived observation' are very much more complex and informative than Lemmo allows.

(ii) The *Discoverie* as literary text and epic fiction

Recent literary commentators, particularly Stephen Greenblatt (1973), have developed a paradigm of 'new historicism' which analyses the cultural construction of Ralegh by stressing the performance and 'theatricalism' that was (and is) a form of public and political life. Such a line of analysis carries over the tension between word and deed so evident from the historians' understanding of Ralegh, but sees this slippage as being produced by the general attempt of Europeans to impose meanings on a 'new world' (see also Pagden 1993). Ralegh in particular is shown to be a master of this arena of ambiguous cultural negotiation and projection. As such the emphasis of the 'new historicists', including those who discuss more limited aspects of the *Discoverie* (Fuller 1993, Montrose 1993), is upon the role of such texts in the ideological work of conquest and colonial expansion, as well as in the intrigues of the Elizabethan court. For Greenblatt, the iteration of place names, native terms and titles and the personal names of native leaders functions to build the credibility and the epic-romantic qualities of the text. Ralegh is seen as the last in a long line of mystical adventurers in the 'New World', projecting the cosmographies and ethnographies of the medieval mind on to the realities of native cultures, finding redemption in discovery and possession. Although Ralegh himself makes the suggestion that he is carrying on the 'discoveries' of earlier *doradistas*, he is quite explicit that *El Dorado* is 'not his own invention'. So even as Ralegh intends to scoop the 'great and golden citie' from the clutches of the Spaniards, he does so by direct diplomacy and questioning of the native population, not the epic-heroic search for an already-known location in which unwilling and uncomprehending natives must be enlisted and made to serve. However, Greenblatt's engagement with the text of the *Discoverie* is minimal and he largely sees it as one among many other contemporary texts that were intended to seduce others to support the colonial enterprise. The occurrence of 'marvels' is seen as part of a persistent failure to maintain the boundaries of life and art, and Ralegh's narrative ethnography as a form of 'primitivism' that stands in opposition to the colonial purposes of both textual and actual 'discoverie'. It is something of a surprise then to find that in Greenblatt's work *Marvelous Possessions* (1991), which even features the engraving by de Bry representing the meeting of Ralegh and Topiawari as cover art (see Plate III), Ralegh is mentioned only once; and then only in reference to his capacity for marvel, despite his scepticism as to those medieval wonders of Mandeville, the *Acephali*. In any case, as is evident from the annotation of the text itself, the vast majority of native words that Ralegh cites are either directly intelligible as, or lexically consistent with, known languages of the Cariban linguistic family.

In contrast, for Mary Campbell (1988) Ralegh exemplifies the cusp between the medieval and archaic world of Plinian marvels and the modern realities of cultural variety and a universal humanity. As a writer of 'travel literature' that emphasises geographical verisimilitude over fictional Utopias[12] and personal experience over specious comprehensiveness, Ralegh is necessarily also concerned with issues of veracity. As a result Ralegh perforce acknowledges his own context and position in events, and the *Discoverie* may be considered at least proto-ethnographic in this regard. The new cultural demands of writing meant that Ralegh had to struggle for new forms and terms of description, which moved on from the allegorical map of earlier European imagination. In this light the long lists of names and inclusion of a wide array of native terms appears as an advance in literary technique, not a retrograde rosary of the exotic, as Greenblatt suggests. This use of narrativity in the *Discoverie*, as opposed to the epic or encyclopedic form, also necessarily involves a dialogic form of representation of the Orinocan

II *How the nobility of Guiana would cover themselves in gold when feasting*

natives. In stark contrast to earlier writers Ralegh thus makes the 'savages' human and accessible, possessed of 'inward feeling' that is accessible from Ralegh's text.[13]

However, this struggle for descriptive terms with which to render new and exotic experience has been taken as evidence of the wholly self-referential nature of such linguistic acts of possession (Greenblatt 1991, Fuller 1993), but this seems to confuse objective and subjective classifications. All description and classification obviously has a metonymic relation with that which is so described, but the crucial difference is whether the object or the subject is that which is so described or classified. As Campbell (1988: 233) suggests, 'Ralegh's verisimilitude refers to inner experiences, but those experiences are of phenomena and people outside himself, and thus their written reality is co-extensive with his [. . .] The narration of Columbus is occluded by a dense veil of preconceptions: he has a word for everything, and an imaginary map to whose features everything he finds can be made to correspond'.[14]

A subjective description is phenomenological, an objective one empirical, but this does not invalidate classificatory or descriptive procedures, only the range of inference that we might make from descriptions, both objective and subjective (or 'object-driven' and 'subject-driven'). The understanding here is that Ralegh's text exemplifies empiricism rather than phenomenology, and as such stands in contrast to the earlier reliance on the inherited cultural forms of pastoral and heroic romance, or the sacred geography of earlier descriptions of the New World. However, this contrast emerges through an act of literary comparison, and Ralegh's text still expresses, as we shall see, some of those prior features of travel writing, as well as the new elements of ethnography and ethnology. Accordingly, just as Schomburgk showed for geography, this edition will show for anthropology the ways in which such implicit classifications, as well as the overt judgments Ralegh makes on native culture and society, are quite successful attempts to depict native practice. This may be gauged from how such native practice was recorded by others or has even persisted up to the present day. As a result we must abandon the easy assumptions that the *Discoverie* is merely self-referential or largely invented, but in so doing it also becomes possible to reclaim this text, and by implication a broad range of colonial documentation, for the insight it offers into native, not just colonial, practice. This issue is discussed further in section (iii) below, but suffice it to say here that colonial texts are complex products, reflecting not only the desire of the conqueror but the recalcitrance of the conquered. In this way native conceptions and metaphors have become embedded in colonial texts, sometimes quite directly, since native intellectuals also worked within colonial idioms of literary and intellectual production.

Montrose (1993) has considerably advanced this task by providing an astute reading of the *Discoverie* with a view to revealing the discursive importance of gender categories, not just in a metonymic representation of the landscape of Guiana but in the representation of the native population in that landscape as well, as in Ralegh's [42-3] description of the 'manlie' speech and disposition of the Warao. At the same time Montrose shows how both Spanish and English are gendered with regard to this sexualised ethnology, allowing Ralegh to discursively suggest a superiority of the restrained, continent English over the lascivious, incontinent Spanish who 'used them for the satisfying of their owne lusts' [51].

Ralegh's ethnographic interest and delineation of natives as persons is not, therefore, a token of a progressive morality, but rather partly a narrative response to this otherwise empty space of Guiana – since *El Dorado* is not actually encountered – and partly a result of the narrative style itself, which invites the accumulation of gratuitous detail. None the less, as Campbell (1988: 251) has also pointed out, it is possible to extrapolate and make substantive inference from the information with which Ralegh infuses his account, and which he orders as the narrative of incident and event. This is because, for Ralegh, the use of simile and analogy does not function to deny radical differences and assimilate them to requirements of medieval travel literatures, but rather allows the expression of difference without requiring falsification. The landscapes of Orinoco are assimilated to the meadows of England, not the pastures of Paradise.

Thus, just as the text of the *Discoverie* already anticipates the grounds of its contemporary critique through an overt mimesis of the 'discoveries' of both Columbus and Mandeville, so too our contemporary concern as to the constructed nature of self through an other that is itself constituted through a projection of self is anticipated by Ralegh through a covert mimesis of native Orinocan socio-cultural forms. This is seen in the explicit political analogy that is made between native and colonial chieftaincy as in the functional isomorphism of the terms 'capitayn' and 'cacique' (See Chapter 2 (i)), allusions to native female eminence *pace* Elizabeth I, and military opposition to the Spanish presence in Orinoco and Trinidad.[15] Thus perhaps the most striking aspect of Ralegh's *Discoverie* is the degree of equivalences between English and 'Guianian' socio-cultural forms that he suggests. Clearly this may in part be an aspect of the invention of an 'Empyre' – for even the 'borderers' of an 'Empyre' must shown signs of its proximity as reflected in their capacity for polity and hierarchy – much as Columbus saw the 'Canibals' as soldiers of the 'Great Khan' in order to preserve the allegorical geography of 'Cipangu' as 'Antilles'. However, the *Discoverie* has to be driven by more than the trope of *first* encounter since the prior Spanish presence in Orinoco is key to the production of the idea that the English can act as rescuers of the 'mayden' Guiana. In order to establish the political legitimacy of usurping Spanish claims to 'discovery' and thus dominion, an equivalence, an appropriate complementarity, even mimesis, between the Virgin Queen Elizabeth I and the colonially 'virgin' Guiana has to be discursively suggested (see Montrose 1993). From this emerges the detailed interest in the dynasty, diplomacy and dynamics of native political life which can then be assimilated to a grand narrative of imperial destiny via the collapse and flight of the Inca and the prophecy that the 'Inga' would be rescued by those from 'Ing[l]a-terra', with the result of pre-empting the establishment of the *Nuevo reyno* of the Spanish.

Literary interpretation of this kind is thus indispensable to the critical reading of such texts, since changes and choices of literary form are often indicative of unexpressed or implicit epistemological values – and it is knowledge of others through text that the *Discoverie* invites. However, from the point of view of anthropology such exercises are also incomplete, since the work of discovery and conquest must also be carried out in fact, as well as expectation – that is in the context of Guiana, as well as that of England. Although we may be more immediately aware of the results of Ralegh's Guiana voyage on the politics of the English court, and although Ralegh's actions in Guiana were clearly influenced by how they might be understood on his return, it would be preposterous to suggest that he acted without regard to the situations actually encountered, indeed his narrative shows us otherwise. This much being the case, it follows that a proper evaluation of the claims and descriptions of the *Discoverie* must also evaluate other contemporary texts and material remains; not just because the *Discoverie* itself overtly synthesises a wide range of descriptive material but also because the *Discoverie* was only one of a whole slew of descriptions of 'Guiana' that emerged in the years 1596-1618 as a series of English, French, Dutch and Spanish adventurers sought to establish outposts for trade and dominion of the interior of South America.

It is precisely the negotiation between such forms of implicit or overt expectation and actual experience, as expressed in the literary form of text, that determines what observations are finally inscribed into that text. Therefore, it is an examination of the character of that negotiation of expectation and experience which forms the basis for the exegesis presented here. Moreover, in so far as the *Discoverie* as text emerges from a dialogic encounter between Ralegh and the indigenes of Orinoco it becomes ethnographic in character, and it is this anthropological aspect of the *Discoverie* which justifies and occasions this present edition.

Ralegh continues also to register as a literary icon of the moment of discovery and the process of colonial conquest. Recently both Robert Nye (1982) and V. S. Naipaul (1969, 1994) have used Ralegh iconographically for the production of literary texts as has, most recently, Charles Nicholl (1995).[16] As was discussed above, the ironies and agonies of Ralegh's decision to return to England to face execution at the end of the second voyage to Guiana allow the invention of a literary character, even as Ralegh invented himself: for what other process of decision and expectation could have permitted him to set sail on that fateful last journey in a ship named *The Destiny*, if not his own appreciation of the necessity of performance and the irrelevance of practical consequence? The fictional form therefore becomes a dynamic arena for the discussion of the idioms of negotiation between expectation and experience that were mentioned above.

Naipaul (1969) uses the *El Dorado* theme to represent, like Ralegh himself, the idea of a pristine native Guiana whose loss signals the death of epic-romance and inaugurates the age of modernity. As in the analysis of Mary Campbell, Ralegh forms a bridge between the deconstruction of one world and the invention of another. The first half of the novel *The Loss of El Dorado* basically synthesises in précis form the narratives of Spanish attempts on *El Dorado* (familiar also from the editions of the *Discoverie* by Harlow and Schomburgk) and the events and incidents narrated in the *Discoverie*. The story is then continued, using primary materials, beyond Ralegh's departure in 1595, through to his return in 1618 and the end of the *El Dorado* dream with the death of the son of Antonio de Berrio, Fernando.

Naipaul's evident familiarity with the primary materials infuses his account with a convincing verisimilitude, and arguably represents a viable form of historiography, as Richard Price (1990) has recently showed, and as has been suggested above. Naipaul's intelligent manipulation of the inferences and implication of such texts thus allows him to make a number of telling points with regard to the coherence of the text of the *Discoverie* and its consistency with other documentation of the period – just as is the case for Spanish and Venezuelan historiography discussed above. Naipaul astutely suggests that Ralegh was, unlike Berrio, 'exact where he appeared fanciful' but 'got all the hard names right, and all the complex intrigue' and so 'got truth mixed with medieval fantasy'. Of the *Discoverie* itself he writes (1969: 88): 'The book is part of the world's romance. But its details are precise and true', the poignancy of Ralegh's situation on his return in 1617 being then that 'The Indians had changed. They had been dulled by defeat and disappointments'. However, the legacy of Harlow's critique is evident in the repetition of the notion that Ralegh was an 'unskilled' and 'timorous' explorer, with the passage in the *Discoverie* where Ralegh confesses to being 'a very ill footeman' once again being dredged up as evidence. Moreover, just as Harlow emphasised that Ralegh had actually discovered very little that was not already known, especially to the Spanish, so Naipaul piercingly observes that Ralegh departs, after having spent only six days actually in the company of native leaders on the Orinoco.

A number of features of Ralegh's actions, subsequent to the point at which the narrative of the *Discoverie* leaves off, become critical in the eyes of Naipaul – for he returns to these same issues in his later novel *A Way in the World* (1994). Principally Naipaul sees it as significant that Ralegh suppresses further mention of his Spanish captive Antonio de Berrio and how he, and his lieutenant, were finally exchanged for English prisoners. These were taken during the disastrous attack on Cumaná as Ralegh's fleet left Trinidad, bound for England. Some forty or more of Ralegh's men were killed in the attack and many died agonisingly aboard ship from the effects of arrow-poison used by the Cumanágotos. As Naipaul suggests, the inclusion of a somewhat digressionary paragraph in the *Discoverie* on the topic of arrow-poison and possible remedies, is the only reflection of those horrors in the *Discoverie*. Ralegh [59-60] even turns the discussion to sly self-promotion by suggesting that a cure had been revealed to him by the *caciques* of Orinoco as token of their trust in him.[17] In a further callous act, Ralegh [80] leaves behind two English youths, Francis Sparry and Hugh Goodwin, in order to continue his 'discoverie' and learn the local languages. This is seen by Naipaul as a monstrous abuse, evidenced by the prompt capture of Sparry by the Spanish, and the killing of Goodwin, who 'going out into the country in English dress, was attacked by four jaguars who tore him to pieces' (BL Add. MS 36317 f. 62, my translation). This strange incident has been taken as evidence of the cruel abandonment of Goodwin (Naipaul 1994, Nicholl 1995) and an indication that he was not in fact killed (Harlow 1928: 122, Lacey 1973: 244, Ojer 1966: 549, Perez 1973: 619). The various accounts (AGI Indifferente 747, in Ramos-Perez 1973: 671-7; AGI Simancas, BL Add. MS 36317 f. 61 *et seqq.*, in Harlow 1928: 120-5; AGI Simancas, BL Add. MS 36317, f 83, Report of Roque de Montes, 18 April 1596) appear to make no sense, since 'jaguars' (*tiguere*) do not hunt in packs and are not known for their sartorial prejudice. So Harlow suggests that this was a story spread around by Sparry and the natives to discourage Spanish efforts to capture Goodwin. However, there are actually cultural circumstances in which 'jaguars' might become enraged at European clothes. The four *tiguere* who dismembered Goodwin may have been 'were-jaguars' or *kanaimas*; that is ritual assassins who 'become' jaguars as they hunt their victims.[18]

However, Ralegh in turn had taken back Topiawari's only son, Cayoworaco (also named as *Iwiakanarie Gualtero* in Keymis 1596: 16), as well as others. Cayoworaco returned to rule Arromaia briefly, and both Leonard Ragapo and Harry spent time with Ralegh in the Tower before their own return, presumably on one of the many trading vessels that had begun to appear in the Guiana coastal region in the early 1600's.[19]

Naipaul is still concerned with these same set of incidents and circumstances, in the later novel, *A Way in the World* (1994). Here the focus is exclusively on Ralegh's inauspicious return to Guiana in 1617, as is the case for Robert Nye's *Voyage of the Destiny*. For Nye, the pathos and intensity of Ralegh's situation, as an all-but-dead, disgraced dreamer whose incontinent desires bring the death of his son and suicide of Keymis, is seen as a spiritual preparation for a final voyage to meet with destiny. The words and deeds of a life are reworked to determine and reveal the destiny which he then enacts, as metaphor and literal truth. Interestingly in view of the narrative significance that Campbell rightly assigns to Ralegh's representation of the native leader Topiawari as a man of 'inward feeling', Nye likewise gives Ralegh an 'Indian muse' who acts as interrogator of his motives and gently suborns his cultural perceptions. Ralegh's aptitude for adopting native customs was most evident in the matter of smoking tobacco, but in the Tower Ralegh was also accompanied for at least some of his imprisonment by Leonard Ragapo and Harry, who, along with Cayoworaco the son of Topiawari, had returned with him from the 1595 voyage. They had lodgings near the Tower and frequently visited Ralegh who busied himself with teaching them English and various experiments in medicinal preparations, for which the native drugs *chincona* (quinine), and possibly *coca*, were important.[20] After their return to Guiana these individuals were met with by Harcourt in 1608 and Ralegh in 1617 (see n. 18).

In contrast, for Naipaul in *A Way in the World*, Ralegh has neither real understanding nor personal engagement with the native population, much less the spiritual need for an 'Indian muse'. In Naipaul's construction the place of this native voice is taken by a Spanish interrogator, and Ralegh emerges through this device as a typical icon of colonial absurdity, engaged in fantasies of discovery that force the indigenes to become both the audience and the actors in the performance of an imperial dream. For Naipaul, Ralegh sits impotently aboard *The Destiny*, lost in the refractions from his own fantastic projections of twenty years ago, unable to recreate the moment of first 'Discoverie' and unwilling to acknowledge its illusory quality until the deaths of Wat Ralegh and Lawrence Keymis. Ralegh becomes a dark shadow in the colonial mirror of cultural production unable to reproduce himself through the invention of the 'Empyre of Guiana' he has no option but to then die physically, being already dead performatively. None the less, there is no necessity to accept the idea that Ralegh's last performance was doomed. Naipaul makes much, as other commentators have done, of the supposed non-existence of the Caroni gold-mine. Keymis's failure to re-identify its location then also casts doubt on Keymis's own integrity (Naipaul 1994: 86). But here the incommensurability of fiction and historiography becomes evident, for the explorations of Robert Dudley, Robert Harcourt, Charles Leigh and Thomas Roe, as well as the activities of the Dutch, certainly attest to the existence of indigenous gold working and circulation, if not a location for the city of *Manoa* – see Chapter 2 (ii). Yet Naipaul chooses to represent this otherwise, in order to produce the marvellous fiction of Ralegh's final voyage. In the specific case of the Caroni mine we now know that it did exist (Lorimer 1983), that it was known to the Spanish in 1595 (Ojer 1966: 548), and that it was still known and considered for exploitation at the end of the eighteenth century (Whitehead 1990a). Despite such empirical grounding it is the 'theatricalism' of Ralegh's self-presentation in text, plus wider questions of the ethnographic authority of colonial observers, that, as we have seen, dominate most interpretations of Ralegh's *Discoverie*.

Charles Nicholl's novel-cum-travelogue *The Creature in the Map: A Journey to El Dorado* (1995) is no exception[21] to this, but he interrogates the text of *Discoverie* and Ralegh's reputation through an imitation of scholarly methodology. A journey with a television film crew from

Trinidad to El Callao, on the Caroni (Nicholl's candidate for the location of Ralegh's *Macureguarai*), stands for the eyewitness 'authority' of the field geographer or anthropologist. Similarly, Nicholl's claims to deal in previously unpublished materials, and his interviews with professional historians and anthropologists, take the place of actual scholarly debate. Finally, a textual study of literary scholars provides 'theory' with which to evaluate Ralegh's claims as based on 'fantasy' and 'projection'. However, as with Naipaul, although such commentary is necessarily unsystematic and prone to error, Nicholl does produce some valid and interesting interpretations. In particular, his suggestion that Sarmiento de Gamboa's *La Historia de las Incas* (Seville, 1572) may have had a strong influence on the development of Ralegh's theory of Incan invasion is well made. Like Naipaul, Nicholl is also keen to point out the lack of reference in the *Discoverie* to a possible initial hostility between the English and the *Orinoqueponi*, the unsuccessful attack on Cumaná as the English departed, and the 'abandonment' of Hugh Goodwin and Francis Sparry. Although, despite claims to the contrary, Nicholl brings no new materials to these issues, he does spot the canard that Hugh Goodwin survived to be encountered by Ralegh in 1617. None the less, Nicholl's brief encounters with *criollo* and *indio* tempt him into a variety of ethnological speculations, including mistaken linguistic etymologies for 'cairi', 'tivitives', 'arowacai' (see fn. 16, 28), the identification of the *Orinoqueponi* with the Macuxi (after Schomburgk – see fn. 37), and the suggestion (my favourite) that 'top' is a common element to native names to indicate 'chief' (presumably as in 'top-dog'!), and so on through arrow-poisons, place names and ethnonyms. This free association of ideas and words works well towards the end of the volume where Ralegh is situated in the context of such associates as John Dee and others interested in alchemy, and 'chymistry'. Even the emergent Rosicrucians are brought into the story, in virtue of Ralegh's naming of the Caño Manamo as 'the riuer of the *Red crosse,* our selues being the first *Christians* that euer came therein'. Certainly there will be reason below to call attention to Ralegh's fascination with native America, and the mimetic qualities to colonial relationships, and it may be that Nicholl's inferences as to the mystical and psychological pursuits of the 'creature' (i.e. lake of Manoa) represented in the map attributed to Ralegh (BL Add MS. 17940, A – see Plate VIII) more adequately illumine Ralegh's personal psychology. However, the idea that the search for *El Dorado* was but a search for the 'Golden King' of Jungian psychic wholeness, or that the pursuit of this 'creature in the map' was but the desire to slay some interior beast on the part of Ralegh, seems necessarily to locate him and his times in a safe haven of unknowable and uninterpretable motivation, as is all too often the case for accounts of native actors (see this chapter (section iii). In contrast, the approach here, by paying close attention to how native socio-cultural forms are registered in Ralegh's text, allows the *Discoverie* itself to become a vehicle for the discussion and analysis of how others are represented and understood through written text. Previous commentators have tended to see this as unproblematic, either in the sense that there was little of use to be known about obscure and extinct Orinoco tribes, especially as they had no more gold, or because all attempts at representation finish in depicting the same object – European selves. In either case native people are erased from consideration. But there are ways of appreciating the role of political power and dominance in acts of representation which do not simultaneously disable our ability to interpret representations, or to make new, valid, even credible ones. For these same reasons the issue of representation is fundamental not just for anthropology but also for the intellectual and theoretical interactions of the humanities and the social sciences in general, and so forms the topic of the next section.

(iii) Anthropology and colonial text

Put simply, issues of the cultural and behavioural interpretation and representation of others through the medium of written text are fundamental to all the branches of anthropology. Accordingly, such issues have been at the centre of recent debates on the intellectual directions that anthropology should, or can, follow. The analysis carried out here fully employs the suggestions of Ricoeur (1971) and Foucault (1969) as to the model of the text and the textual inscription of power. However, if the objects of anthropological analysis are written and communicated as text, and if text encodes the relationships of power and domination that pertain between the student and the studied, then this situation as much *enables* an integrative analysis of others as it *disables* the denial of difference. Thus, it is not the relation between texts and referents which is the issue, but the way in which anthropology understands the ideological contexts of colonial intellectual and textual production.[22] Primary among these newly appreciated contexts is a realisation of the importance of native cultural tropes, as much as European ones, in the colonial construction of particular ethnographic descriptions and anthropological categories. Ralegh's *Discoverie*, like the texts attributed to Columbus or deriving from the French encounter in Brazil, is therefore precisely the kind of text for which anthropology must necessarily establish a competent commentary. Sahlins (1985, 1995) and others, for example, have done much in this regard with the *Journals* of Captain Cook and other historical documentation in the Pacific region. None the less an unrealisable

III *How Ralegh made alliance with the King of Arromaia*

historicist ambition, just as with the literary 'new historicists', drives this type of analysis – that is the illusion that the past and others might be understood 'in their own terms'. The simple fallacy of logic that this illusion involves is shown by the fact that if historicism indeed achieved the aim of understanding a past culture 'in its own terms', the result of course would be totally unintelligible, except to that culture and that moment. Nothing would have been explained, and rather than the past being made 'present' it would have been rendered impenetrable. Such strictures apply equally to ethnographic writing that would attempt to render the native 'point of view' or understand a culture in 'native terms'. Whatever literary technique or rhetorical device is employed – polyphonic/hegemonic, celebratory/valedictory – the intelligibility of representation for one and meaning it has for another are indeed incommensurable.

None the less there are firmer philosophical grounds for the recovery of historical praxis, and, in particular, for treating native trope as an inseparable part of the production of colonial text. This mutuality is exemplified by the evidence as to the mimetic and symbiotic character of conceptual production in a broad range of 'encounters with others' (Sider 1987, Taussig 1993) and has already been theoretically applied within the literary analysis of colonial texts (Pratt 1992). One might add that such texts were anyway sometimes the product of co-authorship of native and coloniser, or of native peoples working within colonial idioms.

The relevance of this exercise in the analysis of forms of representation for the writing of anthropology is that it combines the insights on textual production of the last few years, particularly the notion that 'science' writing conforms to the rules of literary genre, with a renewed insistence on the significance of 'anthropological' genre itself. This significance derives from the fact that the writing of others is not simply a token of colonial hegemony but emerges as the critical arena for the mediation of similarity and difference. The issue for anthropology is *not* the veracity of ethnographic representation and translation but its *intelligibility* – that is, how well such representations explain others to us. The veracity or 'realism' of ethnographic writing is analytically an aesthetic and literary issue. Certainly it is this aesthetic that establishes 'authority', and so we have indeed come to appreciate the culturally contingent basis of even 'science' writing. But, to use Clifford's phrase (1988), a *reformulated* cultural science has to test itself concretely through the task of actually showing how issues of ethnographic authority might be resolved.

Some of the reasons why Ralegh's text makes an appropriate proving ground have already been indicated, but it would be well to stress here that issues of historiographic representation and interpretation do not really differ from those that affect ethnography. Moreover, ethnographic representation, if not anthropology itself, is a very ancient human activity so that any proper assessment of the development of a professional anthropology will have to confront the epistemological character of texts both ancient and modern. But it remains the relation of text to testimony, observation to experience, and authority to intelligibility that is at the centre of any hermeneutic exercise in regard to both ethnographic and historical texts. Such an exercise with regard to early modern colonial texts on America indicates that the rhetorical conventions of historical-ethnographic texts show considerable stability within the western tradition (Hulme and Whitehead 1992), as do the topoi with which 'America' in particular was written (Rabasa 1993).

However, we do not just need to consider the specific rhetorical and figurative devices that are used in historical ethnographic texts, although the *Amazons*, *Acephali* and other monstrous races will be discussed below; we should also confront the texture of the text itself. The notion of 'texture' is given a particular definition here to mean any syntactical anomaly, semantic contradiction or logical inconsistency, as well as the physical properties of the document, including alterations, margin notes, format and the existence of multiple editions. All such textual, as opposed to intellectual, features are also potential indicators of the relations between text and testimony. We have already become aware in the case of the *Discoverie* that such textual features are vital to the evaluation of Ralegh's sources for his descriptive claims. This documentary 'texture' then also needs to be considered along with the meta-commentary or rhetorical devices through which ethnographic authority is otherwise established. Recent debate in anthropology concerning the interpretation of other cultures, particularly as they might be revealed in 'pristine' historical contexts such as 'first contact', has been overwhelmingly concerned with this kind of issue, deriving directly from the earlier insights of literary theory. In the hands of the anthropologists the issue has been formulated as follows: given the culturally dependent nature of historical and ethnographic representation, evidence of cultural bias necessarily entails a 'hegemonic' representation of others. Accordingly this is a feature of European writing on non-Europeans that needs to be factored out, accounted for or otherwise made overt before the ethnological claims of colonial texts can be taken seriously. Apart from the irony that it was precisely this kind of activity that first created the literary convention of an 'ethnographic present' which had then to be 're-historicised' by subsequent commentators, such a view vastly over-privileges the colonisers' moment of 'first contact'. The historical significance of such colonially iconic moments for the indigenes is entirely a matter for investigation, and such an investigation certainly requires consideration of a much greater range of text and testament than the *Journals* of Cook, the *Diario* of Columbus or the *Discoverie* of Ralegh. Thus it is epistemologically significant that the *locus* of many anthropological and literary exercises in the deconstruction of anthropological thought is on these beach-heads of an ever expanding European colonial system. Columbus in the Caribbean, Cook in the Pacific or Ralegh on the Orinoco. These are situations in which, by definition, the issues of interpretation and translation are at their most acute. This is not to say that such 'first contact' situations are not relevant to an understanding of the genesis of anthropology's problematic. Rather, they represent a special class of historical event which was a much more limited and rare situation than their iconography in current debates would suggest.[23] My contention here is that an understanding of the internal tropes through which western historiography has been constructed represents only one element in the methodology of interpretation which an historical anthropology must bring to its sources of data. Along with this critical reading of text itself, we must also consider native social and cultural practice, particularly as expressed in native tropes.

Such practice must of course be retrospectively constructed through the artefactual, textual, and oral records. Nevertheless, while the description of

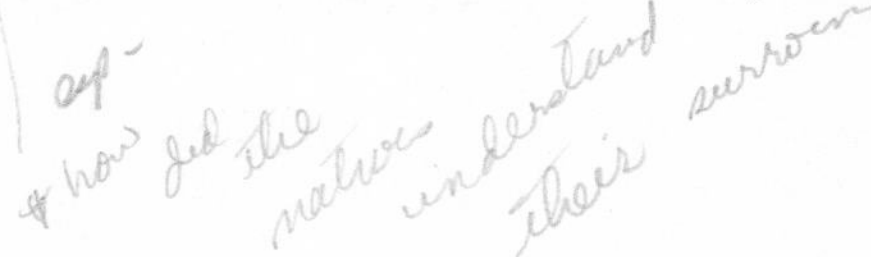

this native practice is obviously an aspect of European textual description, that native practice is itself an equally necessary and knowable context for the interpretation and analysis of European text itself. The question of our knowledge of others therefore cannot be assessed adequately by the critique of a limited selection of colonial text, although this is the kind of analysis usually offered for Columbus's *Diario*, Cook's *Journals* or Ralegh's *Discoverie.* To avoid circular argumentation such readings must at the least address the wider range of textual production that took place during European colonial expansion, and the place of particular texts within that overall literary production. Without this exercise it becomes quite impossible, by definition, to say what the relationship to native practice may have been – although this seems to suit some commentators rather well as it accords with their wider suppositions as to the negative possibilities for cultural translation (Greenblatt 1991, Mason 1990, Todorov 1982, Pagden 1993).

Intertwined with this debate on the epistemology of other cultures is the issue of ethnographic practice, exemplified in the call for the production of 'reflexive' ethnography (Geertz 1988). The antecedents of this debate are partly internal to anthropological theory, as in Lévi-Strauss's (1968: 16-17, 362-3) discussion of 'otherness' in time and space and its replication in the dichotomy of the 'observer' and 'observed'. The essays by various anthropologists collected by Asad (1973) and Hymes (1969) in turn brought to the fore issues of colonialism and political power in ethnographic representation. As a result, a 're-historicised' anthropology seems uniquely placed to offer an improved formulation of the anthropological programme, as well as the epistemological and representational theories and methods to carry out that programme. The consequences of such a re-formulation also challenge literary theories of representation, precisely because anthropology uniquely deals with 'others' who are distant in time or place. By doing so historical anthropology thus directly confronts the difficulties inherent in the literary convention of an ethnographic present,[24] as well as being uniquely placed to understand the forms of the re-presentation of ethnographic categories through time.

Therefore the purpose is to show how the reading of Ralegh's *Discoverie*, if sufficiently informed from the anthropological literature, can extend not only cultural and historical interpretation of Guiana in 1595 but also a better appreciation of that text itself. The problems of theory alluded to above are not thereby automatically resolved. However, the implicit assumption that such a text is to be primarily understood as an act of colonial appropriation of another culture is not borne out by close acquaintance with that text and the conditions, both European and American, of its production. A wholly self-referential purpose to such a text (Fuller 1993) is belied by the way in which native cultures are actually registered in the text, as part of its 'texture'. In this light the various descriptive devices which Ralegh employs appear as suggestive of native American contexts as they are seen to be of European ones, which very much accords with novel trends in anthropological analysis. This new analysis emerges from a growing appreciation of the *symbiotic* nature of cultural construction and the two-way, *mutualistic*, character of cultural transmission, even from colonised to coloniser. This trend is exemplified elsewhere by studies of the 'entangled objects' (Thomas 1991) that are produced by the ideologies of the 'contact zone' (Pratt 1992) and the socio-political transformations of the 'tribal zone' (Ferguson and Whitehead 1992). The key common element to these various notions is therefore the idea that there are no culturally 'pure' productions, that objects of material and intellectual culture emerge already 'entangled' in the ascribed meanings of both producer and potential consumer. In turn those meanings themselves may substantially derive from the cultural and political contacts generated by the literal physical proximity of colonial agents and institutions, within 'zones' of encounter that radiate out from the sites of initial colonial intrusion. In this way ethnographic realities are often re-constituted and re-ordered even in advance of direct face-to-face encounters between coloniser and indigene. Underlying these kinds of transformations, and providing us with insight into how such cultural symbiosis is actually achieved, are the cultural practices of mimesis and alterity, which are now more clearly recognised by anthropological theorists (e.g. Taussig 1995).

Most earlier cultural understandings of colonialism have tended to stress the differentiation that occurs between the colonising 'us' and the colonised 'them', without stopping to consider how these acts of differentiation imply and invite acts of *identification.* This is not to suggest that such acts of identification are any more valid or securely grounded in cultural appreciation than acts of differentiation. Indeed, as Taussig (1987) has demonstrated in the context of the rubber-boom along the Putumayo river, the projection of wild and savage qualities and characteristics onto the colonised leads to the mimetic reflection of that projection in the acts of the brutality of the colonisers. Indian 'savagery' or Caribbean 'cannibalism' thus justify Spanish massacres and punitive raids *a fuego y sangre.* In the socio-political confusions and radical change of the tribal zone the establishment of cultural order may require a mimetic savagery of the civilisers towards those that the colonisers construct as savage. Similarly, the textual reflections of these actions produce new forms of description and analysis, such as ethnography, that meet the linguistic emptiness of an undiscovered place, with a mimetic adoption of indigenous terms that simultaneously populates and locates the experience. It is to a detailed consideration of how Ralegh populates and locates *The Large, Rich, and Bewtiful Empyre of Guiana* that we now turn.

(iv) Text and testament: the *Discoverie* in context

In order to be able to evaluate the claims and veracity of the *Discoverie*, at least as concerns its ethnographic reportage and ethnological synthesis of contemporary materials, Ralegh's account needs to be situated in the wider literature and documentation of the period. Some of these claims and reports are quite consistent with the many other general observations of the native life made in this period; the inventory of resources, crops and manufactures, or the description of appearance, dress and ornamentation, are part of the verisimilitude of the text as a whole. Similarly, the narration of events tells a story that is largely recognisable from other sources, and so the suggestion that Ralegh may have lurked in Cornwall all the while [*Epistle Dedicatorie* -A3], or the suspicion that the whole description was simply culled from other materials, can be discounted. However, there are differences in Spanish and English narrations of Ralegh's actions, there are ethnographic and ethnological elements to the *Discoverie* that are quite distinct from any other accounts, and there are some very important and unique claims with regard to the native polity of the Guiana highlands. In particular, the question of the existence of *El Dorado*, of which, as Ralegh's rival Antonio de Berrio himself noted, 'all speak badly, yet everyone attempts [to discover] by exceptional efforts' (BL Add. MS 36317, f135, in Harlow 1928: 112) needs to be evaluated here, as do Ralegh's claims concerning *Amazons* and Incan invasions. At the same time it is necessary that some sense of the distinctiveness of the *Discoverie*, as well as of the performance of Ralegh himself, be given by putting his actions and words into the contemporary context of other colonising attempts in Guiana, especially those of Robert Harcourt and Charles Leigh. These discussions will then serve to provide an overall evaluation of the social and cultural assumptions about native people implicit in the *Discoverie*, which in turn allows a forward glance at the emergence of professional anthropology and the role that Renaissance ethnologies had in that process – for it is such intellectual continuities that make the *Discoverie* an anthropological document of continuing importance.

The Discoverie *in context: Spanish materials*

We have already seen that, in the views of Venezuelan and Spanish historiography, the original ethnographic content of the *Discoverie* is minimal and in fact directly reflects the extensive knowledge that the Spanish in Trinidad and Margarita had already gained of the indigenous population of the Orinoco. This knowledge was garnered as a result of trade with the Cumanágoto and *aruacas* to supply the pearl fisheries of Margarita with food, and even water. By the time of Ralegh's arrival this trade had already lasted some eighty years, having begun around 1512 with the initial Spanish occupation of the pearl fisheries along the Venezuelan coast. This persistent if limited interaction was occasionally interrupted by new attempts to locate the land of *Meta*, the domain of *El Dorado*, and a number of military expeditions went south from Cumaná with this intention. In the early 1530s Diego de Ordás led a number of *entradas*, as these armed reconnaissances were called, which led to the first military confrontations with the people of Orinoco, particularly the Warao. Trinidad was also first occupied at this moment, by Antonio de Sedeño. It was quickly realised, as subsequent events showed, that a base on Trinidad was the key to occupation of the Orinoco and this strategy culminated in the foundation of San José de Oruña by Antonio de Berrio, again just prior to the arrival of Ralegh. A compendium of these various expeditions is given by Ralegh, to emphasise the pedigree of his own survey, and both Schomburgk and Harlow amplified his basic account of these Spanish explorations and conquests (see Chapter 2 (ii) and n. 9).

As was indicated above, subsequent research, especially by Pablo Ojer and Demetrio Ramos-Perez, suggests that Ralegh had the benefit of inheriting much of the information garnered through these expeditions as a result of his capture of Antonio de Berrio, as well as his own research on the literature of discovery then published in Europe. However, it needs to be stressed that it was not just these better-publicised, full-scale *entradas* that were the effective source of Spanish knowledge of the uncolonised interior. In point of fact many of these expeditionaries, like Ralegh, relied on the local contacts that were already established with the native population for the initial logistics and intelligence required to lead an armed force into native territories.

Something of the tensions and conflicts arising from the differing interests of the local settlers (*vecinos*) and the incoming high-profile expeditionaries (*doradistas*) is reflected in the faction fighting amongst the Spanish. The claims of the Berrio family to the governorship of 'El Dorado and Guayana' were certainly disputed by Governor Vides of Margarita with the support of the Magariteños, as was the succession of Berrio's son by the new appointee to the governorship of Trinidad, Phelippe de Santiago. The key role of Lucas Fajardo, in both the manoeuvring of the *caciques* Carapana and Morequito and of the *capitaynes* Ralegh and Berrio, perfectly expresses these differences as they particularly relate to the *Discoverie*. In

1593 Fajardo was directly responsible for undermining the alliance that Berrio initially attempted with the *cacique* Morequito, Topiawari's predecessor, probably at the behest of Governor Vides. Failing to come to the aid of Berrio, who had been residing with Morequito some seven months, he went to Orinoco on his own account and 'carried off about three hundred stolen souls whom they sold like negroes' (BL Add. MS 363155, f189, Harlow 1928: 100). As a result, when Berrio later returned to Orinoco and freed Morequito, the latter tried to attack the Spanish. Consequently, Berrio was forced to seek alliance with the Nepoyo lord, Carapana, who allowed them to travel inland (BL Add. MS 36316, f65). From these incidents developed the political situation that Ralegh found on his arrival two years later, and it is in this context that Ralegh's diplomatic encounters with Topiawari and Carapana should be assessed. This suggests that Ralegh would have especially impressed Topiawari and his followers, since he had captured the man held responsible for Fajardo's slaving and for Morequito's death (as Ralegh himself explains). The ambiguity of Carapana towards Ralegh also becomes more intelligible in this light, as does the positive hearing, amongst many native leaders, that Ralegh's calls for alliance against the Spanish received and the expectation they engendered. The initial taking of San José on Trinidad was facilitated by the local *cacique*, Cantyman who knew Jacob Whiddon, but wider native support was also encouraged by the display of English military force – as in the occupation by two hundred soldiers of the village of the *cacique* Wannawanare, who had been displaced by the Spanish enclave at San José de Oruña. However, the notion that all the natives were eagerly awaiting a liberation, even though the alliances with English and Dutch were to prove important to the persistence of native autonomy, is belied by the Spanish materials. The Spanish had loyal native allies as well and the English failed to understand this properly. Indeed, the Governor of Margarita, Pedro de Salazaar, was able to send 'two Indian spies, who were in the habit of going among the English; and they declared that although *they had frequently been aboard the Flagship* and other ships, they had not been able to see Governor Berrio or Captain Alvaro Jorge, nor knew anything about them' (BL Add. MS 36316,f 152 – my emphasis). In the same way, part of the reason for the heavy English losses in their parting attack on Cumaná was the fact that, according to Spanish sources, their native guide, Juan Caraca, 'knew what he had to do, he led them by a devilish road overlooked by two forts' (BL Add. MS 36316 f177) and so the English advance was cut to pieces. However, ultimately the issue of native 'loyalty' is important only for a European historiography, since the political independence of native people is well demonstrated by the Spanish observation (Bolivar to King, 8 July 1595 – BL Add. MS 36316 f170) that the natives of Trinidad,

IV *How the Guianans cast gold*

'although very friendly to the enemy and inciting ours to disobedience, were induced by gifts and bribes to tell that they [the English] were waiting for the boats which had been sent to discover Orinoco . . . After this they were more careful.' Trade, bribes, gifts, truck, barter were all opening gambits in the strategy of colonial conquest for they were but an alternative to the direct exchange and violent exploitation of war. As Berrio wrote to the King (1 January 1593 – BL Add. MS 36315, f191) of his attempts to discover more of the interior of Guiana; 'With these few Spaniards and *a host of friendly Indians* I intend to draw them into war, which I will endeavour to maintain for a few days. By these means and with the aid of barter I shall try to see and learn what there is in the interior.'

Ironically, the major ethnological elements that Ralegh incorporated from the intelligence that the Spanish had already gathered were exactly those for which his account has been most pilloried by subsequent generations: *El Dorado*, the invasion of the *Epuremei*, the headless *Ewaipanoma*, women-warriors-without-men, the *Amazons*, and the *Canibals*. However, if the claims of Ojer and others are correct, as they appear to be, then these are actually the elements to Ralegh's account that should be considered the *most* credible; precisely because they were based on a far more extensive and enduring series of relationships between the Spanish and indigenous population than Ralegh's own brief reconnaissance of the lower Orinoco and interview with Topiawari.

This does not mean that Ralegh made a precise or disinterested presentation of that knowledge. It seems to be the case that he used his extensive preliminary research to amplify and enhance the ethnographic reports he makes (as will be discussed below) and that he inflated the Spanish accounts which are printed in translation at the end of the *Discoverie*. Although Harlow (1928: 79) in his edition of the *Discoverie* notes the lack of correspondence between Ralegh's translation of a copy of the original *Actas de las Tomas de Posesion Efectuadas por La Expedicion Española de 1593* made by Berrio's *Maestre de Campo* Domingo de Vera in the territory of Morequito and captured 'at Sea' by Captain Popham, he sees this as simply a result of the 'abbreviation of the more detailed and formal depositions which constitute the original' or as being due to Ralegh having omitted the ' . . . less interesting passages which merely described the same procedure repeated in other Indian villages'. Rather, it would seem that Harlow failed to consult this source properly or even the transcription available in the British Library (BL Add. MS 36316, f30) to which he himself alludes. A comparison of the original in Seville (AGI Escriviania de Camera 1011 A, 6, f11-15) with Ralegh's version of the copy that was captured suggests that a more complex motive was at work.

As can be readily seen from the version of the original published by Ramos-Perez (1973), Ralegh in fact reproduced about a third of the original entirely accurately but inserted two wholly fictional vignettes; of an encounter between Domingo de Vera and a *cacique* called Renato (the entry of 4 May), and the information allegedly given in an encounter with a *cacique* Arataco (the entry for 8 May). As will be seen from these passages, as Ralegh [108-10] published them, the information reputedly given by these individuals bears directly on the most controversial elements of the text as a whole – *El Dorado* and the ritual of anointment with gold, the 'headless-men', the existence of the Caroni gold-mine and the prevalence of gold objects amongst even the 'borderers' to the 'Empyre', along the Orinoco.

None the less, it is hard to see this textual discrepancy as just the result of a cynical manipulation of information on Ralegh's part, and a number of possibilities might explain this addition of gratuitous material. Ralegh, for example, may have independently garnered this information ethnographically – although it might then have easily appeared in the body of the text of the *Discoverie* – or may well have had other oral or documentary materials available that had been taken from Berrio on Trinidad, and which he did not wish to acknowledge, consistent with his own claims to 'discoverie'.[25] Either way it is significant that the greater 'authority' of the Spanish sources would be relevant to either of these possibilities. However, the specifics of Ralegh's additions seem extraneous to both Spanish experience and native cultural practice in this region.

Ultimately Ralegh badly serves himself by trying to inflate the indications of gold working and socio-political complexity in order, one supposes, to conform more clearly to the motifs of the *El Dorado* legend, and especially Ralegh's key narrative themes of Incan invasion and the ritual of anointment of a 'Golden King'. As we shall see in the more detailed discussions below, this misrepresentation of native cultural practice is *not* evidence against the existence of gold working in Guiana, or of the political integration of its peoples. However, it *is* this blending and conflation of the empirical and rhetorical which makes such texts as Ralegh's so problematical. But the web of other contemporary evidence makes possible both this critique of Ralegh's text and so a better appreciation of its intelligibility. The issue here is not how Ralegh's authorship of the *Discoverie* affects our evaluation of his character (biography), or of English imperialism (historiography), but rather how the text of the *Discoverie* was constructed from experience, observation and interrogation of both the Spanish and the indigenous population, as well as the texts and artefacts they produced (anthropology). In this way the past experience and practice of others may be made accessible to ourselves. Accordingly, in the following sections each of these past native practices will be closely reviewed, as will the nature of indigenous polity and economy at the turn of the sixteenth century in order to delineate the ethnographic and ethnological aspects of Ralegh's account.

The distinction between ethnography and ethnology is crucial to a better appreciation of the *Discoverie*, since the nature of the text is an issue separate from the ethnographic abilities and credibilities of Ralegh. Until now it has been assumed that, since Ralegh's ethnographic experience was minimal, then his wider ethnological claims must be suspect. But the issue is not the personality of Ralegh but the meaning of the text of the *Discoverie* and the sources for its construction. In this light we can say that the *Discoverie* synthesises a wide range of ethnographic information garnered principally by the Spanish, to which Ralegh's ethnographic encounter on the lower Orinoco in 1595 adds some critical details. These include the interview with Topiawari, the description of the people and places of the region, and the information on gold working and élite, long-distance exchange. This regional ethnology, which situates the lower Orinoco in the wider context of Guiana, may not be wholly original to Ralegh but he made it accessible and suggested ethnological connections that are not evident from Spanish accounts; in particular the trade in 'green-stones' and the socio-political articulation between the coastal zone, the lower Orinoco and the Amazon basin. Undoubtedly these connections were known to the Spanish (see Ojer 1966: 161-235) but they did not appreciate their regional significance, or at least did not exploit them, largely as a result of persistent native enmity. Thus, whatever, the abstract knowledge the Spanish may have had, their own policies had most certainly created sustained and organised opposition to their presence south of Trinidad, and even their close alliance with the *aruacas* has to be set alongside the hostility of other native groups to the *aruacas*, precisely on account of this alliance with the Spanish.

The Discoverie *in context: English and Dutch materials*

As a direct result of these prior developments in Spanish colonial politics towards the indigenous population Lawrence Keymis, for example, was explicitly asked for military assistance against the *aruacas* and Spanish. In his *A Relation of the Second Voyage to Guiana* (1596: 4) Keymis tells us that on the arrival of his fleet off the coast at the Caw river (French Guiana), at first he could get no one to come aboard, since they thought them to be Spanish, but that, eventually having done so, the *cacique* Wareo

> declared unto us, that he was latelie chased by the *Spanish* from *Moruga*, one of the neighbouring rivers to *Raleana*, or *Orenoque*: and that having burnt his own houses, and destroyed his fruites and gardens, he had left his countrey and townes to be possessed by the *Arwaccas*, who are a vagabound nation of *Indians*, which finding no certaine place of abode of their owne, do for the most part serve and follow the *Spaniardes*.

Wareo adds that the same had also happened to the Yao of Trinidad who, because the Spaniards started to 'borrow' their wives, 'with general consent' decamped towards the Amazon. None the less, the intimate involvement of Ralegh with native regional politics is amply testified to by the fact that the pilot for Ralegh's journey down the Amana channel in the Orinoco delta, Ferdinando, was actually one of Wareo's followers. Although he had moved to the upper Essequibo river, rather than follow Wareo to the southern coastal region, he had told Wareo about Ralegh and this was the reason that Wareo had now come to see Keymis. Wareo informed Keymis (1596: 5) that report of Ralegh's visit and of the defeat of the Spanish at Trinidad 'was now so generall, that the nations farre and neere were all agreed to ioyne with vs'. In view of the frequent occurrence of such alliances of colonial interest and native military ambition (Whitehead 1992), there seems no special reason to doubt this report. Wareo concludes their interview by assigning them a pilot for the Orinoco river, who it transpires was a follower of the *cacique* Putijma, whom Keymis had met the previous year and who was responsible for the ambush of a Spanish expedition on their return from *El Dorado* laden with gold (see Plate V and Chapter 2 (iv)).

In these ways then, texts such as that of Lawrence Keymis, but also of Robert Harcourt or of Charles Leigh, being closely connected in time, space and purpose to that of the *Discoverie*, provide a vital context for the evaluation of its claims, and, moreover, one which suggests its general accuracy. Previous commentators have tended to compare the claims of the *Discoverie* with the consequences of Ralegh's last voyage in 1617-18. However, the intervening twenty years saw profound changes in native polity and economy which certainly meant that Ralegh had little chance of reconnecting with key native leaders on his return. What remains impressive is the fact that his name was certainly relevant, and his return certainly expected, during the decade after the first voyage. The political impact Ralegh himself made on native political consciousness and traditions is reflected in the subsequent use of his name as an honorific title, in the form *Waterali* (AR, 1st Afdeling, Sociëteit van Suriname 225: July-December, 1697) and it is even apparent in the eighteenth century, when Bancroft (1769: 258) reported that

> They retain a tradition of an English Chief, who many years since landed amongst them and encouraged them to persevere in enmity of the Spaniards, promising to return and settle amongst them, and afford them assistance: and it is said that they still preserve an English Jack [flag], which he left them, that they might distinguish his countrymen.

The retelling of this tradition by an English author of the colonial period clearly serves wider political purposes than just the individual hagiography of Ralegh, but the historical impact of Ralegh's activities on Orinoco also have this manifest resonance in later native consciousness. However, this political legacy proceeded from an era before the new political and economic forces of colonial occupation had reshaped indigenous leadership, and even within the few months before Keymis's return in 1596, the situation had begun to change. Keymis (1596: 8-9) therefore relays a complex series of incidents in which various native leaders ally with the differing Spanish factions that emerged in the wake of Berrio's capture by Ralegh, and drive out other groups, as in the case of Wareo. Indeed one Arracurri, an *aruaca* from the Barima river, willingly led Spanish troops to various native villages that were then destroyed. It was during one such armed *entrada* that Francis Sparry was captured. Ralegh [40] also describes an incident in which extreme hostility was shown to his *aruaca* pilot, Ferdinand from the Barima river, precisely because of this fear on the part of the Warao *cacique* that Ferdinand's presence presaged violent invasion by a 'strange nation'. In terms of the *Discoverie*, the discursive presence of various strange and invasive nations – Spanish, Incan and Orinocan – thus serve to ratify Ralegh's own incursion, which he justifies by a textual self-presentation as more diplomat than conqueror.

As a result of these interests and purposes in the text of *A Relation of the Second Voyage* Keymis is necessarily more ethnographic than ethnological in his observations. In the first century of contacts between Europe and America the inscription of native society and culture with characteristics derived from a European repertoire of signs, symbols and myths was feasible, for it went largely unchallenged. However, by the end of this period, and as noted in the writing of Ralegh, this medieval mentality was vying with a need to acknowledge more properly the alterity of 'America'. In the socio-political sphere this is reflected in the vagaries of Ralegh's political legacy in Guiana, and more generally it can be said that the successful initiation of a colonial project required, by the beginning of the sixteenth century, a pragmatic understanding of native polity and leadership. This obviously means that such texts as Keymis's are only partial representations of native society and culture, but, just as with professionalised ethnography, a dialogical interrogation of subjects and a defined agenda of explanation, whether implicit or explicit, creates the structure of representation. These criteria for ethnographic practice might in turn provide us with a basis for the literary distinction of a genre of 'travel writing' from that of 'ethnography'. What appears to be crucial to ethnography is that both a direct and personal interaction and dialogical interrogation of other people (in whatever way that 'otherness' may come to be defined) and an explanation of those other people, according to a defined agenda of ethnological speculation, must take place. Travel writing shares with ethnography the characteristic of attempting to order and make systematic the unfamiliar (Stagl 1995) and so it easily incorporates ethnographic, as well as geographical, zoological and botanical forms of reporting. Indeed, ethnography as a component of travel writing is clearly prior to European expansion after 1500, and arguably much more ancient than that, being a facet of any culturally external interactions. However, a travelogue *per se* need not make any special claims to authority based on the form and purposes of encounter with others. The fact that ethnography needs to make such claims does not, of course, mean that ethnographic authority is thereby established, as the discussion in section (iii) showed.

If there is a lack of equivalent ethnographic, as opposed to ethnological, writings by the Spanish and it is notorious that both published and archival government sources relevant to Orinoco unfailingly elide most political and ethnic distinctions into a handful of cultural categories, *aruaca*, *caribe*, *indio* – then it is tempting to interpret this as partly due to the absence of this need to establish a colonial toehold. As Ralegh and others found out, the Spanish presence in this region, however minimal or unwanted, was of sufficient antiquity that it had been a persistent factor in native life for over a hundred years, and so already was constitutive of elements of native sociocultural practice. The emergence of *caribes* and *aruacas* as revolutionary political movements in the face of this Spanish presence was the most obvious result of this historical situation.

European cultural and political divisions thus became part of native calculation, not least because the Spanish were themselves divided over the control of Trinidad and Orinoco as the Spanish Crown gave out ambiguous titles to the governorships of ill-defined provinces. The faction of Antonio Berrio and his Campmaster, Domingo de Vera, bitterly opposed the faction of the Governor of Margarita, Phellipe de Santiago, for influence and control of the native population of Trinidad and the lower Orinoco. It was while in pursuit of Berrio, who had tried to escape Santiago's troops by hiding with his native allies in Trinidad and Orinoco, that Francis Sparry was taken and the killing of Goodwin by four *tiguere* reported (see n. 18). An account of this incident was also given to Keymis by a Yao, who had been raised by Berrio (see below).

The account given by Sparry himself, in Purchas (1906: XVI, 301-8), adds hardly any details not already appearing in the text of the *Discoverie* but his deposition made to the Spanish authorities in Madrid (AGI Indiferente General 747, printed in Ramos-Perez 1973: 671-7), apart from declaring his conversion to Catholicism, is of interest since it suggests that Ralegh may have had an initially hostile reception (not mentioned in the *Discoverie*) from the native groups in Orinoco. Beyond this the other notable feature to Sparry's deposition is the confirmation of native gold working on the Caroni. The Yao informant of Keymis even suggested that Sparry had ransomed his life from the Spanish 'with plentie of gold'. Sparry himself describes both sources of gold on the upper Caroni as well as the ways in which it was worked and the forms of object (chest-plates and nose-pieces) that were produced.

As Keymis finally comes to anchor in Orinoco itself, he is greeted by twelve war-canoes, commanded by Anawra and Apawra, who are eager for military assistance, and from them receives further confirmation of the way to *Manoa* via various rivers. Keymis was also able to get further intelligence on the approaches to *El Dorado* from the upper Essequibo, as well as Orinoco.[26] Perhaps even more significantly for the outcome of Ralegh's plans, as expressed in the *Discoverie*, was the news that '*Topiawarie* is dead: the Indians of the coast all fled, and dispersed . . . That *Iwiakanarie Gualtero* [Cayoworaco] his neere kinsman, hath held the countrey to his use by his fathers appointment, ever since you being in the river . . . And that *Berreo* has sent for sixe peeces of ordinance' (1596: 16) In short the putative alliance of Topiawari, and other native leaders, with the English against the Spanish was no longer sustainable because of the way in which the Spanish had re-occupied Orinoco after Ralegh's departure. To this end they had promoted one *Don Juan*, also known by the native name *Eparacano*, the baptised nephew of Topiawari and cousin to *Iwiakanarie Gualtero*,[27] as their favoured leader for the *Orinoqueponi* (or *Guayanos*, in the Spanish sources). Moreover, *aruacas* had already been 'planted' in Orinoco by the Spanish and had received black slaves to work their tobacco plantations. Most revealing of all for this new political situation, as well as for our assessment of Ralegh's ethnographic reportage, was the attitude of the *acarewana* ('King') Carapana. When Ralegh had originally arrived on Orinoco Carapana was already an active ally of the Spanish but Ralegh [96 *sic*/86] reports in the *Discoverie*; 'But in mine opinion, or rather I assure myself that *Carapana* [. . .] if hee finde that wee returne strong, hee will bee ours, if not, hee will excuse his departure to the Spanyardes, and say it was for fear of our comming'.

This proved to be a very accurate assessment since Carapana was again 'absent' when Keymis sends for him and it is only after seven days that finally one of his 'aged followers' appears to make various excuses for his *cacique*; that he is powerless to act independently because his authority amongst the Orinoqueponi has been undermined by Eparacarno and he can trust only a few of his men, that in order to preserve his authority and extend his political influence he must consent to his people trading with the Spanish, and that the necessity for allying with one or other of the European powers was all too evident to him but unless the English could offer military protection there was no possibility that he could break with the Spanish. As we have seen, the growing power of the *aruacas* on Orinoco was already evident to Keymis and, although he indicates that there are still important groups prepared to ally with the English, it is clear enough that, without some concrete commitment of men and *matériel*, promises and fine words will achieve very little (Keymis 1596: 20-3). To this particular analysis is appended the general lessons (1596: 25-6) that the key element of the colonial enterprise is to 'steale the first blessing of an untraded place' and that the indigenous population 'are impacient of such a wrong, as to have anie of their people perforce taken from them, and will doubtlesse seek revenge'. In this light Ralegh's documentation of both the anti-Spanish proclivities of native leaders and Ralegh's claims to wield influence with them (in so far as he could produce military and economic support) seem perfectly plausible.

In the event no messianic 'King of the Indians'[28] was needed to organise and sustain fierce opposition to the Spanish. Even before Ralegh appeared, probably around the year 1584, fundamental changes in native polity and leadership were evident from the emergence of the *caribes*, as a political and cultural counterpoint to the *aruacas* (Whitehead 1992, Whitehead 1995a 1995b). These indigenous groupings were a direct response to the Spanish *conquista*, encapsulating through their oppositional identities the inevitable consequences of foreign invasion: resist or co-operate. Spanish military superiority, a complex consequence of various logistical and technical factors rather than a simplistic expression of a supposed cultural superiority, necessarily set this political agenda for native leadership and the vacillations of the ancient élite, as in the cases of Carapana or Morequito, were terminated by the succeeding generation, represented by individuals such as Eparacarno, or the war-chiefs of the *aruacas* and *caribes*. Moreover, the Spanish were justly alarmed at the increasing intervention of the Dutch and English in the region in which Ralegh's journey represented only an episode.

Robert Dudley had in fact preceded Ralegh in Trinidad by only a few weeks and his reconnaissance of Trinidad and the lower Orinoco very much confirms the account of Ralegh, especially as regards native gold working. This evidence is treated below in the discussion of *El Dorado* so it need only be noted here, otherwise Dudley's account and the other narratives (Warner 1899) serve to verify Ralegh's description of the Warao of the delta region.

The Dutch reconnoitered Orinoco in 1597 (*Verclaringe van de onbekende ende onbeseylde voiage van America – A. Cabeliau*, 3 February 1599, in Jonge 1862: I, 153-60) and had private traders operating widely across the whole region until the formal founding of the *West-Indische Compagnie* in 1621, which operated out of the fort *Kyk-over-al* on the Essequibo river for the next 150 years. Fundamental in the success of this operation was the alliance and support of the native population which the first Governor of Essequibo secured through a marriage-exchange with *caribe* chieftains. The subsequent conflicts of Spanish:Dutch *aruaca*:*caribe* thus broadly characterise the history of colonialism in the region. English interests, which anyway were not perfectly separated either financially or politically from those in the Netherlands, might well have replaced the Dutch in this role, and it should be remembered that the English did indeed originally possess what was to become Surinam under the title of 'Willoughby-Land' (see Whitehead 1996c). This territory was conceded to the Dutch only in return for *Nieuw Amsterdam* (New York). However, the point is not to speculate on moot possibilities but to illustrate that the political potential which

Ralegh outlines might well have been realised, even if his attempt to do so in 1618 had become anachronistic.

The materials relating to the attempts made under Charles Leigh in 1604 to settle the coastal region – collected in Purchas (1906: XVI, 309-51) – underline the way in which Ralegh's particular political connections with native leaders were being made irrelevant by the emergence of new native groupings in response to this flurry of Spanish, Dutch and English colonial activity. None the less, Leigh's expedition benefited from the genuine expectation among the native population that he would return and assist them militarily against their enemies. However, the Spanish occupation of Trinidad and the Orinoco mouth continued apace in Ralegh's absence; so too, Ralegh's connections with the older generation of Yao, Orinoqueponi and Nepoyo leaders, such as Topiawari, Carapana or Wareo counted for less. The Yao, as we have seen, had anyway abandoned Trinidad by around 1600, Topiawari was dead, Carapana isolated, Wareo driven out from Moruca, and Putijma had been forced to retreat into the interior. Both Keymis and Sparry also mention 'Curmatoi' or 'Caramatoi', as an emerging Orinoqueponi leader of some account and of 'special note' (Keymis 1596: 16) amongst other native groups, but he was already hunted by the Spanish.

This dispersion of the Yao, Suppoyo, Nepoyo and Orinoqueponi leaders and the resettlement of some of their village populations did not go unopposed by the indigenous groups of the areas into which they went. The southerly part of the coast between Orinoco and Amazon was occupied by the Palikur and the Karinya and both groups bitterly opposed the intrusion of the Yao nobility. In consequence the English, committed to, or searching for, alliance with the leaders identified by Ralegh, then necessarily came into potential conflict with the indigenous groups of Oyapock, Cayenne and the Maroni. Moreover, since the eventual political outcome of the conflicts amongst indigenous groups, resulting from the re-locations provoked by the European occupation of the Orinoco, was the absorption or disappearance of the Yao, Suppoyo and Nepoyo as distinct identities, English diplomatic orientations were utterly inappropriate. The understanding of native politics in Orinoco that Ralegh offered could not simply be transplanted to the Guiana coast, and the failure of the English Surinam colony, as well as the attempts to settle the Oyapock, may be seen as a consequence of this failure to stay in touch with a highly dynamic period of social and political change. In contrast, the Dutch, as mentioned above, dealt with the emergent class of *caribe* or *aruaca* leaders and were not encumbered by an outmoded analysis of native polity.

This new political reality is again reflected in Robert Harcourt's *Relation of Guiana* (1613), even though, as Harlow (1928: 9) noticed, Harcourt used the name of Ralegh to establish his credentials with local leaders and had the benefit of encountering other native individuals who had travelled to England, as well as actually returning with two persons who had been in England for four years. [29] However, the price of continued assistance for the English colony was protection for Yao, Suppoyo, Paragoto and *aruacas* against the *caribes*, or Karinya. Harcourt's (1613: 15) account gives a detailed description of political relations in the region at this time and he noted that Leonard Ragapo, who was in the Tower with Ralegh, now held the 'Signiory of *Cooshebery*': 'Captaine *Leonard* came to *Wiapoco* [Oyapock], (being above an hundred miles from his owne Countrey) only to visite mee and my company; for the great love hee did beare to Sr. *Walter Raleigh*, and our nation.' But Harcourt's (1613: 19-21) own intelligence revealed that the fidelity of given individuals was beside the point. This was because the political refugees from the Spanish in Orinoco, even though the paramount chief of the Yao, Anacajoury, was with them and had temporarily enforced an acquiescence by the *caribes* to their settlement in the southern zone, none the less clung to their new 'Signiories' by dint of military force. Leonard Ragapo in fact claimed that he had seized his 'Signiory' in Cooshebery because it was 'slenderly inhabited' – a case of a native colonialism, even as it is a textual mimesis of native voice to mask Harcourt's own colonial intent.

Harcourt did attempt to lay the ground for future English interests by making diplomatic overtures to the *caribe* warlord Arrawicary at Cayenne, and by leaving a man behind to learn the language. However, prior political entanglements with the Yao, especially Leonard Ragapo, meant that Harcourt simultaneously agreed to joint military action against other groups of *caribes*; specifically those dispersed by Ragapo's 'colonial' occupation to the south and west, whose counter-attack, with a force of two hundred warriors, was witnessed by Harcourt's own men (Harcourt 1613: 21-3). Fortunately for Harcourt and his men, they did not appear to have immediate communication with the *caribes* at Cayenne, but observations of indigenous military formation, among both foes and allies, were noted, foreshadowing plans for later colonial occupation.

A further consequence of English, as well as Dutch and French,[30] interest in coastal Guiana was that putative alternative routes to *El Dorado*, other than the Caroni one first mentioned by Ralegh, began to be researched. The Maroni and Surinam rivers were broadly identified as particularly promising and the possibility of an Incan presence in the hills of Tumuc-Humuc (French Guiana) was first broached, and lingers on as a nagging historiographical footnote (Chapter 2, n. 7).

Notes

1 Schomburgk produced a highly useful map to accompany the 1848 edition of the *Discoverie* which very effectively demonstrates the accuracy of Ralegh's geographical reportage of the lower Orinoco. However, Schomburgk seems to have lacked sufficient information to make much of Ralegh's wider allusions to political and geographical features and so tends to assimilate such information more to parochial contexts, or to dismiss it as unintelligible – for further discussion of Maps (I) and (II) see Chapter 2 (iv).

2 In the 1928 edition by the Argonaut Press N. M. Penzer is listed as 'Editor' under the title lines facing the Preface, although on the title-page the *Discoverie* is apparently 'Edited from the Original Text, with *Introduction, Notes and Appendixes* of hitherto unpublished documents by V. T. Harlow'

3 The illustrations to the German edition are reproduced here, and are discussed in Chapter 2 (iv).

4 In the *Tabula Locorum quorum in libello hoc mentio fit.* Schomburgk (1848: 1xvi) notes that the degrees of longitude are reckoned eastwards from the island of Ferro (Portugal), itself 18° 7′30″ west of Greenwich. According to this table the position of *Manoa* is firmly fixed with regard to other known locations, such as the Amazon, Orinoco and Essequibo rivers, at 320° longitude, 1° latitude.

5 A Dutch reconnaissance of the lower Caroni in 1597 was even carried out 'according to our description (made by Sir Walther Halley)' and in the company of a Spanish refiner sent with them by Fernando de Berrio. They did not locate the mines but came away convinced that they existed (as indeed it transpires). Both the accuracy of Ralegh's reportage, whatever its sources, and the specific issue of the Caroni mine (see also Lorimer 1982) are thus important for assessing the reliability of other aspects of the *Discoverie.*

6 A copy of these *Actas de las Tomas de Posesion,* which were legally required recordings of the 'fact' of having received native consensus to Spanish sovereignty, appears among the materials seized by Popham and printed at the end of the *Discoverie* (105). See below for discussion of how they were manipulated by Ralegh and for further discussion of such European rituals of possession.

7 From his role in the punitive campaigns in Ireland Ralegh emerges as quite a different character to that of the witty and enlightened author of the *Discoverie.* In 1580 Ralegh was sent to Ireland as a captain of a company of soldiers, following a landing in Ireland under Lord Fitzmaurice with a commission from the Pope to liberate Ireland from the excommunicant Elizabeth I. Lord Grey, overall commander of the English forces, had trapped Fitzmaurice's mercenary and rebel force at Smerwick. On 10 November the garrison surrendered and Grey sent in two companies, one of which was Ralegh's, to kill everyone – Spanish, mercenaries, Irish rebels, women and children – which they did without demur. As Quinn (1947: 35) suggests, it has remained controversial as to whether Grey had agreed to any conditions for surrender, for if he had not then the practice of war at this time would condone these killings. Both Berrio's killing of a group of Jacob Whiddon's men in 1594, and Ralegh's own tactics in taking San José, were equally brutal by modern ethics.

8 The revelation of the Caroni mine of course will have a fundamental significance by the time of the second voyage in 1617-18, as it becomes converted 'into a true obsession of Ralegh's' (Ojer 1966: 548) and see further discussion below.

9 The *quinto real* was the 'royal fifth' collected on all precious metals and jewels taken as war-booty, mining, duties on good entering the Indies and tribute levied from the native population (Parry 1966: 40). Those licensed as *conquistadores* were under legal obligation to secure their possession of new territories taken in the name of the Spanish Crown through a *Requerimiento,* a mandatory ceremony that had to be recorded and notarised. A principal element was that the native population should freely accept this Spanish sovereignty and understand what it was they were doing. As Seed (1995) has recently shown, the Spanish were not alone in this procedure and all the European colonial powers had similar ceremonies of possession. For example, Robert Harcourt (1613: 42) recounts that he 'tooke possession of the Land by Turfe and Twigge, in behalfe of our Sovereigne Lord King James I: I tooke the saide possession of a part, in the name of the whole Continent of Guiana [. . .] ; wherewith the Indians seem to be well content and pleased'. He adds that 'having taken possession at *Gomeribo* [. . .] I delivered the possession [. . .] to my Indian *Anthony Canabre, To have, hold, possesse, and enjoy* the same, to him, and to his heires [. . .] *Yeelding and paying* yeerely the tenth part of all Tobacco, Cotton, wooll, Annoto, and other commodities' (1613: 45-6). In this way native leaders became enmeshed in the political forms of the colonial powers. However, it remains open as to whether native participation in these rituals can be taken to indicate knowledgeable consent to European settlement.

10 See Lemmo (1986: 22-3) and Lorimer (1979). The Dutch, who were also colonially active in this region, were similarly engaged in the tobacco trade and, indeed, Fernando de Berrio, son of Ralegh's famous captive, was himself deprived of his father's titles as a result of his involvement with this commerce in tobacco (see Whitehead 1988: 85). The *aruacas* on the Orinoco, in return for their support for the Spanish, were given black slaves to work their tobacco fields, as were the *Guayanos* the term by which the Spanish denoted the 'Orinoqueponi' (Keymis 1596: 19, Archief Staten van Zeeland, Journal van een reis naar Orinoco, etc. 24 January 1629 – 1 May 1630).

11 For an analysis of the origins and intellectual influence of Bartolomé de Las Casas's advocacy for indigenous people see Anthony Pagden's *The Fall of Natural Man* (1982). More broadly Spanish historiography tends to associate Las Casas with the production of the *leyenda negra* (black legend) of Spanish despoliation of the New World. In 1583 the first English edition of Las Casas's *Brevissima relación de la destruyción de las Indias* (Seville, 1552), was published and focused attention on the ruthless plundering of indigenous cultures that had accompanied much of the early Spanish occupation in Mexico, Peru and the Caribbean. Further editions appeared in the 1600s, as well as being included in Samuel Purchas's *Purchas his Pilgrimage: Or Relations of the World and Religions in all Ages and Places* . . . (London, 1613). The *Brevíssima relación*, entitled 'Tears of the Indians' in the edition of 1656, thus served to establish the 'black' image of Spain and was often used to justify colonial activity by the English in the New World (see Steele 1975).

12 Campbell's (1988: 212-16) stimulating discussion of the role of Utopian vision is marred by a curiously orthodox notion of the potential 'reality' of western geographical description. 'Utopia' as a rhetorical device for expressing desire for a different world is contrasted to the 'practical geographical knowledge' of the Elizabethans that produced a 'gradual division of the geographical world into real and unreal places'. But this division is a cultural product of colonialism itself and is of concern to geography only by virtue of the way in which such depiction is of practical use. The fact that it was commercial rather than cosmological desire which was inscribed into the landscape of new worlds seems no reason to privilege one or other geographical expression of those desires as the less fictive.

13 The emergence of this genre of travel writing and its attendant ethnographic narrativity is driven by more than literary sensibility, however. The changing political and economic relations between Spain's colonial rivals and the native populations is a key reason why ethnological detail and the rudiments of linguistic expression begin to appear with increasing frequency in travel texts. This thirst for detail was born of the persistent need of the interlopers to trade and ally with the native population in the face of Spanish hegemony, and such texts were, at the very least, offered as a testament to the author's capacity for such negotiations.

14 However, Campbell's (1988: 254) notion that for Ralegh 'Personal experience is the primary content of his knowledge' is belied by his dependence on prior Spanish ethnology and geography. Ralegh's text presents ethnology gained elsewhere as being the result of an ethnographic encounter; thus the style is one which emphasises dialogical encounters with the native élite but how personal it is to Ralegh is disputable, as discussed above.

15 A personal cultural mimesis by Ralegh is perhaps reflected in his promotion of smoking or 'tobacco drinking' in England, following his experiences in both Virginia and Guiana, whatever the commercial rewards that also accrued. Thus, Thomas Hariot was responsible for inducting Ralegh into the mysteries of smoking and was himself a heavy user. As Schomburgk (1848: xxxiv) noted, soon after smoking became more popular a proclamation was issued against 'this imitation of the manners of savage people', while the chronicler Camden observed that in the practice of smoking tobacco *'Anglorum corpora in barbarorum degenerasse videantur,* (Ann. Elizabeth 1585). Certainly this adoption of 'savage manners' particularly repulsed James I, a notorious opponent of the divine weed who in his *Counterblaste to Tobacco* (1604) asked 'shall we [. . .] abase ourselves so farre, as to imitate these beastly *Indians*? Ralegh's smoking can have done little to endear Ralegh to his already hostile sovereign and so even on the scaffold Ralegh smoked (see Corti 1931).

16 Ralegh also makes a literary resurrection in the mystery novel by L.B. Greenwood *Sherlock Holmes and the Case of the Raleigh Legacy* (New York, 1986). The 'legacy' in this case transpires to be his severed head! Other recent inventions include the 'dramatic fantasy' by Samuel A. Tannenbaum *The Knight & the Crystal Sphere* (New York, 1946) in which Ralegh and a host of other eminent Elizabethans play out their stereotypical historical personae and Ralegh is made privelege to a 'crystal sphere', which is in the possession of John Dee, that can 'see' the future. By means of this crystal Ralegh witnesses, amongst the other scenes of world war and civic reconstruction, 'people [. . .] sitting in their homes and looking at screens hanging on the walls; they are watching a play brought to them by radio and television', to which Ralegh remarks 'This is incredible, nay, impossible', but Dee then rebukes him that 'your knowledge of history should have taught you that much that was thought impossible has come to pass', which neatly echoes Ralegh's [70] own sentiments as to the 'fables' of Mandeville.

17 It certainly was the case that an antidote to the native arrow-poison, *curare/ouralli,* was much desired by the Europeans and the tactical military value of these arrows was enhanced by this fear of their toxicity – a fear which was well grounded in view of the potency of curare preparations. Robert Harcourt (1613: 31, 25) therefore also recounted that manatee hide was an effective armour against native arrows, noting that Ralegh had brought a supply into England, and that the juice of a leaf called *uppee* would cure poison arrow wounds. Likewise, Jean Mocquet (1696: 57) was shown this antidote to arrow poison by the grandson of the Yao king, Anacajoury, but 'the Indians who were with him, seemed to be very angry he had shown me this Plant, which they prised and esteemed above all others'. The composition of *curare* was the subject of many European fables that alluded to snake and ant poisons, but it is the use of the *Strychnos* roots and bark of various species that is the key defining ingredient and the *toxifera* the most potent, taking only a few minutes to act. Other poisons existed for arrow-points but are far more rare, including one made from dried fish *Chelichthyus pssittacus,* another from the fruit of the Manceniller tree and used in the Caribbean islands, and a poison additive called *pougouly,* which is said to gnaw at and inflame the flesh around the wound. This latter concoction seems to have prompted the following estimation by Dutch observers on Orinoco that 'if any one is hit by them [Carib poisoned arrows] so that the blood flows, he will die in 24 hours, and all his flesh would drop from his bones, so that the Spaniards greatly fear that nation and their arrows' (*Verclaringe van de onbekende ende onbeseylde voiage van America – A. Cabeliau,* 3 February 1599, printed in Jonge 1862: I, 153-60). Keymis (1596: 43) lists four poisons, *ourari, carassi, apareepo, parapara* and four antidotes, *turara, cutarapama, wapo, macatto,* which would seem to reflect the information we have from these other sources, though no precise identifications can be made at this time.

18 As practitioners of an ancient form of shamanism such killers are ultra-traditionalists and even in the present day still refuse all tokens of contact with outsiders, such as metal tools, guns, matches and particularly, clothing. Kanaimas also always hunt in 'packs' of five to ten men. Any suggestion as to why *kanaimas* might have killed

Goodwin is pure speculation but we can at least note that conflicts over mimesis of European cultural signs remain a constant in native political calculation. Moreover, as mentioned, the idea that Goodwin was still alive in 1617 has led numerous authorities to err in identifying him with 'Harry the Indian' whom Ralegh encounters at Cayenne in 1617. Harry was in the Tower with Ralegh and was mentioned in the letter that he wrote from Cayenne to his wife in 1617 (Harlow 1932: 158-9). For Naipaul (1994: 169) Harry 'wanted to take back a lot' of English clothes, but Goodwin's only 'maddened the tigers' (176). The fact that Harry was erroneously thought to have been Hugh Goodwin, because he couldn't speak English but was wearing English clothes, is then attributed to his long sojourn among the natives! These bizarre misreadings are provoked by an inability to interpret anthropologically the original killing of Goodwin and the native semiotics of English clothing – see also n. 29 below.

19 Though not at the Spanish outpost on Orinoco, Santo Tomé where, according to a report of Sancho de Alquiza, dated to the King 11 February 1612, 'It is more needful here to go with musket on shoulder than with pen in hand, for there are so few men, and so many enemies, and I must say, it is necessary to sleep like a heron, on one foot' (BL Add. MS 36319, 38).

20 Thus indigenous knowledge of the botanical pharmacopoeia was not limited to cures for arrow-poison (n. 17) and this medical knowledge was of political significance. For example, John Wilson (in Purchas 1906: VI, 342), reported of Charles Leigh's attempts to settle in the Oyapock in 1604 (at the same moment as Mocquet) that 'divers of them died of the *Fluxe:* which the Indians. . . know right well for to cure, yet concealed it from our Generall'. Indeed, the local population of the lower Oyapock began distancing itself from Leigh's expedition as soon it was evident that they were carrying disease and it was this situation that caused the Yao king, Anacajoury, to plan an attack on the English. In this context Ralegh's researches (BL Sloane 359, 640, Bodleian Tanner 169) seem very much in tune with current hopes that the bio-diversity of the rainforest may eventually reveal many useful medicines, through the search for the 'secret' or 'esoteric' native knowledge that can unlock the botanic pharmacopoeia. Ralegh's activities in chemical and pharmaceutical research produced a much-famed cordial that was celebrated by Nicaise Le Febvre in his 1665 *Discours sur le Grand Cordial de Sr Walter Rawleigh par N. le Febvre.* Unfortunately the cordial failed to effect a cure for King James's son, Prince Henry, although it did briefly rouse him from his deathbed. Nevertheless, Lefranc (1968: 681-2) assesses Ralegh's experimentation as both useful and of an advanced level for the age, although he remains sceptical of Ralegh's [24] endorsement of the curative power of the greenstone *takua,* called 'spleen stones' or *piedras hijadas* (liver stones) by the Europeans, that were prominent in indigenous notions of healing and cosmology – see also Nicholl's (1995: 278-87) lively account. Many of Ralegh's contemporaries and successors continued to bring back such amulets, and the French missionaries in Guyane reported as late as 1721 on the sources for such objects, interpolating that they were excellent for epilepsy among other ailments and were 'en vogue' in Paris where they were known as 'pierres divines' (AN Serie C 14 Guyane, XII *f*.288, Memoire Générale sur la Guyane, 1721).

21 Indeed, the form and intent of Nicholl's book seems very close both to Stephen Minta's reprise of Lope de Aguirre's descent of the Amazon in the 1560s, *Aguirre. the Re-Creation of a Sixteenth Century Journey Across South America* (New York: Henry Holt, 1993) and to Bruce Chatwin's quest in *The Viceroy of Ouidah* (London: Jonathan Cape, 1980) or *In Patagonia* (Jonathan Cape, 1977).

22 To some extent anthropologists have become paralysingly aware of the impossibility of neutral presentation and have even despaired of the idea of 'context' as being necessarily wrought from the same ideological materials as the text it supports (see Brown and Vibert 1996, Fabian 1995, Galloway 1992). While it is philosophically the case that text and context may be linked logically, this does not entail that text and context may not be usefully distinguished, not least since multiple texts can arise from single contexts. Such a procedure is often employed in this essay on Ralegh's *Discoverie* and is demonstrably helpful in delineating both the forms of ethnological representation and the native practices to which the text refers. That such an exercise is difficult or occasionally impossible does not invalidate the procedure as such.

23 The encounters of Columbus, Cook and Ralegh are all represented as pristine contacts with unspoilt indigenes. Except perhaps in the case of Columbus this was not so. More important here is the self-representation of 'discoverers' and the way in which anthropology has uncritically assimilated this viewpoint as an ethnographic trope. For further discussion and references to the anthropological literature on historical ethnography and its relation to literary analyses, see Whitehead 1995c.

24 The concept of an 'ethnographic present' is necessary to all forms of writing ethnography and is not just a fallacy of functionalist forms of explanation. Any attempt at description must necessarily use the ideal of functional connection between phenomena, but, since the entire range of cultural meanings is never apparent in any given episode of the fieldwork encounter, ethnographic representation is necessarily ahistorical – precisely because of the necessary functionalist assumption that meaning of an action is fully present in the observed context of cultural performance. Bourdieu's (1977) *habitus,* the theoretical projection of a psychological 'black box', or 'deep structure' of unconscious cultural motivations, which, in Chomskian manner, is supposed to generate cultural performance, might equally be seen as merely the means by which ethnographers historicise their accumulated, successive, observations, not an historical structure of performance itself.

25 Antonio de Berrio himself had already reported to the King that 'it is said as a certainty that the Inca Kings of these provinces set out to conquer Peru, and afterwards on account of the disagreements between two brothers, the one, from fear of the other, fled back to these provinces' (AGI Consejo – Escriviania de Camera Pleitos, años 1597, Legajo 1011 1 January 1593, BL Add. MS 36315, *f*.186). Although Ralegh's idea of an Incan connection may therefore derive from this Spanish oral tradition learnt through Berrio, the Spanish theory actually posits a prior Guianan invasion of Peru. Ironically, such a reversal in the flow of historical causality also emerges from recent archaeological findings which suggests that the

ceramic cultures in the Amazon emerged *before* those in Peru and are therefore the oldest in the whole of the Americas (Roosevelt *et al.* 1991, Roosevelt 1996).

26 Keymis (1596: 8) writes of the Essequibo route: 'and from the mouth of it unto the head, they passe in twentie dayes: then taking their provision they carie it on their shoulders one dayes journey: afterwards they returne for their Canoas, and beare them likewise to the side of a lake, which the *Iaos* call *Roponowini* and the *Caribes, Parime:* which is of such bignesse that they know no difference between it and the maine sea. There be infinite numbers of Canoas in this lake, and (as I suppose) it is not other then that, whereon *Manoa* standeth'. Whether or not a 'golden city' was to be found it is perfectly evident from this passage that the highlands were well travelled and of commercial and political significance.

27 The exchange and use of personal names was an important token of alliance, be it marital, commercial or political, and so the occurrence of forms of 'Ralegh' as native names or titles – *Gualtero, Waterali* – was certainly significant. For an excellent discussion of the politics of personal names among the contemporary Sanumá (Sierra Parima) see Ramos (1995) – also Chapter 2, n.2.

28 This phrase is Ralegh's own, occurring in the letter written to his wife from off the Cayenne river dated 14 November 1617 (in Harlow 1932). The passage reads: 'To tell you that I might be here King of the Indians were a vanitie; but my name hath lived among them. Here they feed me with fresh meat, and all that countrey yields; all offer to obey me'.

29 Among the individuals mentioned by Harcourt (1613: 6-7) were 'John', who had been in the service of Sir John Gilbert, as well as 'Martin' and 'Anthony Canabre' who were returning to the Oyapock. Other individuals were wearing English clothes but despite these tokens there was a long debate as to whether the English should be allowed to settle, both because of the labour of having to supply food to them and because they had often promised military assistance but never yet given it.

30 The account of the Frenchman Jean Mocquet (1696: 68) confirms this changing political scene in Cayenne and Oyapock. Indeed, Mocquet even encountered a native whom Ralegh had taken to England – probably 'Harry' (though *not* Hugh Goodwin, see Chapter 1, n.18) – and employed as an interpreter, although he didn't appear to understand the Yao language very well.

2 • The *Discoverie* as ethnological text

(i) Capitaynes, cassiques and Incan imperialists

Recent work in the anthropology of colonial contact and the texts it generates has emphasised the way in which political, economic and social assumptions are implicit within categories of explanation (see Dirks 1992, Hulme and Whitehead 1992, Schwartz 1994 and Chapter 1 (iii) above). At the same time texts, such as Ralegh's, may be quite overtly concerned to deliver a certain kind of impression of the political, economic and social capacities of the native population, in order to facilitate the colonial enterprise itself. Both features are present in Ralegh's *Discoverie,* which, as has been mentioned already, breaks with earlier forms of ethnographic reportage by giving a real significance to the forms of native voice presented in the text. This does not mean that the way in which supposed native opinion and feeling is used is straightforward, but it opens the possibility that, in the absence of any other sort of record, the voices of that native past may still be heard.

There are therefore two levels at which the text of the *Discoverie* works anthropologically – at the level of an overt statement of ethnographic observation or ethnological inference and an implicit level of anthropological assumption and ethnographic recording that requires an informed contextual reading to make explicit. In many ways it is this implicit material which is most interesting since the hand of Ralegh's authorship must necessarily be less evident and the transmission of past practice more direct, even if apparently less intelligible. A good example of this latter issue is Ralegh's [7] recording of the phrase '*Ezrabeta Cassipuna Aquerewana*' which he partially translates correctly as meaning '*Elizabeth* the great princesse or greatest commaunder'. However, quite apart from the way in which Ralegh wishes to imply a mimesis between native and colonial politics, this phrase is actually much more interesting than his overt reporting of it indicates. Ralegh does not translate the word 'cassipuna' but its occurrence bears on a critical issue in the historical anthropology of the region – who were the *caribes,* and what is their relation to the *aruacas*? This is because the word '*cassipuna*' is a ethnonym that has been associated exclusively with *caribe* populations of the Caribbean, but here Ralegh's implicit reportage reveals to us the conti-

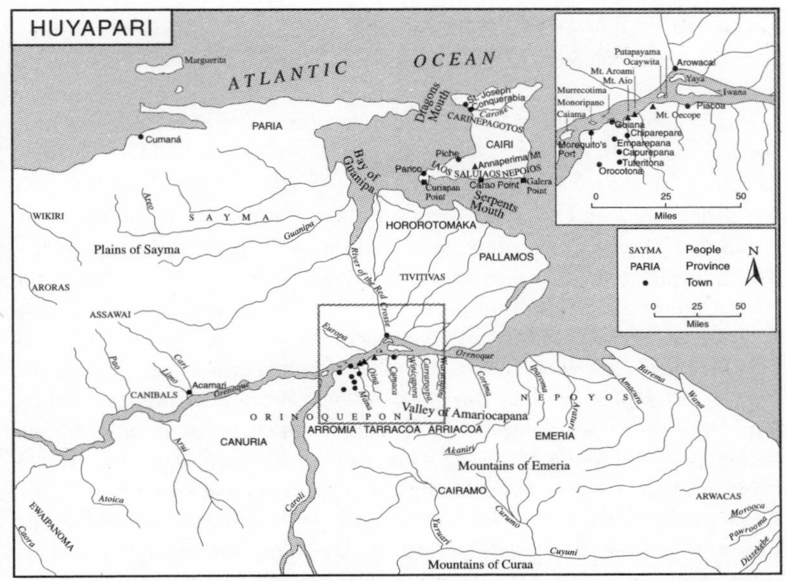

Map I *Huyapari: Locations and people mentioned in the* Discoverie

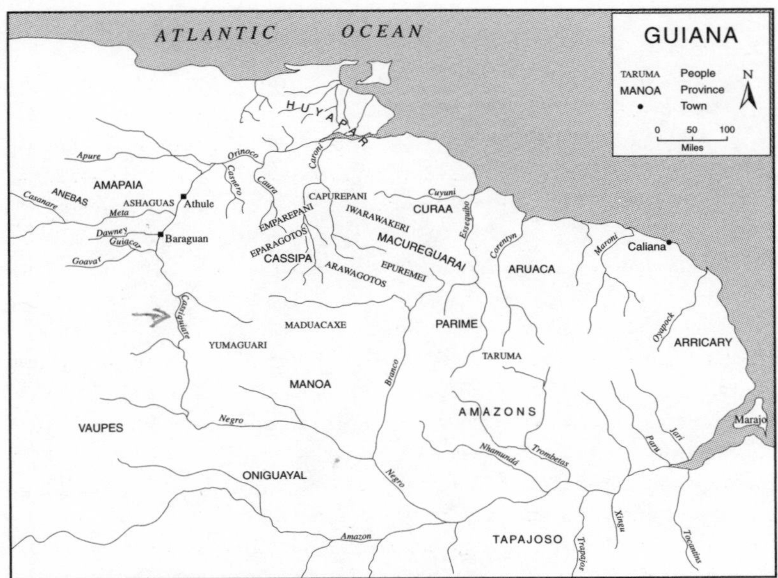

Map II *Guiana: Native polities according to the* Discoverie

nental distribution of this ethnonym and so makes possible a better interpretation of *caribe* and *aruaca* ethnogenesis. Moreover, without this specific instance, it would be difficult, in the absence of other evidence, to connect the '*cassipuna*' of Orinoco, with a different occurrence of the ethnonym in the account of the voyage of Jean Mocquet to the Oyapock. Here Mocquet designates all the inhabitants of the coast as '*Caripou*' when all other sources (reviewed above) indicate only *caribes*, Palikur and Yao. It might then be inferred that Mocquet's use of the term 'caripou' was a garbled attempt to render 'Palicour' since the substitution of 'p' for 'b' and 'r' for 'l' is common in the European transcription of native American languages. However, thanks to Ralegh's inclusion of the term for quite other reasons we are able to say that Mocquet's '*Caripou*' are the Yao of the English sources (see above). But even more important than this positive identification of historical native populations is the revelation as to the broader usage of the term '*cassipuna*' that is contained in the *Discoverie*. This suggests that there were different levels of auto-denomination with 'cassipuna' referring to a wider ethnic, linguistic and cultural base than the more specific and politically charged terms, such as Yao, *caribe*, *aruaca* and so forth. This insight vastly improves our ability to analyse the historical emergence of successive identities and so the dynamism of native political structures through the colonial period.

V *How ten Spaniards fell at the hands of the Indians and their treasure was taken*

These native political structures in turn reflected the unfolding of colonialism in the region and, as has already been suggested, Ralegh's text refers to a moment of particularly rapid development – the transition from the ancient élite rulerships to new forms of political and military association – represented by *caribes* and *aruacas*. In fact the *Discoverie* is quite notable for its almost complete absence of reference to *caribes* and *aruacas*, especially since the lower Orinoco and Guiana coast was the historic site of the emergence of this powerful native political phenomenon. One might take this to be evidence of the limitations of ethnographic coverage in the *Discoverie* but it actually reflects the highly time-dependent nature of ethnographic observation, as Ralegh was to find out on his return in 1618. This is not to say there are no such references but the political centrality of the *caribes* and *aruacas* is not at all evident yet, as Topiawari and Carapana try to cling desperately to the old forms of leadership and power, hoping no doubt that Ralegh will ensure their political continuance if not the rout of the Spaniards.

The particular moment at which Ralegh's text captures native society and polity does not tell us then of certain important developments, but it does tells us what preceded those developments. Many other accounts tend to project these burgeoning native identities on to the sixteenth-century material, much as Columbus used the distinction *caribe-guatiao* to simplify his own and subsequent Spanish ethnologies. Of course these ideological frameworks were themselves influential in bringing about those changes in native society which they claimed to already be describing. However, Ralegh, by dint of his access to Spanish intelligence on the lower Orinoco, was necessarily directed to the extant leaderships with which the Spanish had been struggling since the 1530s. The tendency of Spanish accounts to elide and simplify native distinctions, as in the prescriptive use of the categories *caribe* and *aruaca*, meant that such accounts have not left us with the detailed information that Ralegh's drive to narrativity in the *Discoverie* requires (see above). In consequence, Ralegh emerges as our most intricate source for understanding the lower Orinoco, notwithstanding the fact that he may have culled much from Spanish informants and published or captured texts. Without the *Discoverie* it would be difficult, perhaps impossible, to reconstruct the polities of Carapana, Morequito/Topiawari and their connections to Trinidad. Similarly, modern ethnography has been aware of the ancient nature of the Warao occupation of the delta and coastlands, but has been unaware of the kinds of political divisions that both Ralegh and Dudley refer to. Such information might be recoverable from Spanish records but it would require a major archival project to know whether this was so or not – if nothing else Ralegh then suggests why such an effort could be productive and what sort of research strategies should be followed.

Precisely because Ralegh's ethnology looks back into the sixteenth century it has an imaginary and fabulous appearance to commentators whose own historical ethnology is formulated via materials of the seventeenth century onwards. This, unfortunately, therefore applies to most anthropologists, especially the archaeologists, who have studied the Caribbean and Amazonia.[1] This comes across most clearly in the matter of *El Dorado* and native gold working, which is why these topics are subject to extended treatment below. But because of this kind of issue in the interpretation of the *Discoverie* other kinds of evidence for the complexity and scale of native polity on Orinoco have been dismissed out of hand. Ralegh's diplomacy to the 'king' of Arromaia, Topiawari (see Plate III), his construction of the event as a courtly encounter and the delineation of the 'lords' and 'captains' that are subject to such as Carapana, all build the feeling of being in the presence of persons of significance and developed polity. More cynically it might be said that this presentation is no more than an attempt to dress up as 'imperial discovery' what was in fact no more than a touristic sojourn of some thirty days among the petty tribal chiefs of Orinoco, enlivened by tales of monstrosity and marvel, and made credible by the lucky happenstance of Berrio's capture and the plagiarism of his sources. This interpretation would work for those unconcerned with the indigenous population except for the fact that, even if derivative, those sources, as well as others, are consistent in their description of native social scale and political complexity.

Another way to view this issue is to notice the mimesis in political forms implied in the analogy between 'capitaynes' and 'cassiques'. Ralegh [6] suggests that native usage had changed under European influence such that the term 'capitayne' had become the more common. Native practice then makes licit the inference that the equivalence was perceived only in performance of that role, not in a theoretical and historical understanding of naval leadership in Europe. The latter inference would pertain to a situation where the term 'capitayne' is given by the Europeans to those whom native practice designates as 'cacique'. Indeed, Ralegh even seems to implicitly acknowledge this since he uses the term 'captaine' to refer to the rank of his officers, such as Preston, Calfeild and Gifford, reserving 'capitayne' as descriptive of native leaders; although his usage is not consistent enough to make this a certain distinction. None the less, if we understand the captaincy of Ralegh and others as a 'feudalism of the sea' (Ojer 1966), then the analogy is apt in making accessible to us the feudal dynamics of native leadership as well. Ralegh [4] thus defines 'cacique' as a 'lord of people' with implicit contrast to ownership of a resource as property (things) or vassals (slaves).

This returns us to a consideration of Ralegh's phrase '*Ezrabeta Cassipuna Aquerewana*' – for the element 'aquerewana' or 'acarewana' [6] has yet to be analysed. It was not an equivalent for 'cacique' but implied another level of hierarchy and so was entirely appropriate for a queen or princess, though again, as in the case of 'capitayne' it must be seen as a limited analogy from native practice since royal ritual and history was quite different. However, the force of the analogy is such as to reveal to us the existence of paramount chieftaincy, an important theoretical category for political anthropology. Moreover Ralegh himself, as has been pointed out above, even toyed with the idea of becoming an *acarewana* on his final return in 1617 (Chapter 1, n. 28).

However, the colonial cultural and social conquest of indigenous people destroyed the basis for the *acarewana*, since their large polities were easy targets for successive invasion. Rather colonial conditions of trade and warfare engendered, even as Ralegh's observation confirms, a mimetic elaboration of the role of 'capitayne' – for it was this political form of leadership that was key to the development of the *caribes* and *aruacas*. Colonial authorities right across the region thus promoted their favoured trading partners and allies in war on an individual basis, which over time crystallised out these oppositional identities, even as the same process of colonial conflict engendered the idea of the 'nation-state' in Europe.

A close reading of Ralegh's account, in addition to a survey of the toponymic evidence available in other sources, suggests that the basic political and spatial entities of lower Orinoco were constituted in a hierarchical fashion with, at the base, a group of villages sharing a section of river being called a 'countrey' by Ralegh, and being indicated by the linguistic element 'cai' in the native terms he records. A number of such 'countreys' went to form a 'province'. These political units are also directly indicated in Spanish sources via the name of their principal *cacique*, which is why Topiawari, for example, is sometimes referred to as 'Morequite' in Spanish sources.[2] Finally, at the highest level there was a maximal 'lordship' (*acarewana*) which comprised a number of such river systems, as in Topiawari's dominance of the Orinoco south bank as 'King of Arromaia', or Carapana's 'Kingdom of Emeria'. Thus political authority was held at all levels by hereditary chieftains belonging to Topiawari's immediate family (i.e. son or nephews) and so may be considered a truly dynastic form of political organisation. The accuracy of Ralegh's description of native political hierarchy is demonstrated by the fact that the Spanish explicitly followed such rules of succession when attempting to usurp Topiawari's accession as *acarewana* of the Orinoqueponi, by promoting the candidacy of Topiawari's nephew, Eparacano, having first baptised him as *Don Juan*. They also, according to what Topiawari told Ralegh [76], 'apparelled and armed' Eparacano's son and baptised him as *Don Pedro*, 'by whome they seeke to make a partie against mee, in mine owne countrey', to which end Don Pedro married 'one Louiana of a strong familie, which are my borderers and neighbours'.

Similar political structures were also directly instituted by the Yao settled at the Oyapock mouth in the early seventeenth century, as was outlined in the discussion of Leonard Ragapo's 'Signiory' of Cooshebery. Besides Leonard Ragapo the Yao *acarewana*, Anacajoury, had four other 'signiories' in the region between the Amazon and Oyapock. Since these political arrangements were quite consciously created as part of an act of indigenous colonialism this is perhaps our clearest demonstration of a sophisticated native capacity for political organisation of some complexity and scale. It is also possible to sense the strongly mimetic element that was present in the political performances of *Capitayne* and *Cacique*, as such individuals were variously, but in a similar structural manner, displaced from their familiar arenas of political action. In this way both indigenous and colonial leaders were faced with analogous problems of sustaining their authority over their fellows in the face of the unknown and unpredictable conditions of contact and for this reason we can observe the emergence of symbiotic and mimetic social forms (Whitehead 1992, 1996a).

The search for meaningful analogy between native political proclivity and colonial ambition is also expressed in the *Discoverie* through the idea of an invasion of upland Guiana by the remnants of the Incan royal house. Ralegh [100] suggests that Berrio had confessed to him that, when the Spanish seized the major 'temples' in Peru, a series of prophecies were uncovered that included the promise that 'from *Inglatierra* those *Ingas* should be againe in time to come restored, and delivered from the servitude of the said Conquerors'. Of course Ralegh is not unusual in searching for a justification for colonial occupation that proceeds from some supposed desire of the colonised themselves (see Chapter 1 (iv)).

In both Mexico and Peru there were various suggestions by the Spanish, as well as their native allies, that Cortéz or Pizarro were returning gods.[3] The *Viracoa* of Peruvian myth-cycles, an ancestral creator, bearded and white, left the Andes towards the east promising to return, and so provided an opportunity for the identification of Spanish colonialism with the fulfilment of that prophecy. Along the Orinoco the culture-hero *Amalivaca* likewise disappears to the east, promising to return at the end of time. He was often noted by the missionaries as an apparent native prefiguring of the coming of Christian religion. In Amazonia and coastal Brazil native Tupi prophets, who led messianic migrations in search of *Guayupia* ('The-Land-Without-Evil'), were known as the *Carai* (Clastres 1995). This term is used to this day to describe 'whites', but in its original application would have referred to the extraneous origins, religious proclivities and 'shining whiteness' (skin and/or armour) of the Europeans.[4] In Orinoco Ralegh's call to fight the Spanish, in the context of increasing Dutch, French and English activity in the region, produced a similar prophetic vision. As mentioned before, in 1597 a Dutch reconnaissance of Orinoco gleaned the remarkable information that a native leader had 'spoken with the spirit *Wattopa*' and thereby prophesied the liberation of the native population by the English and Dutch. Of course the recording of this prophecy was utterly self-serving in the matter of the colonial project, and the British Government in the nineteenth century did not fail to massage even this early account in order to enhance its later claims to influence amongst the people of Orinoco.[5] None the less, traditions of prophetic political leadership are deeply ingrained in native practice and this will be relevant to the interpretation of Topiawari's reported interview with Ralegh, where the scale and complexity of native polity are laid out.

According to Ralegh's report, Topiawari told him of a fundamental division in the societies of Guiana. From the Orinoco south as far as *Wacarima*, that is the beginning of the upland sierras (*La Gran Sabana* in Venezuela, *Rupununi* in Guyana), the people were all of the same 'cast and appellation'. This accords with the distribution of peoples sharing Cariban language which is mutually intelligible amongst many of its modern variants (Pemon, Kapon, Karinya, Macuxi). Schomburgk (1848: 75) thought that *Wacarima* was a direct reference to the Pakaraima mountains and that *Amariocapana* was 'inhabited by the Epuremei', but this is inconsistent on the part of Schomburgk since Ralegh says [62] that they were 'in sight' from Orinoco, and the map to accompany Schomburgk's edition of the *Discoverie* clearly marks *Amariocapana* as on the northern flanks of the Sierra Imataca. But Ralegh is also inconsistent as we are told later [84-5] that *Wacarima* is the name of the 'mountaine of Christall', first mentioned earlier [69] when the Orinoqueponi agree to take Ralegh there. According to Ralegh [85] Berrio confirmed the mineral richness of this mountain but was unable to approach it because of the Orinoqueponi's hostility. This confusion suggests either that Ralegh simply misunderstood the referent for Topiawari's name or that Topiawari was referring to the Sierra Imataca with the term *Wacarima*, which Schomburgk then illicitly assimilated to the modern usage. However, while there is reason to be sceptical of Ralegh's understanding of Topiawari, that the term *Wacarima* might function as a toponym for both a basket-shaped mountain (see fn. 87) and as the name for a region of mountains displaying such characteristics is undoubtedly a fertile source for the misapprehension of Ralegh and inconsistency of Schomburgk. In either case the issue of the geographical scale and reference in Topiawari's reported description is critical for assessing the accuracy of

Ralegh's understanding of Topiawari, and Schomburgk's ambiguousness at this point may well be related to an unspoken scepticism of Ralegh on this issue. However, the continent-wide nature of native political geographies is amply demonstrated by both European report and native oral tradition (Vidal 1993, Whitehead 1997 – see also fn. 49 and section (iv) below) and so we can be confident of Topiawari's ability to relate events and locations that were deep into the interior. In which case it is this latter context, until now underappreciated, that should be considered as the context for Topiawari's allusions, if not for Ralegh's interpretations of those allusions. Accordingly the valley of *Amariocapana* would refer to the Yuruari–Cuyuni river basins, in which case the first 'civill towne' of the Empire called *Macureguarai* would be situated in the Mazaruni river basin, which also accords with the other internal evidence of the *Discoverie* (see below).

Topiawari, at the time of his meeting with Ralegh [61], was supposedly 110 years old,[6] so that his own recall of the invasion into Guiana places the event at the beginning of the fifteenth century. The flight of the Manco-Inca, brother of the reigning Inca, Atahualpa, did not occur until the spring of 1532 so accepting Ralegh's report of Topiawari's recall would seem at best uncertain. In any case modern research has definitively established the direction of Manco-Inca's escape as south of the Amazon, to the region of the fortress city of Vilcabamba. Moreover, Manco-Inca was to the south of the Amazon at the time of his flight, making a north-easterly route of escape very unlikely. [7]

So if the identification of the *Epuremei* with the royal Incan house can be dismissed as Ralegh's misunderstanding or misrepresentation of Topiawari's discourse, to what else might Topiawari have been referring? Goeje (1939) was the first to suggest that what Ralegh took to be references to the invasion of Incan *orejones*, led by a remnant élite, the *Epuremei*, were in fact poetic allusions on the part of Topiawari to the *oriyu* and *pululima*, the spirits of water and rain in the Arawakan and Cariban language-families respectively. This suggestion certainly accords with the practice of anthropology to be alert to native tropes and metaphors that lie behind apparently culturally transparent propositions and, certainly, colonial history is replete with examples of such misconstruals.[8] In this case, however, such an interpretation is complicated by the way in which Ralegh works the master-trope of Incan invasion and makes it appear that Topiawari was speaking in more than one language at the same time. Significantly then there is reference to the *Epuremei* in other sources, both Spanish and English, but not to the *Orejones*. This suggests that this latter element is evidence of Ralegh's wish to derive ethnographically an Incan connection from the discourse of Topiawari, perhaps to conceal his Spanish sources (see Chapter 1 (iv)).

Nevertheless, Topiawari may yet have been accurately telling of a fundamental change in the upland polities in the period since Spanish contact. Recent work by Vidal (1993) on the sacred histories of the Bare, an Arawakan people of the upper Río Negro region in western Amazonia, startlingly amplifies inferences already made from the colonial material (Whitehead 1989: maps a and b, 1993, 1994). Vidal records that the *Epuremei* appear in Bare history as the *Maduacaxes*, part of a once extensive Arawakan macro-polity. As indicated on Map II, the political intrusion of the *Epuremei* from the south, and their construction of a major settlement or province in the Orinoco basin, *Macureguarai*, is a key context for understanding Ralegh's reportage of Topiawari's analysis. Indeed the very name *Macureguarai* seems highly apposite for the military outpost which was the source of Topiawari's suffering, since it may be glossed in the Bare language as *Maculewawa* (Scorpion). Moreover, in so far as the effects of colonial contacts far outrun in time and space the face-to-face encounter of coloniser and colonised we should remember that the advent of European activity in the Amazon valley from the 1540s onwards could also have played into these emergent conflicts among native polities. The oral history of modern groups living in the Pakaraima mountains, the archaeological pattern of military sites and the contrasting cultural ecology of groups living in the upland savannas to those of the forest and low valleys, also indicate that these regions dividing the drainage basins of Amazon and Orinoco form a 'natural' frontier (Whitehead 1996d). A socio-economic orientation to either the Amazon or Orinoco would then carry political implications for an involvement in various networks of trade, marriage, and alliance in war, as would the broad cultural-linguistic contrasts between Arawakans and Caribans that this frontier also partly descries.

So there are excellent reasons to think that much of the reportage Ralegh supplies directly reflects the complexity and sophistication of native Guiana polities at the end of the sixteenth century, including their production of gold work and its distribution across the western Amazon–Orinoco river basins. Even the legendary 'city' of *Manoa* and the lake *Parime* on which it stood may be located as cultural, if not physical, phenomena once Ralegh's descriptions have been contextualised in respect of both native praxis and the history of the European myth-cycle of *El Dorado*. Such contextualisation necessarily takes us beyond the immediate limits of Ralegh's text by requiring a broad discussion of the nature of past socio-cultural praxis in northern South America. It is worth emphasising now, however, that Ralegh's Incan framework to explain the existence of a large, rich and beautiful empire in the highlands foreshadows the early archaeological interpretation of complexity in Amazonia by deriving the source of this complexity from outside the region itself (see Whitehead 1996b). It was this early paradigm in Amazonian anthropology that led to an almost complete disregard for the documentary record, precisely because texts such as Ralegh's were uninterpretable to those with an ethnology derived from the post-1600 era.

(ii) Golden metals

As was remarked in Chapter 1 (iii), it is plausible to claim that anthropology is hopelessly contaminated by its colonial origins, continually conceptualising others according to a set of categories originally generated by the exigencies of colonial conquest. In consequence the discipline of anthropology is seen as wedded to an exotic presentation of others – for without such culturally unfamiliar behaviours and institutions why would we need anthropology to explain them? Ralegh's Incan version of the *El Dorado* legend seemed to anthropology's critics a perfect example of this process, and one which neatly accorded anyway with a professional lack of interest on the part of anthropologists in textual materials. 'Fieldwork' was the redemptive totem of anthropology's intellectual transgressions as a handmaiden to colonialism. However, the contextualisation of Ralegh's descriptions with native practice undertaken here uses a very different kind of hermeneutic, which stresses similarity over difference, symbiosis over isolation, and coevalness over cultural time, as was suggested above. This is because the standard approaches of culture theory are inadequate for understanding of convergent, mimetic, and negotiated meanings which emerge in the course of colonial encounters (see Whitehead 1996a), and, as we have partly seen, are strongly present in Ralegh's text. If mimesis is simultaneously present and logically connected to the production of difference in the colonial process, this would contradict the anthropological presumption of some theorists and commentators (e.g. Greenblatt 1991, Mason 1990, Pagden 1993, Sahlins 1995, Todorov 1982) who seem to stress only the alterity and the incommensurability of cultural forms. We may wonder then if subtle rhetorics of identity, revealed in mimetic borrowing from native forms, are not themselves as much a product of encounter as the production of difference. If so, then this facet of colonialism is at least as important as the rather obvious analytical discovery of 'marvellous monstrosity'. As is evident from the *Discoverie*, colonial interaction engenders a process of *mimetic elaboration*, and so the putative 'discovery' of *El Dorado* and his Guianan 'Empyre' becomes an opportunity for the cultural elaboration of various ideological motifs, by both indigenes and colonials alike.

The negative case confirms this since the relative importance of *Sciopodi* and *Acephali* in the European writing on the New World is directly connected to the relative importance of those icons in native thought. The dog-headed people, centaurs, and minotaurs do not appear with the same frequency as other monstrous/marvellous motifs in the colonial records because they were not part of the native repertoire. In any case various monstrosities were already present in native ethnologies prior to European contacts, and so cannot be dealt with as an aspect of European ideological projection, or indigenous acculturation to these projections. This holds true even if any given text cannot be relied upon historiographically or ethnographically, since, as already mentioned, the evidence is also archaeological.

Golden metals and colonial desire

The legend or myth of *El Dorado* refers to a diversity of native cultural practices that are related only by virtue of being grouped together by European compilation, and there is no reason to think that such practices were uniform for native people themselves. Nor should it be forgotten that, whatever the apparent absurdities of European accounts of *El Dorado*, an ancient tradition of gold working in northern South America is amply attested to in both the archaeological and the historical record. Specifically that record tells of both the production of native gold work, with all the attendant metallurgical knowledge that this implies, and the diverse symbolic and ritual uses to which such golden metals were put. Given the vast metallic wealth extracted by the Europeans from both Central and South America, it is not surprising that the notion of *El Dorado* should have seemed most credible at the time. For, although the *El Dorado* motif was not prefigured in European ethnologies in the specific way that both 'Cannibals' and 'Amazons' were, it is none the less the case that there existed a general expectation, partly deriving from the encounter with Africa, that gold was especially engendered as a geophysical property of the 'torrid zone', or equatorial latitudes. In Ralegh's case his personal interests in, and connections with, alchemists and mystics, such as John Dee, suggest that he also may have had further reasons to anticipate and seek out a 'golden king'.

Earlier editions of the *Discoverie* have tended to focus only on the absurdities and failures of the Spanish quest for the 'Golden One' as have commentators on early European expeditions more generally, and so it will not be necessary to supply such a review here.[9] Rather, by considering native ritual and symbolic uses for golden metals, not only the 'rationality' of the European mystic quest but more particularly the credibility of the reportage in the *Discoverie* can be better assessed. For this reason a clear distinction must be made between colonial and native understandings of *El Dorado*.

The European *El Dorado* myth refers to the existence of a 'Golden One' –

that is a 'king' or 'high chief' – who once a year was anointed by the sprinkling of gold dust on to his body. He was then paddled to the centre of a vast lake where he would deposit votive offerings of gold work. A further subsidiary element in this tale concerns the names of this lake – variously given as *Paytiti, Parime* or *Rupununi* – and the great and golden city which stood on its edge, called *Manoa*. This city was held to lie in an upland area, perhaps recalling locations such as Tenotchticlan and Cuzco, and so it was that in the high sierras of the upper Amazon, Colombia, Venezuela, Guyana and Surinam the *El Dorado* legend came successively to rest. In trying to uncover the extent to which such reports may have also reflected actual cultural practices, it is therefore important to remember that these variations in the European legends relate as much to the expansion of cultural and geographical knowledge in the sixteenth century as they do to any inherent inconsistency and prejudice in European discourse about the native population. There were plausible reasons for seeking *El Dorado* in these three regions, and these reasons remain valid whatever the cultural rapacity and geographical ignorance of the early expeditionaries who acted on them.

For example, in the case of Colombia where the native tradition of gold working is well attested to from the archaeological record, the European myth of *El Dorado* accurately reflected elements of past cultural practices of the Muisca who lived in the highland region. Just outside of Bogotá lies Guatavita, a deep freshwater lake, formed by the impact crater of a meteor. Repeated dredging operations, beginning in the last century, have been carried out at this site and, *tunjos* (golden votive objects) have been recovered from the lake bottom. More significantly a *tunjo* recovered from Lake Siecha, also in the Muisca region, depicts *El Dorado* himself, aboard the raft and surrounded by his retinue, paddled annually to the center of a lake, there to cast in the *tunjos*, as an offering to divinity. No city has been discovered on the shores of the lake, but the proto-urban scale of the culture of Muisca people, at the heart of whose territories Lake Guatavita and Lake Siecha are situated, is strongly attested to by the historical record (Ramos-Perez 1973, Langebaek 1987, 1990).

So here the *El Dorado* myth as the Europeans presented it is precisely confirmed by native practice, but it is also significant that this only led to the belief that there would be yet more *El Dorados* to be encountered – especially as the Muisca store of gold work was quickly plundered by the Spanish. This unwillingness to abandon the idea of an *El Dorado* shows the irreducibly mythic aspect of the tale in the service of the ideology of colonial expansion. Early encounter with the Muisca, and the other Colombian gold working cultures, could not completely satisfy all the elements or promise of the *El Dorado* myth, and so only encouraged the search for another location.

Accordingly *Manoa*, the supposed 'golden city' on the shores of a great lake, was transposed to the upper Amazon during the 1530-40s and latterly to the Guiana highlands, during the 1580-90s; these transpositions closely match the chronology of the expansion of European geographical understanding and colonial ambition. As a result, Gonzalo Pizarro, conquistador of Peru, wrote to the Spanish King in 1542 that, following assurances from native leaders as to the wealth of this region, he had led an expedition to *La Canela*, or the Land of Cinnamon, and the region around the lake of *El Dorado*, an area known today as the Río Napo, in the upper Amazon. Although Pizarro did not ultimately locate this source of native gold work during his incursion, one of his captains, whom he sent to reconnoitre further downstream, Francisco de Orellana, found it impossible to return upriver to the main party and so became the first Spaniard to descend the full length of the Amazon river. It was following Orellana's encounters on the lower Amazon, which will be discussed below, that the myth of the American Amazons originated – a conjuncture of historical circumstance which also brightly illumines the interplay of myth and reality for the Europeans.

Despite Pizarro's failures in the Land of Cinnamon, the mythic apparatus of the Amazonian *El Dorado* continued to grow. The lake on which he resided was now said to be called *Paytiti* and various locations, subject to the annual flooding of the Amazon river, were investigated. Native gold work was also persistently encountered but the identification of a single source repeatedly frustrated. This was undoubtedly partly due to the fact that the key elements of the *El Dorado* myth had been transposed by the Europeans from the Colombian context, and that gold sources in north-eastern Amazonia are rarely to be found in geological contexts like those in Colombia, but rather are alluvial and dispersed in character. However, the annual formation of 'lakes', due to the flooding of the Amazon river, as well as the cultural pattern of the working and wearing of gold as élite activities, meant that any one of the chiefdoms of the Amazon basin could have provided an empirical context for European readings of the *El Dorado* legend.

The final, and still controversial, location for *El Dorado* was in the uplands of Guiana and, while we may rule out the possibility of uncovering an urban-scale settlement in this region, its significance as major intra-continental trading crossroads should alert us to the past ritual and political significance of upland peoples. Obviously such a location for the *El Dorado* legend seems unlikely given an absence of direct archaeological confirmation, but the importance of the flooded savannas of Rupununi in facilitating and inviting communication across the Orinoco and Amazon watersheds, principally via the Río Branco and Essequibo or Río Negro and Casiquiare, certainly validates the emphasis given to the upland region in

Ralegh's understanding of native politics. As mentioned above, recent work by Vidal (1993) on Bare oral history has illustrated how the Guiana region was politically and ritually integrated through the encoding of key trade routes and ritual sites in the mythologies of Bare culture heroes, and we may expect that native tales both of the *Aikeam-Benano* (Amazons) and of élite display of gold (*El Dorado*) relate to this past integration in a similar way. Moreover, the connection of the Guiana region with the production of gold work can now be better understood in material terms also since, in 1990, a sample of such gold work was recovered from precisely the area that Ralegh [19, 30, 63, 75, 91] records as the site of the 'first civill towne' of the *Epuremei*, the Mazaruni river.

None the less, recent cultural-ecological perspectives in anthropology have held this region to be generally poor or marginal to human settlement in South America with a corresponding scepticism as to the potential of this region for producing complex societies. Accordingly what traces there were of such complexity were thought to derive from the Andean and/or Colombian regions, just as Ralegh's Incan theory represents an early example of this intellectual trend to deny autonomous socio-cultural complexity in Guiana. The Guiana area is relatively little studied anthropologically: this is not just due to the finite resources that are available but also, as mentioned previously (n. 1), due to the negative evaluation of the potential of this region for significant cultural development. Consequently the intellectual projection of an ethnographic record, itself historically constituted from the categories of seventeenth- and eighteenth-century ethnologies that actually reflected the decimation which colonial occupation had wreaked on native societies, back into the pre-European and early contact periods has seemed to justify the derivation of any advanced archaeological and cultural features in Amazonian societies from outside the region altogether. In turn this has produced a deep, but unwarranted, scepticism of the historical record, in which the problematic aspects of such texts of the *Discoverie* are held up as exemplars of the general unreliability of colonial documentary evidence. However, with the benefit of modern archaeological techniques and a critical use of the written records, as in this edition of the *Discoverie,* important features of ancient Amazonian society are at last beginning to emerge.

Just as a proper anthropological understanding of this region has only now begun to develop, so too Guiana was the last place that *El Dorado* was pursued. This final pursuit began in the 1580-90s and really ended only in the eighteenth century as Europeans finally traversed the upland savannas that connect the Amazon and Orinoco river basins. Moreover, as this was the geographical context for the final version of the *El Dorado* myth it has also often been taken to stand for all other versions, with the result that the failure to extract significant native gold work from this region was thought to invalidate the *El Dorado* myth-cycle as a whole – notwithstanding the extensive plunder of gold in Colombia and the upper Amazon. This persistent ideological desire for an *El Dorado* reveals the functions it served for the Europeans: that is, it acted as a constant stimulus to further colonial conquest and occupation of the continent – just as was the case for Orellana's descent of the Amazon – in a way that abstract appeals for 'exploration' or 'discovery' could never have been. In turn such an ideological motif could become a constant stimulus to high political ambition as much as for low greed, since the political significance of the power of 'Indian Golde' in Europe was explicitly alluded to in contemporary debate, and by Ralegh [*To the Reader* 3 verso] with regard to Charles V, King of Spain. However, to show the role that European ideas of an *El Dorado* had in facilitating colonial conquest is not to answer the question – was there ever an *El Dorado* in the Guiana highlands?

Golden metals in native practice

The interpretative tradition in history, anthropology and geography to date has been to see the *Discoverie* as no more than a spurious reworking of the *El Dorado* legend or an 'exuberant flight of fancy' (Hemming 1978: 166). None the less, both Robert Schomburgk (1848: lxii–lxiv) and Paul Rivet (1923) were notable early exceptions to this consensus, as are Warwick Bray (1972) and Adam Nagy (1982) more recently. As Bray (1972: 25) rightly notes in relation to Walter Ralegh's extensive reports on native metallurgy, deriving from his reconnaissances of the lower Orinoco and Guiana coast in 1595, 'it comes as an anticlimax to learn that no pre-European metal objects of any kind have been preserved from Guyana or the eastern parts of Venezuela'. The discovery of just such an object would therefore clearly require a profound re-examination, not just of Ralegh's account in the *Discoverie* but also of the many other historical sources, and ambiguous archaeological finds, that testify to a native metallurgical tradition in Guiana.

In 1990 gold-miners brought a golden chest-pendant[10] in the form of a two-headed 'eagle' which they had dredged from the mid-Mazaruni river bottom, to the Walter Roth Museum of Anthropology in Georgetown, Guyana. It would thus appear that the persistent testimony of the historical record as to the existence of a native tradition of gold working and usage, in the region of *Macureguarai*, should no longer simply be dismissed as the ideological product of the gold-fevered brains of the *conquistadores* and their English, Dutch and French contemporaries. The more so since the Guyana discovery has been recently paralleled by the find of an example of native

VI *How during winter people lived on trees and large rocks. Their ceremonies for the dead*

gold work from the Antilles (Siegel and Severin 1993). However, there are two key reasons why more extensive archaeological evidence of this tradition is so far absent.

Firstly, there seems a strong likelihood that European trade and plunder had exhausted the native store of gold by the end of the seventeenth century. Some native leaders were perfectly content, notwithstanding the ritual significance of golden objects, to exchange them for the powerful political potentialities inherent in the control of the distribution of European manufactures. In Orinoco both the *acarewana*, Morequito and Carapana, traded their store of gold work to the Spanish in anticipation of political or commercial advantages. Since, as we have seen, these individuals were also political opponents in a protracted struggle for the favour of the Europeans, one may infer that such exchanges were not considered detrimental to the authority of their leadership. Emphasis on this issue is important because of the supposed secrecy that surrounded the location of gold sources – was this part of a native tradition of élite control that preceded the interest of the Europeans, or was it a response to the Europeans' obsessive interest in gold? In the latter case native 'secrecy' cannot be seen as indicative of the actual presence of gold at all, but rather as evidence of native attempts to deal with the violent obsessions of the Europeans. In practice the issue is further complicated by the fact that both motivations are likely to have been present, but until now it was assumed that the latter analysis was sufficient explanation of native practice.

For example, Morequito forbade his people from revealing or trading gold as much because it would (and did) undermine his authority as for reasons of cultural scruple, given its use to adorn sacred caves and the bones of the ancestors (see Berrio in Relaciónes 1964: 237; Ralegh [42]). Moreover, given the ritual and symbolic substitution of native gold by European metals, particularly brass or bronze bells and rattles which mimicked the most desirable features of native forms (smell, brilliance and voice), native production itself may have anyway have fallen into decline, or turned to other less dangerous materials such as silver. In which case it is probable that the native store was quickly exhausted, especially where trade became plunder and ransom. Morequito, according to Ralegh [32], tried to escape execution by the Spanish with the offer of three 'quintals' of gold (approximately 300 to 336 lbs), and his mother's brother and designated successor, Topiawari, survived only through the ransom of '100 plates of gold and diverse spleenstones [*takua*]'.

A second reason for the absence of archaeological finds of native gold in Guiana is suggested by the cultural context of the better-known Colombian examples. The bulk of the native gold work that the Spanish and their modern successors have recovered in the territories of such groups as the Sinu, Tairona and Muisca has been looted from élite burials or sites of votive offerings. Neither of these kinds of site has yet been encountered in the region under discussion. However, Ralegh [92-3] suggests that such sites might yet be found.

Accordingly, it will be the purpose of this section to outline and discuss the content of the *Discoverie* as regards the production of native gold work in the Guiana region, with particular attention to the upper Mazaruni and Caroni rivers, since these are significant within Ralegh's account and in the subsequent commentary on the credibility of Ralegh's claims. This exercise is critically different from the reviews of the *El Dorado* legend in the editions of the *Discoverie* by Harlow and Schomburgk since the information is reviewed in the context of indigenous ritual and symbolic uses of golden metals. By these means it is hoped that the symbolic convergence of native and non-native traditions as to *El Dorado* can be better appreciated and so the general veracity of the accounts in the *Discoverie* be established.

Not surprisingly the first extensive accounts of the existence of native gold work, often simply called *joyas de oro* ('jewels of gold'), come from the Caribbean region during the Spanish occupation of Hispaniola. It is clear from these descriptions that such objects are to be distinguished from the gold alloy (Arawakan *guanin*, Cariban *caracoli*) pieces that originated in Guiana. There is no evidence either that naturally occurring gold-copper alloys are present in the Caribbean islands or that the indigenous population at contact had knowledge of the metallurgical techniques to produce such alloys. For such pieces as were produced in the Greater Antilles the technique of beating relatively pure nuggets of gold (called *caona* or *tuob*) into thin sheets was the prevalent practice.[11] However, the Spaniards often encountered *guanin* objects as well as simple gold-leaf decoration which indicates that, whatever technical limitations there may have been to gold working in the islands, they were more than offset by the close political and economic connections of the islanders with the southern continent.[12] The importance of this relationship was also strongly reflected in the myth and symbolism of the fifteenth-century Antilleans who identified the southern continent with the legendary *isla de Guanin*, the ancestral source of gold alloys.

The source of the relatively well documented Antillean *guanin* was, according to native testimony, to the south east and, indeed, it is to the region to south of the Orinoco and east of the Caroni that the early accounts most consistently refer in their discussions of native gold working in Guiana.

On the basis of Ralegh's [22, 24] testimony it appears that two kinds of manufacture, gold 'plates' and carved nephrite or *takua*, which were usually rendered in the form of frog-shaped pendants, had a key role to play in the long-distance exchanges of élite groups from the Antilles to the Amazon. It is therefore significant that the initial establishment of many of the Spanish colonial enclaves mimicked this native political process through the exchanges made between Spanish and native leaders, matching these gold objects against steel tools and 'European *guanin*' in the form of hawk bells, rattles and buckles made of brass.

Along the Atlantic coast, even into the seventeenth century, golden artefacts were an important medium of exchange in both the surviving native economy and the burgeoning colonial one; suggesting that native willingness to exchange gold work at rates the Europeans perceived as laughably favourable to themselves was less an expression of native commercial naivety and more an indication of alternative economic values, deriving from their contrasting cultural attitudes to metals. In native terms gold alloys were particularly valued for their brilliance and smell – *guanin* objects being sometimes referred to as *taguagua* after the odoriferous Caribbean plant of the same name – rather than their absolute gold content. For the same reasons European alloys, especially brass, were valued as much as, or more than, their native equivalents.

As a medium of exchange within the surviving native economy, Ralegh [43] notes that the ancestral Warao exchanged their carpentry for tobacco out of Trinidad and gold work out of Guiana. Lawrence Keymis (1596: 44), also advised that on the Corentyn river

> Some images of gold, spleen-stones, and others, may be gotten on this coast, but they do somewhat extraordinarily esteem of them, because *everywhere they are current money*. They get their Moons, and other pieces of gold by exchange, taking for each one of their greater Canoas, one piece or image of gold, with three heads, and after that rate for their lesser Canoas, they receive pieces of gold of less value. One hatchet is the ordinary price for a Canoa.[my emphasis]

In the experience of another English traveller, Unton Fisher (Purchas 1906: XVI, 407), Dutch metal tools were considered an even better exchange:

> He showed me before his departure from me a piece of metal fashioned like an Eagle, and as I guess, it was about the weight of eight or nine ounces troy weight, it seemed to be gold or at leastwise two parts gold and one copper, I offered him an axe, which he refused; to which I added four knives, but could not get it of him: but I imagine the Dutch at *Selinama* [Surinam] have bought it of him, for their only coming was for axes, as he said, hearing that the Dutch were at *Selinama*. I demanded where he had that Eagle, his answer was, he had it of his uncle, who dwelt among the *Weearapoyns* [?] in the country called *Sherumerrimary* [Charuma?] near the *Cassipagotos* country [western Pakaraimas] where is great store of these images. Further he said, that at the head of *Selinama* and *Marwin* [Maroni] there were great store of half moons, which he called by the name *Unnaton*.

Moreover, the native store of gold in the sixteenth century was considerable enough to be used to finance the Spanish conquests in Orinoco, as Ralegh [34] tells us was the case for Berrio. Berrio's Campmaster, Domingo de Vera, was certainly successful in this enterprise, winning financial support from both Philip II and the city of Seville. Vera's own testimony as to the nature of native metallurgy also serves to underline the control exercised by members of the native élite, such as Morequito, over the production of *caracoli*, as well as its ritual and symbolic functions. Vera (*Colleción* VI: 562) wrote:

> further inland there is an infinite quantity of gold, and in the mines there nothing is taken out licitly except by the caciques and their wives, and they take it with great superstition, fasting first

> three days;[13] but in the rivers, which carry much, it can be taken out by whoever wishes to, with which tribute is given to the lord or cacique of the grains which are as large as those of maize, or larger.

Overall the early descriptions of the region make it clear that gold work, in the form of pectorals and other bodily adornments, was common on the lower Orinoco. Good illustrations of this are the fact that large quantities were used to ransom eminent individuals seized by the Spanish, and the frequency with which it could be traded for, at least before the Spanish occupation of the region. As Vera indicated, there was a degree of control of the production of gold work by the ruling élite, further strengthened by the political constraints of trading gold with the Europeans. As the Treasurer of Cumaná reported to the Spanish King in 1595 (BL Add. MS 36317, No.30), 'the Indians are very watchful, and always try to conceal and hide it, from the fear and suspicion that they have that the Spaniards may settle there'; a practice also mentioned by both Ralegh [36] and Berrio (*Relaciónes* 1964: 237).

Keymis (1596: 17) explains native political calculation concerning a source on the lower Caroni river in the following manner, and introduces us to the Mazaruni Dragon, *esak* for gold on that river:

> Gilbert, my pilot [. . .] farther told me, that he was with Putijma, at what time Morekito was to be executed by the Spaniards, & that then the chief of Morekito his friends were in consultation, to show this mine unto them, if so they might redeem their Captains life, but upon better advice, supposing them in this case to be implacable, and that this might prove a means to lose not only their king, but their country also: they have to this day concealed it from them, being of all others the richest, and most plentiful. The aged sort, to keep this from common knowledge, have devised a fable of a dangerous Dragon that haunteth this place and devoureth all that come near it. But our Indian, if when we return, we do bring store of strong wine (which they love beyond measure) with it will undertake so to charm this Dragon, that he shall do us no harm.

This latter condition may not have merely been a ruse to induce Keymis to supply alcohol, since Vera also indicated that spirits (*esak*) required propitiation before gold could be removed. Equally, that Keymis chooses to mention the existence of a 'dragon' may have been designed to support further the idea that gold was to be found here, since Ralegh's alchemical circle of supporters would certainly have seen the presence of this dragon as a confirmation of their own mystic quest. In any case, in view of Spanish ruthlessness in the pursuit of gold, the desire to keep secret the sources for gold, while still using finished pieces to trade for European goods, seems plausible enough. Thus Keymis (1596: 23) also reported that the Spanish had killed twenty of the *Cywannas* (Warao clan) 'and burnt their houses, because they refused to trade with them for certain images of gold made with many heads, which they had gotten out of Guiana'.

It is reasonable to suppose, therefore, that the wish to secure a European alliance led to a less guarded attitude as to sources of gold. This was the case for Carapana, who, as we have seen, twisted and turned under pressure of successive English and Spanish overtures for his allegiance. Keymis (1596: 21-3) informs us that an

> old man, follower of Carapana, showed me whence most of their gold cometh, that it is formed in so many & diverse fashions: whence their Spleen-stones [*takua*] and all other sorts are to be had in plenty: where gold is to be gathered in the sands of their rivers: from what parts the Spaniards, both by trade, and otherwise, have returned much gold. This he uttered with Carapana his consent (I doubt not) hoping thereby to induce us to return again. For contrary to their law of secrecy, which in this case they do all generally observe, sharply punishing the breakers thereof, as enemies unto their native country: I found this man no whit scrupulous, but very free and liberal of speech in all things [. . .] I sent a present of Iron to Carapana, and then set sail.

Similarly, Topiawari showed the location of a gold source to Ralegh (BN 18684/18, 1612 – in Lorimer 1982), which he was not exploiting himself since 'if it should be discovered and reach the ears of the Spaniards, he would not get away with less than his life, and thus he did not trust even his own son in this case [. . .] the cacique [acted] with great caution, replacing the clod and turf that they had taken out in such a way that it might not be noticed'.

So the issue of 'secrecy' bears strongly on our interpretations of reported native knowledge of gold sources and the Europeans became, of course, acutely aware of the difficulties of uncovering such 'secret' knowledge.

Once colonies had been established, the Europeans themselves, in a political mimesis of native symbols of power (see above and Chapter 1, n. 20), became suppliers of their versions of both *caracoli* and *takua*. This is also good evidence of the continuing vivacity of these native exchange systems well into colonial times, and, from the evidence of the non-Spanish sources, it would also appear that elements of native metallurgical traditions persisted into the seventeenth and eighteenth centuries. Scott (Bodleian Rawl. 175, f356, c. 1670) informs us that gold, silver and 'emeralds' (*takua*) were still to be had from the sources of the Río Negro in the west, as well as from the northern Amazon tributaries of Curapanema and Genipapo in the east. He relays the account of one Captain Matteson, a Ghentoise, who had also been employed as captain of Pedro Texeira's own vessel in his ascent of the Amazon in 1637. Matteson subsequently led a successful Spanish trade expedition from Santo Tomé to 'fifty leagues from the head of Dessekeebe' (possibly the upper Cuyuni or Mazaruni) in 1655, there trading for gold, 'weapons of silver' and 'emeralds'. After leaving the service of the Spanish, Matteson then joined with Aert Groenewegen, first governor of the Essequibo colony, to make a second foray to the upland region in 1661 but they, and their escort of some four hundred Caribs, were stopped on the Essequibo as a result of a quarrel between the Caribs and 'other Indians they must pass through'.

Writing some hundred years later, the then governor of Essequibo, Storm van's Gravesande (1911: 460-73), noted a continuing disinclination on the part of the native population to allow the whites access to the upper reaches of the Cuyuni and Mazaruni, as well as alluding to the earlier trade in gold dust that was eventually established with the upper Essequibo. The role of the Manoas in so trading gold to the Portuguese and as suppliers for the native economy is an obvious and clear basis for the idea of *Manoa* as the city of *El Dorado*. Gravesande also mentions a native source for copper and notes that they still make their own silver 'collars'. He further writes (1911: 468), echoing Keymis (quoted above) some 150 years earlier, that

> We must have no expectations of getting information concerning any mines from the Indians. The common people themselves know nothing of them, and it is only the Chiefs and Elders, who carefully keep the same secret, and make the other Indians believe that the Jawaho or Devil lives in those places, by which they are frightened from approaching those places.

It would thus seem that, while a knowledge of metallurgical tradition may have persisted among the native élite of Guyana into the eighteenth century, it was largely passive and actively expressed only in the production of silver items, rather than gold ones, given the dangers of displaying the latter in front of the Europeans. Some further force is added to the notion that silver replaced gold in the colonial era by the evidence that silver-like nose, lip and ear plugs continued to be produced, though perhaps not from silver ore, into the nineteenth century. Today silver is preferred over gold, owing to its association with 'spiritual light' and the association of the gold with the yellow jaundice of disease; perhaps due to an earlier association of epidemics with European contacts and the search for gold.

There are distinct sources of gold in Guiana, it being found, as Ralegh [*To the Reader* 2 verso] perfectly correctly points out, 'either in graines separate from the stone (as it is in most of al the rivers in *Guiana*) or else in a kinde of hard stone, which we call the white Sparre'. Given its physical concentration, the latter type of source may have been more suitable for the exercise of élite control, as Vera and Keymis (quoted above) suggest. Although since Topiawari was able to conceal more dispersed alluvial deposits from both the Spanish and his fellow Orinoqueponi, the manner of gold deposit was probably not the only critical factor. Over a number of years the intensity of tropical rains will alter the situation of alluvial deposits, requiring a thorough and continuous knowledge of local topography if these type of deposits are to be consistently exploited. This consideration seems to have been behind the judgment of Dutch merchants that, without the assistance of the indigenous population, or the actual colonisation of an area, 'no riches or profits are to be drawn or gained [. . .] from the mines' (AR Memorial to States General on colonisation of Guiana, 1603, f.3).

The manufacture of the gold 'plates' and 'eagles' was not primarily on the lower Orinoco itself, although, as both Ralegh [22-3, 25, 47] and Keymis (1596: 14, 23) mention, they were widely distributed here and to the west. Ralegh [75] suggests that it was in the uplands of the Caroni, Cuyuni, and Mazaruni at the location called *Macureguarai.* Other sources distinguish between the production and manufacture of *caracoli* in this region and that to the south, in the Branco–Negro area, where Manoa traders were dominant. We are also told, in an account written by a Spanish spy in England (in Lorimer 1982), that gold extraction and refinement, as it was shown to Ralegh in the region of Topiawari's town, did not require alloying techniques, such as in the illustration by de Bry (see Plate IV and section (iv)). Indeed it has already been suggested that this gold working technique was specially inserted by Ralegh into the captured Spanish documents he reproduces (see Chapter 1 (iv)).

A further production centre existed on Trinidad, supplied with ore from the Caroni Mazaruni region. According to Lawrence Keymis (1596: 17) the Mazaruni source was largely alluvial since 'without digging they gather gold in the sand of a final river, named *Macawini*'. The existence of the Caroni mines was noted by the Spanish on Trinidad as early as 1570 (BL Add. MS 36314, 22) following the expeditions of Father Francisco de Ayala in the previous decade (Ojer 1966: 173-6), but it was not until the eighteenth century that they produced a systematic definition of these deposits (AGI Mapas y Planos, Venezuela #89) under the governorship of Carlos Sucre. This exercise directly confirms the location of many of the gold deposits mentioned by Ralegh and his contemporaries, as well as the location of a silver-mine [66] that was evidently also exploited by the natives.[14] One particular site, at mount *Iconuri* [93 *sic/83*] (or *Riconeri* in Purchas 1906: 408) was explicitly shown to Keymis in 1595, by Putijma, 'capitayne' of the town of Orocoa (or Orocotona) in Topiawari's province of Arromaia.

This site seems to have been directly linked to the production of gold work on Trinidad (Keymis 1596: 17), and it is significant to note that this appears to have been primarily due to the presence of a particular skilled individual. From the accounts of Dudley's reconnaissance of Trinidad and the Orinoco in 1594-5 we are given both a general description of the sources of metals and minerals between Trinidad and the Orinoco and an account of attempts to locate this individual. Dudley and his captains were told by the natives of Trinidad of trading sources for '*tacorah*' (*takua*) in the Moruca river, of gold (*calcurey*) in the Orinoco delta region, and gold-copper alloy (*arara*) and silver (*chipperarey*) in the mountains of the Paria peninsula (Dudley 1899: 65, 73). He was also informed of

> a golden mine in a town of this kingdom [Waliame = Guiana] called Orocoa, in the river [. . .] of Owrinoicke, [. . .] that Armago [= Putijma], Captain of the town of Orocoa [. . .], had a mine of gold, *and could refine it*, and would trade with me; for token whereof he sent me 3, or 4, croissants or half moons of gold, weighing a noble a piece or more, and two bracelets of silver. [my emphasis]

Although Dudley actually confuses the name of the captain of Orocoa, Putijma, with the name of the province in which the mine was situated, Arromaia ('Armago'), it is important to note that Putijma could refine the ore (or have it refined). Attempts were also made on Trinidad to locate another native metal worker, named Braio, following the information given by the '7 or 8 of the chief Indians of Trinidad' (Dudley 1899: 44-6).

Overall what appears to emerge from these accounts is that in the region of the lower Orinoco there were a number of possible manufacturing sites, linked to the presence of skilled individuals, like Putijma and Braio, who were 'very expert in the melting of [. . .] ore [. . .] into [. . .] *calcurie*'. They were supplied by specific mines under the control of the local ruling élite, yet serviced a widespread use of golden objects in the north-eastern part of Guiana which were also traded out of this zone, west towards the mid-Orinoco, north to the Antilles and south to the lower Amazon.

The existence of upland sites of manufacture, also indicated by the historical sources reviewed above, could be reflected in the find by Williams (1981: 84) of a pottery vessel at Muri mountain, on the Brazil–Guyana border, that may have functioned as a crucible for melting metals (see n. 11). A further step in giving a native context for Ralegh's information is to suggest that it is the *Taruma* (*Saluma* or *Xurumal / Charuma*), for whom this is an area of long ancestral occupation, are (like the Maduacaxi mentioned above) another key referent for Topiawari's *Epuremei.* They are also referred to as the *Piriamuy* by Berrio (Ramos-Perez 1973: 658) and the *Epeuremei / Yeanderpuremei* after Unton Fisher (in Purchas 1906: 407-8, quoted above), who may actually be more clearly alluding to the Taruma in the name of the country from which he was told gold 'eagles' were said to come – *Sherumerrimary.* Goeje's (1939: 118) suggestion as to the poetic nature of the political information Topiawari relayed to Ralegh may now be better understood. If the *Epuremei* and *orejones* mentioned by Ralegh were figuratively expressed referents to *pululima* and *oriyu* (the spirits of water and rain), then the metaphorical association between water and the *Epuremei* would be symbolically apposite for the supposed controllers of the upland lake or sea of *Parime*, on which the city of *Manoa* was supposed to be located, and whose fish pools and fish stocks are curiously prominent in some accounts. Association of this symbolism with the Taruma is then most appropriate in view of their native image as a people who live in caverns under the water, more like amphibians than people. Other names given to the Taruma include the *tunayana* (water people) or *okoimoyana* (people who formerly slept under the water). European travellers (see Whitehead 1990a) also reported that they reputedly slept under water in pools surrounded by fences and they were the greatest fish-eaters of all, with extensive fish ponds. Study of the petroglyphic repertoire of this region adds further force to this line of interpretation since it has revealed a high concentration of the 'fish-trap' type petroglyph in the ancestral Taruma zone of southern Guyana. These rock carvings were used in the regulation of fish stocks in the riverine pools of the area, to which varying species migrate annually to spawn. As Williams (1985) remarks, 'the variety of fish traps and baiting procedures exhibited in the Kassikaityu assemblage indicates wide knowledge of the habits and haunts of various fish species and their food preferences'. It is just this kind of ecological knowledge, with its wider significance for the native regional economy, in which control of fish stocks and the production of dried fish flour for external trade was of great significance (see Whitehead 1993), that suggests the inference that the managers of such a system, that is the 'water-Indians' (*Epuremei* or *Taruma*), would have appeared as a powerful force to the down-river groups, such as the Orenoqueponi.[15]

The fact that the *Epuremei* were represented to both the Spanish and English as invasive strangers to the northern Pakaraima region, albeit allied to or having conquered groups indigenous to the area, may therefore genuinely reflect a radical change in inter-group relations in upland Guiana in the sixteenth century – possibly provoked by an undocumented migration away from contact with the Europeans in the Amazon–Negro basin, much as was documented for the Yao, Manoa and Wapishiana in the seventeenth and eighteenth centuries (see above and Vidal 1993). Although it is not possible at this point to resolve whether the Maduacaxi or Taruma were exclusive referents in Topiawari's usage of the term '*Epuremei*', it is noteworthy that the Taruma spoke an 'isolated' language, while incorporating Arawakan and Cariban words to some degree amongst western and eastern groups.[16] Thus, in either case, Ralegh's report of Topiawari's discourse on regional politics was not an act of imagination designed to underwrite English invasion ideologically, but rather the attempt to understand indigenous political practice in this light. This is a subtle but important difference since it allows us to appreciate that Ralegh's misrepresentation of this political history, as being linked to that of the Inca, at least partly stemmed from a necessary ignorance of the ethnological context as much as from a likely desire to bolster English colonial ambition. By the same token it is not necessary to posit a mass migration to account for what may have been an event more in line with the penetration of Incan *mindaeles* (itinerant traders) or the Muisca merchants who likewise maintained colonial outposts in the territories with which they traded. In this way one might interpret the tale of Incan invasion as deriving from a situation in which extant trade links were utilised as a prelude to the more permanent occupation of a region by a relatively small group, perhaps a segmentary lineage,[17] who were displaced or whose trade was disrupted by the European conquests to the west in the early sixteenth century.

Although it is not possible to resolve these issues of identification at present, the extensive researches of Edmundson (1906) should also be mentioned since they do suggest another context for the interpretation of the identity of the *Epuremei*, and the sources of the gold work that was coming from the uplands to the Orinoco, as being entirely extraneous to Guiana. Edmundson shows there is reason to believe that there was also an important zone of production to the south-west of Guiana, in the Vaupés, with which the Manoas of the Río Negro are strongly associated as traders in historical times. He also prefers to identify the peoples of the *Apurima* (Ucayali river), such as the Cocama and Shipibo, with the *Epuremei* of Ralegh's account, situating a further source of native gold work in the 'islands of the Omaguas' (*Oniguayal*), between the Solimoes and Japura rivers; as did the famous Jesuit missionary of the Orinoco, José Gumilla, from his own knowledge of the upper Orinoco and its connection to the Amazon basin through the Casiquiare. Once again the Manoas acted as traders of these items along the Amazon and up the Branco, connecting with the Dutch merchants of the Atlantic coast, who deployed *uitleggers* (itinerant traders) to these locations in the early seventeenth century; just as the Inca and Muisca did in other areas, and perhaps even in the Vaupés and Río Negro.[18] These trade routes linking the Amazon, Orinoco, and Atlantic coast are encoded in the sacred and political geographies of the Arawakan Lokono and Bare as the paths of eminent ancestors and mythic heroes, such as *Kuwai, Purunaminali* (Vidal 1993) or *Kororomanna* (Roth 1915).

An argument therefore can be made for the existence of three non-Peruvian areas of gold working and trading in northern South America directly servicing the Guiana native élite, the Negro/Vaupés = *Manoa,* the Japura/Solimoes = *Oniguayal* and Orinoco/Mazaruni = *Parima.* The development of the European *El Dorado* legend also becomes more intelligible, for, in short, all versions are correct. The location of *El Dorado*'s city of *Manoa* on the shores of *Lake Parime* does not move according to the whim of the native informant, bent on deceiving the white man and moving him out of his village, but according to the literal physical standpoint of the interrogator; for example, whether he is in Amazon or Orinoco. Since the searchers for *El Dorado,* as well as latter-day commentators on their efforts, have the *ideé fixe* of a single, urban-scale situation for the production and distribution of the wide range of native artefacts made in gold or silver, there was no possibility that it would be found. This was simply because the native use of gold was widespread and its symbolic significance far broader than the chiefly rituals that were observed from Colombian native custom and projected into the cultures of Amazonia. Indeed, Ralegh [*Epistle Dedicatorie* A3] implicitly tells us as much when he notes that while the Spaniards seek *El Dorado* (a person), the 'naturals' call the source of gold work *Manoa* (a location or group). Thus Ralegh [104] also tells us how one Martines, a Spaniard, gave the name '*El Dorado*' to *Manoa* and so this 'Nuevo Dorado' in Guiana should not be conflated with other '*El Dorados*', such as in Colombia.

Golden metals as signs and symbols

It will be apparent that, whatever the other ritual and symbolic uses of golden objects within native societies may have been, they certainly circulated as items in an élite long-distance trade with other native leaders, and as items for trade or ransom with the Europeans. The use of exotic artefacts, such as *guanin* and *caracoli,* or even polished black-wood carvings, in the development of élite political structures is already well known to the anthropology of the region but the myth-cycles of both the *Amazons* and *El Dorado* are key to the interpretation of the archaeological and historical evidence, especially that concerning the production and exchange of *takua* and *guanin* or *caracoli* as élite activities in the Guiana region. Goeje (1931) has interpreted the symbolic themes of such exchanges by suggesting that the *takua* are representative of the water, nature and woman, and the *caracoli* are representative of the sun, culture and man. This symbolic opposition is also strongly evinced in the gender polarity of the Arawak languages, and most notoriously so for the Antillean *caribes*, or *caraïbe*. Moreover, *caracoli* pectorals and nose-plates were evidently at one time symbols of chiefly authority or élite lineage in a way that the curative greenstones were not; Ralegh [24] also tells us that the *takua* were owned by 'every king or *Casique*' but that they were usually worn by their wives. However, over time, and given the clear dangers of displaying gold, the *takua* became more generally worn as tokens of spiritual power or understanding. So too, native leadership itself became less dynastically based as the old élite genealogical structures were swept away by colonial conquest, and the *takua* rather than *caracoli* became associated with chiefly authority. This association was probably always present in the use of *takua* south of the Amazon, among the Tupian peoples, who called them *murayataka*.

Our understanding of this ritual and symbolic context of the exchange of gold work is deepened by analysis of the native use of gold on the Caribbean islands, especially through the sixteenth-century writings of Father Raymond Pané (1987). His account of native conceptions on the larger islands tells us that in the origin myth of Antillean society *Guahayona*, culture-hero and source of ancestral authority for the native élite, took all the women from the islands to *Matinino* and then travelled on to the island of *Guanin*, 'origin' of metals, i.e. *caona* (pure gold) and *guanin* (gold alloy). In this way a close connection between the ancestors and golden metals is immediately established and was the reason for the noted link between the honorific titles of the élite and the names of metals. Ralegh [43] notes a similar association of chiefly authority and golden metals in the treatment of the skeleton of a *Tivitive* (Warao) chief.

Among the chieftains of Hispaniola we can recognise *Caona-bo* meaning 'he who is like gold', and his wife *Ana-caona*; also *Turei-ga Hobin*, the honorific of the cacique Bohechio, meaning 'king as dazzling and heavenly as guanin'. On Puerto Rico among the names of the native provinces, often treated as equivalent to the personal names of caciques by the Spanish (as noted above) we find *Guaynia*, *Guaynabo*, *Guayama*, and *Guayaney*, all containing the radical for *guanin* and the ancestor *Guahayona*. The 'name' (title) of the *acarewana* of the Yao, *Anacajoury*, reflects both the name of the ancestor who accompanied *Guayahona* to the isle of *guanin*, *Anacacuya*, and the meaning of that name as 'brilliance that guides'. Given the interchangeability of the personal titles and names of leaders with the names of places, there is also a link to toponyms (see Chapter 1, n. 27 and Chapter 2, n. 2). The Arawakan word for gold, *caona*, and the Cariban word in the orthographic version *carocori*, also form linguistic radicals for the place names associated with gold working on Trinidad and in Orinoco recorded by both Dudley and Ralegh; for example, *Carowa*, *Paracow*, *Caroni*, *Caura*, and *Carricurina*. So Ralegh's identification of these places, implying the occurrence of gold, was not suggestive for the reason that we might assume (i.e. there was a connection between naming of place and its geological features), but rather it was suggestive because the toponyms were derived from the native association of political authority with the use of *guanin*.

Despite the scepticism which has generally gone along with the evaluations of the written records, it has to be emphasised that in fact, as well as in mythology, the Europeans were directed by the *caciques* of Cuba and Hispaniola towards the lesser Antilles (*Matinino*) and Guiana (isle of *Guanin*) as the source of gold, also indicating that in this direction lived the *canibales*. In the political ideologies of these island chieftains the first ancestor, *Guayahona*, when he left Hispaniola for *Matinino* and persuaded the women to accompany him, also forced them to abandon their husbands but bring their children, as well as a cargo of the narcotic snuff *digo* with them. They travelled to *Matinino* where they were entranced by the sight of beautiful sea-shells (*cobo*) which, following the example of *Guayahona*'s brother-in-law, they descended into the sea to admire. Here the women were left by *Guayahona* who returned to Hispaniola with the first *guanin* and *cibas* (magic stones, i.e. *takua*). In other versions of this myth-cycle the fate of the children varies – either they are simply abandoned in a ditch at *Matinino* or they become frogs. In this latter version there are strong thematic connections to both the *takua* and the *Amazons* of the continent.

For the islanders the important feature of the myth is that it provides the ideological grounds for taking *Guayahona* to be not only the originator of political authority but also the first to base this authority partly in exchanges with outsiders, the *caribe canibales*. In this light the myth-cycle as a whole may be said to represent the ideological underpinning of an élite trade in which drugs (*digo*), shell money (*cobo*, *quiriquiripa*) and persons (women and children) were exchanged for *guanin* and *takua*, the latter significantly being carved mostly in the form of frogs. In this context *Matinino*, the 'island of women-without-men', represents the site of these exchanges, just as the land of the Amazons is the source for the 'spleen-stones' of Ralegh's account, and the *caribe canibales* emerge as economic or marital, but not gastronomic, consumers of persons. One might also note the further connection of *Matinino* with the Amazon myth-cycle in the manner of origin of the *ciba*, i.e. from female water spirits. The continental *takua* also were said to be made by the 'water-mama', who to this day still supplies the stones for smoothing pottery among native potters.[19]

The Caribbean region was therefore linked by trade and exchange, in both marriage and warfare, to the Orinoco. More distant connections were also present with the Meta, down which Berrio had travelled in his first searches for *El Dorado* [Ralegh 25-6]. At the headwaters of the Meta the Muisca offered gold for *mojas*; that is, young boys who were used as singers and functionaries for ritual events, later being sacrificed at puberty (Langebaek 1990). The Antillean *cacique* Caonoba was, like the *cacique* of the Muisica mines at Dabeiba, called a *canibale*, and, like the Muiscas and *caribes-canibales* of the islands, was a controller of gold sources or finished gold work. We can complete this interpretation by suggesting that the exchange of persons for gold was a common aspect of the élite exchanges that underlay forms of chiefly authority not just in the Caribbean, but also across the whole of northern South America. In this context the suggestion of an invasive and aggressive *Epuremei*, who were 'consuming' the political authority and marriage exchanges of the *Guianians* and Orinoqueponi through their control of worked gold, appear as the *caribes* do in the political discourse of the Antillean élite. Such a framework of native belief and practice also allows us to suggest that Ralegh's description of an Incan invasion, derived from the interview with Topiawari, was embedded in a native cultural trope of cannibalistic conquest and possession which was all but impenetrable to initial observers (see Whitehead 1996a). However, the suggestion here is that Ralegh was not simply projecting the Incan story but also recording elements of native practice in the Guiana region and attaching to it a more 'plausible' and accessible interpretation – that is one that would accord with other known events within native polities. It should not be forgotten that the allusions to the *Epuremei*, in both Spanish and English records, are hardly adequately dealt with just by showing that there was no Incan invasion, or that Ralegh did not completely understand what Topiawari told him.

The evidence reviewed here suggests that golden metals had a critical role to play in the validation of political and social authority, particularly where this involved the exchange of persons, whether by marriage or by some other form of contractual relationship. This need not imply that gold-items were exchanged directly for persons, in the manner of later European slave-trading, but the belief systems that supported the valorisation of golden objects also signalled the appropriateness of persons as items in a wider cycle of exchange. This is very evident from the fact that 'exchanges' were both commercial and military in form, the distinction between trading and raiding being, as ever, a fine one. While there is no evidence to hand that the wearing of golden objects was explicitly reserved for the élite only, ornamentation with golden objects was none the less a symbol of an exalted status and the accumulation of such objects was unlikely to have been achieved by those who were not to the fore in either the external relations of trade and war, or the internal relations of leadership. The various native beliefs that have been conflated into the European myth of *El Dorado* clearly testify to this and, although the ritual parameters that went along with such beliefs are unlikely to have been identical in the Colombian and Guianan contexts, as the Europeans assumed, the likelihood of sustained, if indirect, interaction between the élites of these regions is also amply demonstrated by the antiquity and wide dispersion of culturally related archaeological materials from the lower Orinoco to the western Venezuelan *llanos.* It was these native realities that Ralegh's *Discoverie* of the 'Empyre of Guiana' reflected.

(iii) Amazons, Acephali and Cannibals

If Ralegh transpires to be an imperfect ethnographer of Guianan metallurgical lore and ritual, rather than a mere fabricator of mythic empires of gold, it none the less remains that the *Discoverie* refers to other marvels and wonders of native practice and custom which seem scarcely more credible: men-with-heads-in-their-chests, women-without-men and man-eaters. However, once again, if those elements of European anticipation and projection are carefully delineated then it can be seen that Ralegh records novel elements and additional information derived from observation or interrogation of native people in Orinoco, by himself or others. Moreover, Ralegh engages in the collection of reports of these marvels with a firm scepticism as to their literal existence but a definite appreciation of the importance of establishing the bounds of the possible.

Ralegh [69] says that living 'on that braunch which is called *Caora* are a nation of people, whose heades appeare not aboue their shoulders'. These *Ewaipanoma* were also reported to Ralegh [70] as having 'their eyes in their shoulders, and their mouths in the middle of their breasts, & that a long train of haire groweth backward betwen their shoulders'.

As Schomburgk stressed in his edition of the *Discoverie*, just as Ralegh does in original text, *Acephali* had long been present in European mythic tradition. However, both Ralegh and Schomburgk also stress that an analogous tale was told by the indigenous population, being recorded in subsequent centuries and still being elicited in modern times. For example, the Patamona of the Guyana highlands refer to the *Totopu*, a dwarfish and strangely misshapen race of beings whose original presence in the mountains connects them to a mythic-historical 'first time'. The disappearance of the *Totopu* in this century is understood as judgment on the cultural authenticity

VII *Untitled scene depicting Ralegh's ingress into the Orinoco river*

of the Patamona, with whom they once came to dance and feast (Whitehead 1996d). References to such monstrous, originary beings can readily be found from other times as well, and one of the most striking reports is an eyewitness account of the capture, torture and execution of an *Acephali*, as witnessed by the shipwrecked Dutch sailor Lourens Lourenszoon among the *Arocouros* of the Amapá coast (between the Amazon and Oyapock rivers) in 1623, five years into his captivity. In his deposition before the Directors of the West-Indische Compagnie, made after his rescue in 1625 we are told that Lourens joined a war-party sent against the *Acephali*:

> They [*Arocouros*] came in the afternoon to this country [. . ..] Shortly afterwards Lourens found out that they had told the truth. He saw, at a great distance, more than one hundred of them [*Acephali*] on the beach, busy with fishing [. . .] they found one standing on a pole behind a rock. Approaching him from behind he saw no other way to escape and went in the water. The whole company went after him. They had great difficulty to get him.

> Continuously he moved like a porpoise and was so powerful, that they could hardly catch him. Finally, tired of the long struggle, he was caught. With hands and feet bound, he was thrown into the canoe and carefully taken away [. . .] A great commotion, as never before, started right away when they arrived there [the *Arocouro* village]; each and everyone being afraid of, and wondering about, this monster. He was short of height, thick, corpulent and fat of body. On top, where every human has neck, he has a long lock of black hair. In the middle of his chest, he has a nose. The eyes were a hands-width from each other. The ears close behind the armpit. His small *passagien* [?] could hardly be seen, so everything looked horrible. When they arrived in the evening, they got busy making a forked-gallows. It was planted in the ground and they hung him, his feet at the two branches of the gallows. When they were doing this he ranted, raved and screamed so much it sounded awful. Then they started hitting him, with sticks, on the chest at the place in front of the heart, and against the legs. So he screamed louder and louder. Finally they killed him with great difficulty. When they hit him in the sides, he started bleeding out of his nose and mouth, his tongue hanging outside, so that he passed away. They left him hanging that way [. . .] Lourens had to believe this, which he never could have understood, and will only be believed by a few, unless another one is seen.[20]

These continuing indigenous and colonial expressions of the existence of 'headless men' support the idea that Ralegh's analysis is correct to stress the collective cultural meaning of such ideas, to go beyond a mere positivist discussion of possible referents for a literal existence of such 'monstrous' individuals. As in the case of the *El Dorado* legend, the conflation of many different native expressions under the organising idiom of European expectation produces a false impression of cultural uniformity to native ideas and practice. No one *El Dorado* existed but many, all of which conformed imperfectly with the golden empire of European anticipation. Similarly, a trope of the monstrous, used to express alterity, was already present in native thought before the European arrival, as is shown by the archaeological evidence of *Sciopodi* in ceramic representation. Equally, the 'men-with-heads-in-their-chests' have a number of analogues within native idioms, just as there are a range of monstrosities related to this general idea of acephalism that have been conflated by later commentators. For example, Keymis (1596: 13-14) reports on 'headlesse men, and that their mouthes in their breasts are exceeding wide', called *'Chiparemei'* by the *Charibes* and

'*Ewaipanomas*' by the *Guianians*. But Keymis also sounds a note of caution: 'What I haue heard of a sorte of people more monstrous, I omit to mention, because it is no matter of difficultie to get one of them, and *the report will otherwise appear fabulous*' (1596: 14, my emphasis). In fact Harcourt and others also collected such tales in the region of Oyapock but they subtly introduce a new element that illustrates for us how a variety of native metaphors became constricted by the categories of European expectation. Harcourt (1613: 41) thus mentions '*Charibes* hauing great eares of an extraordinary bignes', quite consistent with Tupian and Incan practices of massively distending the ear cartilage. Likewise the Spanish reports partially reproduced by Ralegh [105-10], though significantly *not* this particular passage, refer to the '*ypurugotá*' speaking people as having 'shoulders so high that they are almost the same height as their heads' (in Ramos-Perez 1973: 659). Ralegh appears to have transposed this information to the Caura river, since he does note just before giving the description of the appearance of the *Ewaipanoma* that 'on that braunch which is called *Caora* are a nation of people, whose heades appeare not above their shoulders' [69]. In just this way the native trope of monstrosity is made to conform to European expectation, generated not just by a knowledge of the Classical canon but also, as in this case, by knowledge of other ethnological information. The account given to Ralegh by Topiawari should therefore be read in this light and so situated in the native politics of the region at the end of the sixteenth century, as follows. The Caura river chieftains, to whom the trope of acephalism is applied, were in latent conflict with Topiawari and his ruling family, over access to the Orinoco and trade routes to the upland regions.[21] Moreover, we may be justly sceptical of the precision of translation and understanding involved in the collection of these tales since, with but a change of preposition in the English gloss on these native concepts, we are able to see that both the native and European tropes of acephalism resonate more fully than this. 'Men with heads *on* their chests' were, and still are, an icon of fierceness, appearing as motifs on golden pectorals, body-paint designs, and ceramics (Roosevelt 1991: 81); just as the *Sciopodi* were part of the ceramic repertoire of the Tapajoso culture of the central Amazon (Guapindaia 1993).

Paradoxically then, it is Ralegh's overt, comparative ethnographic allusion to Mandeville's account of the *Acephali* that distorts rather than clarifies his implicit ethnographic observation of a native trope of 'acephalism'. Notably, Schomburgk uses the same argument when trying to explain this observation, thereby prefiguring much of the modern literature on the 'monstrous races' and their supposed transposition to America (see Friedman 1981, Kappler 1980).

Similar analytical considerations also apply to the tale of the *Amazons* who enter Ralegh's [23] account earlier on. Once again Ralegh explicitly acknowledges the way in which earlier writers had discussed them and it is important to note that key elements of the Classical accounts are utterly absent in the American version, particularly the idea of removing the breast to facilitate military performance.[22] However, if European anticipation is distinguished from the native practice that occasioned the speculation, as to the identity of the Classical Amazons with the eminent females encountered by Ralegh and others, then once again we see that the text of the *Discoverie* contains important information on the structure and functioning of native polity.

Ralegh locates the Amazons, also producers of the *takua*, in the vicinity of the Tapajos river. Ruling out any simple identification with the Amazons of antiquity, Ralegh suggests that, alongside their active trade for gold work, once a year there was a great assembly of 'all the Kings of the borders, and the Queenes of the *Amazones*'. Whether or not the ritual practices involved in this assembly included sexual intercourse and the eventual conserving of female offspring cannot be determined. But the *takua*, as Ralegh says, were exchanged for gold work from the Orinoco basin and it was in upland Guiana that the markets servicing this trade were probably located – undoubtedly reinforcing the notion that *El Dorado* was also to be encountered here.

In other sources the 'Queen' of the Amazons was called *Cuna Ataere* or *Conori*, but unlike *El Dorado*, whose golden empire was subject to successive relocation, the geographical referents for the tale of the Amazons were far more consistent. She was said to rule over seven settlements in the Guiana highlands and, indeed, was there visited by one Irish adventurer who travelled to the headwaters of the Trombetas river for that very purpose (Lorimer 1989). A system of roads, guarded by her warriors, connected these villages. In her capital city stood five large temples, or *caranain*, dedicated to the worship of the sun, whose interiors were lined with painted wooden carvings and featherwork, as well as containing idols of gold and silver in the form of women. Most versions of this myth, deriving from the South American context, were inspired by the account of Gaspar de Carvajal (1934), a cleric who accompanied Orellana on his reluctant descent of the Amazon in 1542. However, 'women-without-men' were already prefigured in European minds by the tales of the Amazon, or warrior-women, such tales having come down from the Greeks via the Romans (see n. 22) and, as Ralegh's allusion indicates, had become popularised through various medieval texts such as Mandeville's *Travels*.

In Amazonia, the meaning of native names for such 'Amazons' was critically different, being given as *Aikeam-Benano* (women-who-live-alone) north of the Amazon river, or *Cougnantaisecouima*[23] (women-without-men) to the south of the Amazon. Secluded 'women-without-men' appear also on *Matinino* in the Caribbean, and at *Calamahala* (n. 19) on the mid-Orinoco; locations which were shown above to have been intimately involved in the patterns of élite exchange across the whole northern part of the continent. While aspects of the European myth are clearly transferred to these novel American contexts, different elements also emerge and old motifs are absent or suppressed, suggesting that in America the interplay between European preconception as to Amazon women and actual experience of native culture developed in a distinct way. This in turn implies that the *Aikeam-Benano* were not simply a recapitulation or retelling of the European Amazon tale in an American context. Such a conjecture is also reinforced by a careful reading of Carvajal's original text, as well as other secondary materials, such as the account in Thevet's (1577-8) description of southern Brazil. This suggests that the category 'Amazon' is used as a figurative device to make observation intelligible, rather than to advance the claim that the Amazons of antiquity had been finally discovered in South America. The fifteenth-century descriptions of Columbus and Chanca concerning the secluded or 'captive' women on the islands of Guadeloupe and Martinique (in Hulme and Whitehead 1992), as well as further such encounters in the territories of the Colombian Muisca and in Orinoco, also suggest that the military element in the medieval European versions was not an invariant element of the encounter with native Amazonian cultural forms. However, Thevet's later reports of women warriors in Brazil, as well as Carvajal's own observation of women war-captains driving on the male warriors as they attacked the Spanish brigantines along the banks of the Amazon, clearly echo themes from the European versions.

Even so, if the American Amazons were not military specialists they were certainly represented as politically dominant women, as certainly occurred in some indigenous societies of the sixteenth century (Sued-Badillo 1979). In regard of the Amazons, Carvajal was told that many of the towns along the banks of the Amazon river were vassals to the Queen *Conori* and that the presence of her captains in the ranks of warriors was to exhort them to the defence of these boundary regions of her domain. One of Caravajal's informants also claimed to have been responsible for carrying the yearly tribute to the city of Conori herself – this tribute consisting of the feathers of macaws and parrots for the decoration of their temples.[24]

The American Amazons thus conformed only in part to European expectations. It also seems undeniable that both European and American males shared anxieties about women that led to a mutual interest in the possibility of an exclusive or secluded female society, and a convergence of symbolic and mythic motifs in its representation. In these terms we appear to be dealing with a cultural convergence in regard of gender relations. However, since there are also clear indications that women did on occasion enjoy higher status within native societies before the European conquest, it may be possible to suggest the elements of native cultural practice from which these mythic motifs arose and to which the European versions ineptly allude. Certainly, archaeological (Roosevelt 1991) and historical (Whitehead 1994) data gathered from the lower Amazon, particularly from Marajó island in the river's mouth, strongly suggest that women also enjoyed élite status, and a social pattern of female eminence could well have occurred in many other locations since, in Marajó iconography, the prevalence of the female form it is thought to derive from the structural centrality of females in the matrifocal, uxorilocal contexts which are common within Amazonian social organisation. Female eminence on Marajó was also economically underwritten by the specialist role women played in providing faunal protein through fishing. Given the importance of fishing in the interpretation of the *El Dorado* story, and the identification of the *Epuremei* with the Taruma, then the location of the Amazon Queen, Conori, at the headwaters of the Trombetas, and so physically proximate to the *Epuremei*, suggests that the annual gathering of 'Kings' and 'Queens' was an aspect of élite ritual and political relationships.[25] The universality of gender antagonism then provides the basis for a mimetic elaboration of the *Amazon* theme by both natives and colonials. The *Discoverie*, of course, negotiates a particular connection to European traditions of gender polarity, through the constant sub-textual presence of that Amazon Queen *par excellence* – Elizabeth I.

The *Discoverie* is undoubtedly a flawed lens through which to view the past, but the text clearly does *refract* something of native cultural praxis in 1595; not least the existence of native tropes of physical and social monstrosity involving acephalism, physical hybridity and 'free' women. That such motifs were already present before European contact indicates that the symbolic convergences involved in recording these native metaphors confused not only observers but also subsequent interpreters of those textual recordings. So, although the native idioms are initially unfamiliar to us, and to Ralegh, the text of the *Discoverie* implicitly, as well as overtly, portrays the political relations among the indigenous inhabitants of the Guiana region, especially the lower Orinoco, with accuracy. However, other commentators have simply avoided analysis of the commensurability of colonial and indigenous cultural forms through a failure to understand these kinds of symbolic convergence, mimetically elaborated. They incorrectly assume that Ralegh was poorly served by his interpreters or unable to effectively communicate with them or any other indigenous people. Yet, as Humboldt (1907: II, 317) observed,

> In every zone intolerance accompanies credulity; and it might be said that the fictions of the ancient geographers had passed from one hemisphere to the other, did we not know that the most fantastic productions of the imagination, like the works of nature, furnish everywhere a certain analogy of aspect and form.

Certainly Ralegh seems to have been at least as concerned with the logical status of his statements as he was with keeping his readership enraptured by authenticating detail and the apparatus of probability – textual and performative forms which Classical theory judged to be powerful factors in inducing belief in otherwise 'fictional' statements (Feeney 1993). However, Ralegh's claims appear only as fictions while they are abstracted from the native practices from which they were derived; other sources, both documentary and archeological, supply a context for the interpretation of those practices. None the less, whatever the nature of native cultural practice, the European myth of the *Amazons* had a role to play in the ideology of colonial occupation by emphasising the exoticism, inversion and femininity of native America, thereby rendering it a fit object for domestication, conversion and invasion. However, the European *Amazon* myth had neither the endurance of the *El Dorado* legend nor the direct, pragmatic political purpose of the discovery of cannibalism.

Ralegh's treatment of anthropophagy, or 'cannibalism', is, in view of the popular assumption that this practice was a convenient invention of colonial ideology, very ambiguous. Although the *Canibals* are alluded to several times [22, 29, 33, 37, 43, 47, 51, 71, 90-1], they are treated as unfortunate exceptions to more typical native cultural practices. But this strongly suggests that *Cannibals* could not have simply functioned as a projection to legitimise European predatory intentions as has been suggested by other commentators (Arens 1979, Montrose 1993), even if this is part of an explanation of the European interest in the phenomenon. Rather, as we have found to be characteristic of Ralegh's text generally, the ethnological observations he records about *Canibals* are well attested to in contemporary and subsequent native practice. In which case our attention is necessarily directed towards the mimetic nature of the claim, which requires a more sophisticated understanding of the ideological role of 'cannibalism' for native and European alike. It therefore needs to be emphasised that for Ralegh and the other English colonisers of this period, unlike their Spanish counterparts, the native population were potential allies, not potential rebels or enemy collaborators. The relative discursive absence of *Canibals* in the *Discoverie* may then be linked to the differing outlooks and colonial policies of the English and the Spanish with regard to the native population, notwithstanding shared predatory intentions.

In Ralegh's text the 'Cannibals' in fact are never linked overtly to anthropophagy but rather to the selling of the 'sonnes and daughters' of their own 'brethren and sisters, and for somewhat more even their own daughters' [33]. Ironically, in view of the way in which Spanish colonial ideology politically and legally distinguished the savage *caribe* from the tractable *aruaca*, Ralegh informs us that this slave-market of the '*Caribas* or *Canibals*' existed primarily to service the export of native bodies to the Antilles by both the *Arwacas* ***and*** the Spaniards. The discursive failure to reproduce this Spanish ideological dualism in the *Discoverie* may then be taken as testimony to the real impact that Ralegh's active engagement with indigenous people of the Orinoco had had on any cultural anticipations he might have arrived with.

Ralegh [51] also tells us the following:

> This Arwacan Pilot with the rest, feared that we would have eaten them, or otherwise have put them to some cruell death, for the Spaniards to the end that none of the people in the passage towards Guiana or in Guiana it selfe might come to speech with us, perswaded all the nations, that we were men eaters, and Canibals: but when the poore men & women had seen us, and that we gave them meate, and to everie one some thing or other, which was rare and strange to them, they began to conceive the deceit and purpose of the Spaniards.

Ralegh [7] also says that the Spanish planted native allies on Trinidad in order to 'eat out' the local population and so neatly reverses the Spanish accusation, as in the presentation of 'meat' to the alarmed natives – a 'marvel' in counterpoint to Spanish monstrosity. The issue here is that neither colonial nor indigene was previously unfamiliar with the trope of cannibalism. It therefore worked as a *mutually intelligible* political idiom and, because of its multiple referents, one which could also serve to obscure, in Ralegh's presentation, the identity of Spanish and English interests in the consumption of the *Guianians* and their land. But this was more than a textual device on Ralegh's part since his action was both felicitous and appropriate in indigenous terms. The gift of meat, not just for the semiotic reasons already outlined but also for political reasons, was an important performance of a claim to authority for native observers. In this way Ralegh established both an implicit critique of Spanish actions and a demonstration of his political potency by means of such an act – a veritable *acarewana*. Similarly, Ralegh's [81] distribution of Elizabethan gold coinage would have been replete with similar meanings for Topiawari and his followers.

In sum, although European accounts of America were strongly prefigured by ideas that had existed since Classical times, there yet remains a residual element in European description that can be taken only to refer to some new reality that was encountered, and this is precisely the case for the text of the *Discoverie*. At times there also appears to have been a convergence between native and European ideas, which certainly confuses the process of interpretation but does not invalidate it. The tales of the *Amazons* and *Canibals* seem to be good examples of this process of symbolic convergence, since native cosmologies were no less concerned with issues of the proper status of women, or the profanity of eating human flesh, than were European ones. It can hardly then be a surprise if the first Europeans in America perceived only themselves in others. This mimetic quality to the relationship of coloniser and colonised is particularly evident in the broad symbolic category of 'cannibalism' (Whitehead 1996a) and works well as an analytical principle for understanding colonial relationships. Moreover, it also accords well with the both the notion of a socio-political 'tribal zone' and the cultural arena of the 'contact zone' (discussed in Chapter 1 (iii)). Ralegh himself appears as a particular adept in the matter of such colonial mimesis of the native and this may help explain the persistent resonance of his name in native consciousness, even to the end of the seventeenth century.[26] This mimesis, perhaps appearing as humanistic scepticism to Eurocentric observation, occurs in a number of ways; his adoption of smoking, the experimentation with biotropic drugs served as 'cordial', the presence of freely captive indigenes with him in the Tower or his possible role as the shaman ('conjuror') in a school of occult, or pagan, 'religion', in which Thomas Hariot, John Dee and the 'Wizard Earl' (i.e. Northumberland) also participated (Lacey 1973: 125-6). Such spiritual interests also accord with Ralegh's [43] textual appreciation of Warao tobacco-shamanism (see also Chapter 1, n. 15, 16, 17, 20).

At the least, this is certainly the profile of a man who would be 'King of the Indians', just as he is captain of his *Destiny* in the feudalism of the sea, paying homage to his Amazon Queen – *Ezrabeta Cassipuna Aquerewana* – as *cacique* of her guard. Even unto death he carried totemic objects from Guiana – a 'stob' of gold (possibly that given him by Topiawari), a Guiana idol of gold, a 'plott' of the river Orinoco – as if possession of these images were to possess Guiana itself.[27] The extent of this mimetic performance of 'Indian-ness' is therefore suggested by both Ralegh's contemporaries, through their rejection of him as a dangerous nonconformer, and ultimately by himself in that greatest performance of all – the snuffing out of his own life.

(iv) The colonial mirror – images from the *Discoverie*

In this final section depictions of scenes from the *Discoverie*, the cartography its reportage suggests and the wider reputation of Ralegh himself, as an icon of the Elizabethan age, will be considered. It is not the intention to offer a close analysis of the content of his various formal portraits, although a tutored eye may well read there aesthetic and cryptic allusions opaque to this author, but rather to briefly indicate the range of such portrait materials, to outline the ethnological basis for Maps I and II in this volume, and to consider the significance of 'Ralegh's Map' as a product of his 1595-6 voyage.

Perhaps the most familiar images of Ralegh are those created by his portraits, particularly that of 1585 by Nicholas Hilliard (National Portrait Gallery); that of 1588 showing, in the top left corner, the moon, emblem of the goddess Cynthia (National Portrait Gallery); that of 1598 or later, known as the 'Cadiz' portrait for the map of the same in the background (National Gallery of Ireland), in which Ralegh stands supported by a walking stick due to his wounds received there; and that of 1602 (National Portrait Gallery) showing him in company with his son Wat, who was later to die in Orinoco. Ralegh is also represented in the plates from de Bry's *America* (reproduced in this volume) which are virtually contemporary with the publication of the *Discoverie* itself. We cannot know if Ralegh in any way 'approved' these representations but they certainly accord with his text. The incidents illustrated may help us derive some sense of those features of the text that were considered most significant, at least by de Bry, but by implication for de Bry's audience also.

The seven plates reproduced in this volume are taken from the Frankfurt edition of *America* (1599, volume VIII). The text to the illustrations is in German and is derived from that of the *Discoverie* itself. Those numbered I–VI appear in all editions of de Bry but the unnumbered illustration depicting the pastoralised scenery of Orinoco is more rare. The English captions are my direct translations of the original German.

Number I (p.9), *How Sir Walter Ralegh conquers a city and captures the Spanish governor*, shows both Alvaro Jorge and Antonio de Berrio being marched to the boats by Ralegh and his troop, following the capture of San José de Oruña. There is no visual reference to the part played by native allies in this victory but to the left we can see an English troop releasing natives, which may allude to the *caciques* that Ralegh found captive and chained in the city.

Number II (p.25), *How the nobility of Guiana would cover themselves in gold when feasting*, envisages a scene inspired by Ralegh's description of the meeting with Toparimaca, *cacique* of *Arowacai* and vassal to Carapana, with a *cacique* higher up Orinoco, and one of Toparimaca's own vassals [54-5]. Were one to substitute other paints or pigments for the gold dust, then both Ralegh's description and de Bry's illustration seem perfectly accurate and non-controversial representations. Indeed, Humboldt (1907) noted that the use of glittering marcasite as body adornment so that even this detail need not be understood as simply imaginary embellishment (see *Discoverie*, fn. 32).

Number III (p.34), *How Ralegh made alliance with the King of Arromaia*, illustrates the famed encounter between Ralegh and Topiawari [61ff.]. This scene has been used in an iconic fashion, stripped of its textual context, to suggest that it represents a colonial desire to possess the marvellous resources and peoples of Guiana on the part of the all-conquering Ralegh (see cover text and illustration for Greenblatt 1991). However, Ralegh himself suggests a more courtly encounter, although de Bry suggests a Machiavellian edge to this diplomacy, as did Sparry in his deposition to his Spanish captors (in Ramos-Perez 1973: 671-7). Thus we may note the soldier to the right of Ralegh with his musket match being kept ready, as well as the soldier to the left of Topiawari with sword drawn but covered by his shield.

Number IV (p.42), *How the Guianans cast gold*: the scene suggests gold working using the lost wax method. Heating the gold ore/alloy by means of a breath-driven furnace was already known of as a Peruvian technique, but the find of a much smaller pottery vessel at Muri mountain in Guyana would seem to suggest that the transposition was not inappropriate (see Chapter 2, n. 11).

Number V (p62.), *How ten Spaniards fell at the hands of the Indians and their treasure was taken*: the text from de Bry suggests that this scene represents an attack on Berrio's men while returning from the city of *Manoa* laden with gold work. Ralegh [32] claims to have stood at this very spot and spoken with the perpetrators. The representation also recalls the killing of nine Spaniards and a cleric, Padre Ayala, during a 1560-1 expedition up the Caroni to *Manoa*. On his return Ayala was killed on the lower Caroni by a war-party led by Morequito's followers Curmatoi and Putijma, who stood with Keymis in 1595 and indicated to him the mountain *Riconeri* below which was situated the Caroni gold-mine. This attack, signalling overt hostility from Morequito, presaged his eventual downfall. After Ralegh's departure, the long-time Campmaster of Berrio, Alvaro Jorge, was also killed while attempting to travel up the Caroni and his party massacred by Topiawari's warriors (BL Add 36317, no.15, Domingo de Vera Ybarguen to the King 27 October 1597).

Number VI (p.76), *How during winter people lived on trees and large rocks. Their ceremonies for the dead.* The text supplied by de Bry reads:

> The *Tivitivas* are a Nation of Indians. During the winter in America they lived in trees and on large rocks because of the River *Orenoque* which would, from May until September, rise 30 feet, making it 20 feet above sea level. They fed on the fish and all the other edible things that are found in the river at this time. Their neighbours, the *Capuri* and *Macuri*, have a particular ceremony for their dead. When the elders died and were buried they had performances with songs and dances to express their grief. After a while, when the flesh had decayed, they dug up the skeletons, which were then held together only by nerves and tendons, and hung them in their houses, in memory of the dead. They decorated their heads with beautiful feathers, their arms and legs with golden plates and all sorts of objects which the deceased had collected in their lifetime. And so these skeletons would be left hanging.

These comments, derived from Ralegh's descriptions [43, 92] are particularly interesting since the custom of secondary burial and the display of ancestral bones were often taken by the Spanish as evidence of 'cannibal' feasting. The stilt houses of the Warao also suggested the name *Venezuela* – 'little Venice' – though they are not built in trees but among them.

Number VII (p.92), This plate is untitled and occurs only in the 1625 Latin edition of de Bry. However, it is packed with incident and significance – firstly for the way in which it visually realises the pastoral aesthetic that drives parts of Ralegh's narrative, especially on the initial ingress to Orinoco proper [48]. One may assume from the facial representation and style of clothing that the figure turned towards us and gesturing is Sir Walter himself; though the figure in the prow of the pinnace might equally be him. The landscape opens before us, as if it were Windsor Great Park or Hampton Court, though other early travellers have used the referent of Port Meadow in Oxford. As was suggested above, these analogies are quite acceptable and at least the Orinoco is flowing in the right direction. Among the quiet grazing of the deer and birds three boats of English precede that of Ralegh and in the distance we can faintly descry four canoes of natives, fleeing into the woods like startled deer at the arrival of the rescuing English. These are the *canoas* of *Arwacas* that Ralegh gave chase to and found to be carrying bread to trade at Margarita. Also aboard were three Spanish, a knight, a soldier and a gold-refiner. However, in the foreground the hidden danger of this deceptively familiar place is suddenly revealed through the exotic *lagartos* (alligators) that, serpent-like, hunt the deep waters for the unwary. In this case Ralegh tells us [48] a Negro leapt from the boat and '. .. was in all our sights taken and devoured'. As V. S. Naipaul (1994: 181) slyly suggests, this incident seems to have been lifted from John Hawkins's account of his voyage to Guinea and the Indies in 1564, and is there to validate Ralegh's experience in Orinoco as truly exotic.

More generally the iconography of indigenous people in de Bry's images replicates a number of well-worn devices that signal, to anyone familiar with de Bry's *America* and other contemporary illustrations, that the people of Guiana were from the tropics of the 'New World' (indicated by the feather skirts and crowns) but that they had traces of cultural complexity (hats, technology, ritual) and polity (killing Spaniards, feasting English). It is perhaps significant then that the plate which represents the ambiguous custom of secondary burial, 'ambiguous' because it was apt to suggest cannibalism to the European observer, shows natives with none of the above characteristics.

The map attributed to Ralegh (BL Add MS. 17940 A, VIII, n.105) is derivative of Spanish sources in the same way as the text of the *Discoverie* as a whole, following the analysis of Ojer (1966). In particular the location of the *Epuremei* and of the lake of *Manoa* were direct borrowings from the information that the *aruacas*, specifically the *cacique* Carivana, had supplied to the Spanish *vecinos* at Margarita (Ojer 1966: 168-9). According to this testimony, the *aruacas* were close neighbours to the *epimeos* (*Epuremei*), who were 'bearded and very small' (like the Taruma), and nearby was reported the domain of the *Amazons*. This certainly accords with both the later intelligence as to the approaches to *Manoa* and the upland distribution of *aruaca* villages gathered by the English, Dutch and French along the Atlantic coast (see *Relation of Marwin River* in Purchas 1906: XVI, 403-13, Keymis 1596), as well as with the prior Spanish cartography (see *Mapa de la Provincia de los Aruacas*, c. 1560, in Ojer 1966: 204-5, and the *Mapa de Diego Sánchez de Sotomayor*, c. 1574, BL Add MS. 13964). But whatever the sources and methods for the construction of this map (Skelton 1963), the inscription of native geographical knowledge is the key feature, since these regions had yet to be physically traversed by the Europeans (see Whitehead 1997). It might also be noted, in support of Ojer's arguments, that the aesthetic style of the map, despite the significance

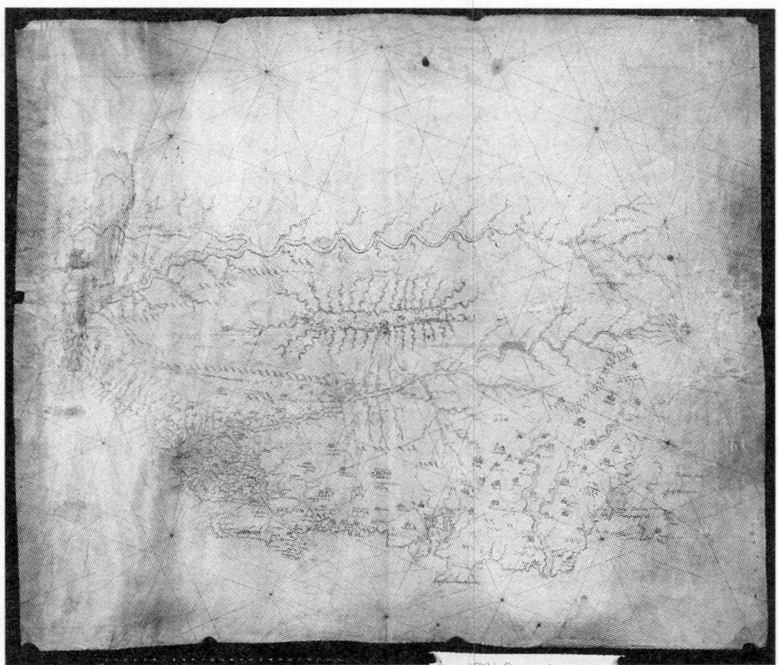

VIII *Map of Guiana attributed to Ralegh*

given it by Nicholl (1995), closely resembles other Spanish hydrological representations of the Amazon, Orinoco and their connections.

Maps I and II in this volume represent the peoples and locations mentioned by Ralegh in the *Discoverie*. Map II also includes other contemporary materials that situates Ralegh's information with regard to native polity in the Amazon basin. Map I is titled *Huyapari* to reflect the fact that the different and even antagonistic groups across this area were nevertheless part of a system of regional interaction (Arvelo and Biord 1994) that was precisely reflected in the indigenous use of this term. In Map I the detail portrayed also maps Ralegh's own route from Trinidad, through the delta (via the 'river of the Red Crosse'), along the Orinoco south bank to the mouth of the Caroni. Beyond this Ralegh fairly accurately reports the disposition of native groups on the lower Orinoco and accurately enumerates the rivers (modern equivalents for Ralegh's place names are given in the Index).

Map II is titled *Guiana* to again reflect the facts of native political and economic interaction; in this frame *Huyapari* appears as one among a number of political formations, along with *Manoa*, *Amapaia*, *Aruaca*, *Oniguayal*,

Amazons, Tapajoso, Arricary, Cassipa, Parime, and *Macureguarai.* Map II, therefore, also includes information derived from Ralegh's Spanish and English contemporaries, particularly Antonio de Berrio, Robert Harcourt, Charles Leigh and Lawrence Keymis. In addition we can see strikingly how Ralegh was utterly dependent on Berrio's earlier journeys from Bogotá for his information on the province of *Amaipa.* The location of the other provinces (except *Parime, Cassipa* and *Macureguarai*) are therefore derived directly from those contemporary sources mentioned above. Generally Ralegh's conceptualisation of the information he was given is compressed into too small a geographical space, possibly because he was too keen to claim an eyewitness status with regard to it. None the less, the region known as *Guiana* was politically integrated in native conceptions and Ralegh's information regarding both long-distance trade and the political intrusion from the south and west certainly accords with the other sources – see Chapter 1 (iv).

The other materials which I wish to briefly consider are highly miscellaneous and bear less directly on the reading of the *Discoverie,* but they do provide a feel for the long-term resonance that Ralegh has as an icon of his moment and its meaning. Although the many literary works and reprints of Ralegh's own writings speak strongly enough of this iconicity, its more diffuse cultural forms are the issue here. Our own cultural consciousness of Ralegh has its roots in the late nineteenth-century invention of Britain's imperial origins, evidenced particularly in a form of English national myth that sought a continuity of ethnic sentiment with the 'Saxon' freemen of pre-Norman England. In this ethnic discourse a 'Saxon' populace is the bedrock of 'Englishness' and the fount of its principal virtues of propertied egalitarianism and insular parochialism. To this is contrasted Norman, Stuart and Hanoverian foreignness, which is domesticated through some form of cultural assimilation or conquest. This process occurs in the iconography of specific historical figures, and the supposed effects of their actions on emergence of the English nation; as, for example, in the key national myths of Robin Hood and Richard the Lionheart (assimilation), Henry VIII and the destruction of the Catholic Church (conquest), Ralegh and James I or Cromwell and Charles I (assimilation), and Wellington, the Hanoverian general, and the defeat of the republican French general, Napoleon (conquest).

Of course Drake, Hawkins or Essex might also fill the Ralegh slot in this cultural motif, but his execution at the hands of the Catholic Scots King has assured him a special place in this national iconography, as Vincent Harlow (1928) first noted. The portrait by Sir J. E. Millais, *The Boyhood of Raleigh,* perfectly encapsulates this. Ralegh and a companion sit enraptured by the tales of an 'old salt', complete with anchor tattoo and earring, who points firmly west across the ocean. Beside him, and validating the tales he spins to the young boys, are a dead toucan and a wicker bowl decorated with feathers, symbolically redolent of the Indies, thanks in part to de Bry's stock imagery. A model ship is beached in the foreground needing nothing more than youthful imagination to turn it into Ralegh's own *Destiny*, and so their own. This notion of Ralegh as a suitable role model for imperial youth is also reflected in the attention paid to Ralegh by such figures as the adventure writer John Buchan (1935), and by his absorption into the Sherlock Holmes cycle, albeit not through the pen of Arthur Conan Doyle (Greenwood 1986). However, if this introductory essay has shown Sir Walter Ralegh and the text of the *Discoverie* to have had social significance and cultural meaning for others besides the consumers[28] of English national myth then its work is done. It remains only to offer, by way of conclusion, a brief reiteration of the key themes that have informed this introductory essay.

The purpose has been to show how a reading of Ralegh's *Discoverie*, if sufficiently informed from the anthropological literature, can improve not only cultural and historical interpretation of native Guiana in 1595 but also an appreciation of the text itself. This anthropological appreciation of the text of the *Discoverie* suggests that it is not simply a literary act of colonial appropriation, but perforce strongly registers native cultures as well. This anthropological analysis itself emerges from a growing theoretical appreciation of the *symbiotic* nature of cultural construction and the two-way, *mutual* character of cultural transmission, even from colonised to coloniser. However, the manner in which native cultures are depicted in the *Discoverie* suggests a process of negotiation between forms of implicit or overt cultural expectation and the actual experience of the Orinoco in 1595. Therefore, it is an examination of the character of that negotiation of expectation and experience which forms the basis for the exegesis presented here. Moreover, in so far as the text of the *Discoverie* emerges from a dialogic encounter between Ralegh and the indigenes of Orinoco, as Ralegh himself claims [28-9], it also may be said to be ethnographic in character. It is these anthropological aspects of the *Discoverie* which necessitate the interpretative framework of this present edition, since it has been shown that historiography and literary theory alone are unable to interpret certain problematic and enigmatic aspects of the text, as in the fate of Hugh Goodwin, or the identity of the *Epuremei*.

This critical approach also implies that the *Discoverie* is itself an exemplar for the discussion and analysis of how others are represented and understood through written text. Moreover, since issues of historiographic representation and interpretation closely match those that affect ethnography, it remains the relation of text to testimony, observation to experience, and authority to intelligibility that is at the centre of any hermeneutic exercise in regard of both ethnographic and historical texts, such as Ralegh's. Accordingly, just as Schomburgk showed for geographical representation and Harlow for historiographical representation, this edition illustrates how Ralegh's ethnological representation, including both implicit classifications, as well as overt judgments, are in fact intelligible attempts to depict native social and cultural practice. This intelligibility was gauged from how forms of native practice were recorded by Ralegh's contemporaries, as well as from the data of modern archaeology and ethnography. As a result of this evaluation it becomes evident that the easy assumptions of many previous commentators, to the effect that the *Discoverie* was merely self-referential or largely invented, must be abandoned. This implies that a broad range of colonial documentation needs to be re-evaluated for the insight it could offer into native, not just colonial, practice. At the same time, close attention to the unique and particular characteristics of the *Discoverie*, especially as regards other English colonising attempts in Guiana, and the prior establishments of the Spanish, allow a much clearer picture to emerge of the social and cultural assumptions about native people implicit in the *Discoverie.* When laid bare these implicit assumptions suggest connections with the emergence of professional anthropology, as in the primacy given to ethnographic testimony, and underline the role that Renaissance ethnologies had in that process. Such intellectual continuities therefore make the *Discoverie* an anthropological document of continuing importance, quite apart from its ethnological data on Orinoco.

It is a matter of some irony then to learn that it was precisely those ethnological elements that Ralegh incorporated from Spanish sources that have caused his account to be mocked by subsequent generations: *El Dorado*, the invasion of Incan *Epuremei*, headless *Ewaipanoma*, *Amazons* and *Canibals.* However, these ethnological elements in Ralegh's account might be considered the *most* credible! Precisely because such elements were derived through the extensive and enduring relationships that the Spanish had with the indigenous population throughout the second half of the sixteenth century, not Ralegh's own brief ethnographic reconnaissance of the lower Orinoco. It therefore seems to be the case that Ralegh used his extensive preliminary research in the literature of discovery, and especially the first-hand discussions he had with Antonio de Berrio, to amplify and enhance the ethnographic reports he makes.

However, the central issue is not how Ralegh's authorship of the *Discoverie* affects our evaluation of his character, nor of English imperialism, but rather how the text of the *Discoverie* was constructed from experience, observation and interrogation of both the Spanish and the indigenous population, as well as the texts and artefacts they produced. It can be seen then that a clear distinction between ethnography and ethnology is crucial to a better appreciation of the *Discoverie*, since the nature of the text is an issue separate from the ethnographic ability and credibility of Ralegh. Until now it has been assumed that, since Ralegh's ethnographic experience was minimal, then his wider ethnological claims must be suspect. But the issue is not the personality of Ralegh but the meaning of the text of the *Discoverie* and the sources for its construction. In this light we can say that the *Discoverie* synthesises a wide range of ethnographic information garnered principally by the Spanish, to which Ralegh's ethnographic encounter on the lower Orinoco in 1595 adds some critical details. These include the interview with Topiawari, the description of the people and places of the lower Orinoco region, and the information on gold working and élite, long-distance exchange. This regional ethnology, which situates the lower Orinoco in the wider context of Guiana, may not be wholly original to Ralegh but he made it accessible and suggested ethnological connections that are not evident from Spanish accounts. In sum, while it is the conflation of the empirical and rhetorical which makes such texts as the *Discoverie* so problematical, the web of other contemporary evidence simultaneously makes possible both this critique of Ralegh's text and a better appreciation of its intelligibility.

There are therefore two levels at which the text of the *Discoverie* works anthropologically, first at the level of an overt statement of ethnographic observation or ethnological inference and second an implicit level of anthropological assumption and ethnographic recording that requires an informed contextual reading to make explicit. As a result, and precisely because Ralegh's ethnology looks back into the sixteenth century, it has a purely imaginary and fabulous appearance to commentators whose own historical ethnology is formulated via materials of the seventeenth century onwards. This, unfortunately, therefore applies to much of the anthropology, including archaeology, of the Caribbean and Amazonia, as well as historians and literary scholars who have depended on these materials for an understanding of native cultures.

So, although Ralegh transpires to be an imperfect ethnographer, if those elements of European anticipation and projection are carefully delineated then it can be seen that Ralegh records novel elements and additional information derived from observation or interrogation of native people in Orinoco, by himself or others. Moreover, Ralegh engages in the collection of reports of the 'marvels' with a firm scepticism as to their literal existence but a definite appreciation of the importance of establishing the bounds of the possible. Continuing indigenous expressions of the existence of 'headless men' support the idea that Ralegh's analysis is correct to stress the collective cultural meaning of such ideas and to go beyond a mere positivist discussion of possible referents for a literal existence of such 'monstrous' individuals. In the case of the *El Dorado* legend, the conflation of many different native expressions under the organising idiom of European expectation produces a false impression of cultural uniformity to native ideas and practice. No one *El Dorado* existed but many, all of which conformed imperfectly with the golden empire of European anticipation. Similarly, a trope of the monstrous, used to express alterity, was already present in native thought well before the European arrival, just as male anxieties as to their control over women found fertile reflection in native ideas of *Amazons.*

Notwithstanding these critical exercises, the enchantment and magic of the *Discoverie* remains potent for, as the text promises, '*there is a way found to answere every mans longing*' ¶(*Epistle*). The constant reiteration of native names and words chants into existence ('enchants') things, persons and places, just as native shamans first created their world through powerful songs. As the Ye'cuana of the Caura river tell us in their creation myth, the *Watunna*, in *Weyana* ('Guiana') there is a mountain where all the good people of the world are still waiting to be born, and will wait unless there is a 'discoverie' of them. So too, in the reading of Sir Walter's *Discoverie*, we might be magically transported to realms of wonder, in quest of visions of exotic possibility. But the prospect of virgin penetration, gratefully invited, also vies with the lure of gold and reputation, as a promised political redemption for colonial desires of complete and sated possession. All this is then delivered to the reader in tones of collusion and familiarity, that silently bind us to the unspoken purposes in the text. By making gaudy show of disinterest and disability in the matter of so large a physical discovery, Ralegh forces forgiveness for the lack of specific achievements. By the telling of a tale of human frailty and lack in the face of opulent opportunity, we can at once share and approve the glorious failures as beauteous textual triumphs.

The golden empire that Ralegh thought snatched from his certain
possession by dint of circumstance may yet be attained in the
dreams of his readers, through which the slim shadow of
Sir Walter forever slips silently, still searching for
those precious proofs of the large, rich and
beautiful empire of *Weyana*, whose final
discovery will be a just rebuke
to our naughty and
faithless
world.

Notes

1 However, recent research has begun to change this and as a result is uncovering a very different picture of the native world that preceded European colonial settlement to that given in the standard compendium of ethnology *The Handbook of South American Indians* (Edited by Julian Steward for the Bureau of American Ethnology, Washington 1945, 7 vols). See Whitehead (1996b) for a review of recent archaeological research in Amazonia, Roosevelt (1994) for an edited collection of essays presenting new perspectives in Amazonian anthropology, and Whitehead (1995a) for a presentation of new research on the native Caribbean.

2 See Harlow (1928: 120) for an example of this transposition of names. However, a number of scholars have wondered at the sequence of events leading up to the death of Morequito, and seeming inconsistencies between Ralegh's and Spanish accounts of Morequito being still alive after his execution (Ramos-Perez 1973: 568-9, n. 142). These inconsistencies are resolved once this transposition in the names of places and their rulers is appreciated – see Chapter 1, n. 27.

3 This was the case in the apparent 'apotheosis' of Captain Cook by the Hawaiian islanders – although this sudden divinity worked to the ultimate detriment of Cook since he was then supposedly killed for violating the terms of his own godhead. The problems in reading others through space and time that the interpretation of the textual evidence of this event has engendered in current anthropology (see Obeyesekere 1992, Sahlins 1995) parallels many of the issues discussed here with regard to Ralegh, or Columbus. One might note here that the attempts by both protagonists to establish whether or not the natives 'really believed' in Cook's identity as *Lono,* Hawaiian culture hero in the mould of *Amalivaca* or the *Viracoa,* seem misplaced given the cultural specificity of the notion of 'belief', as Needham (1972: 146) remarks: 'It [belief] is not a necessary concept, and it is not a distinct capacity or inner state; other languages make no recognition of a mode of consciousness of the kind and other peoples order their lives without reference to such a capacity'. And so, as is the case here, it is necessary to consider a range of cultural meanings that might be found in specific actions in order to reveal the complexity of motivation that is present in a given situation. At this point it may, or may not, be possible to suggest that one or other of those cultural meanings was so dominant or prevalent amongst the historical actors that it fulfils *our* idea of being *their* motivation.

4 The term *caraïbe,* often occurring in the French sources, shows some form of link to the term *caribe* (Whitehead 1995v: 93). Although there have been many suggestions as to the derivation of the term, another semantic resonance in the term *caribe* may be as 'people of prophecy' (*carai-iba),* that is announcing a new vision of native destiny, as with the oracle of the fire-spirit *Wattopa,* also mentioned by Harcourt (1613: 377).

5 The translation made of this document by the British government (*British Guiana Boundary Arbitration, Appendix to the British Case* (I: 21), London: HMSO, 1896) interpolates 'and by the Dutch' into the crucial phrase that reports this prophecy of

liberation by the English. This may be an innocent error but it would also enhance British claims to a continuity of administration with the prior Dutch colony of Essequibo. Since it was also claimed that the Essequibo Dutch outpost predated Spanish settlement this becomes a significant legal point in sustaining the British boundary claim against Venezuela.

6 However, since Carapana was also reputed by Ralegh [29] to have been over a hundred years old we might consider that these reported numerical ages refer less to individual chronology than to Ralegh's desire to represent these native leaders as sagacious and credible. It could also be that the discovery of *Macrobi* (long-lived or gigantic beings) aids in the textual task of establishing a convincing alterity, as was the case for other of the European marvels of encounter with America.

7 Although Ralegh's suggestion as to the presence of Incas in Guiana violates our professional anthropological and historical expectations, the notion that the last free Incas were in this region has remained persistent up to the present day, being evidenced by travellers' tales (see a report of such an encounter with 'De Laatste Vrije Incas?' in *West Indische-Gids 7: 31-4)* and eighteenth-century documentary evidence from the Spanish authorities in Peru. While investigating the shipwreck of the *San Pedro de Alcantara* off the coast of Portugal in 1786, Professor Jean-Yves Blot (personal communication) became aware that among the passengers were seventeen native prisoners associated with the rebellion of the 'false' Inca, José Gabriel Tupac Amaru (see also Brown and Fernandez 1991). While researching the background on these prisoners Professor Blot uncovered evidence that the Spanish authorities in Peru were in communication with the Dutch authorities in Surinam concerning the rumours that several of Tupac Amaru's chief lieutenants had managed to reach Surinam and were living among the local population. The Spanish authorities wanted the Dutch to investigate the possible influence they had over the indigenous population.

8 The historian Clendinnen (1987: vi) quotes the following passage by Antonio de Ciudad Real (1588) describing the Spanish arrival on the coast of Mexico: 'When the Spaniards discovered this island, their leader asked the Indians how it was called; as they did not understand him, they said *uic athan*, which means what do you say or speak, that we do not understand you. And the Spaniard ordered it set down that it be called *Yucatan*'. However, although this neatly illustrates a point that many commentators wish to make about the cultural impenetrability of native Americans by colonising Europeans, the extended and intimate contacts that are evident from this discussion of Ralegh's *Discoverie* suggest that such misconstruals may well be ironical but were not typical. As already discussed, the moments of first contact on the beach-heads of an expansive Europe are a very limited context from which to derive theories of cultural communication.

9 Among the more useful works in English, apart from Harlow's essay in the 1928 edition of the *Discoverie*, is John Hemming's *The Search for El Dorado* (1978). However, although this volume is bibliographically very thorough there is a persistently negative presentation as to possible native meanings for *El Dorado*, and as to the nature of native society itself. The Spanish-language sources are more scholarly and include Ramos-Perez's *El mito del Dorado,* which is discussed frequently in this text, as well as Juan Gil's *Mitos y utopias del descubrimiento.* An interesting discussion of Ralegh's mystical alchemy occurs in Nicholl (1995).

10 The words 'golden', 'gold' and 'gold work' are used here, unless otherwise indicated, in a very general sense. This is because the precise amount of gold in native objects varied somewhat, the absolute purity in terms of gold content not being a primary consideration for the native metalsmith. However, a comparison of two to three parts gold to one part copper with silver traces varying up to twenty-five percent of the whole, could be considered typical. The Mazaruni pectoral was assayed as 12 carats, precisely agreeing with the 'triall of an Image of copper' made by Ralegh [*To the Reader* 2] in Guiana in 1595. The melting point is much lower and the malleability much greater for such alloys and, as Vega (1980: 492) points out, the modern jewellery business has now accepted such native wisdom, predominantly using 18 carat alloys, as a result of which 'the whole world adorns itself with *guanin*'.

11 However, there are some indications that the islanders may at one time have used annealing techniques to permit further working of their relatively pure gold, since the so-called 'Troumassé cylinders', distributed from Martinique to the north coast of Venezuela, and currently thought to be a form of incense burner, could have been used to heat metals, as could the vessel found at Muri mountain, on the Guyana–Brazil border – for further discussion see Whitehead 1990a.

12 Such connections were still very evident even in the seventeenth century, as the remnant native populations of the Lesser Antilles, such as the *caribes (Karipuna* or 'Island Carib'), continued to raid the *aruacas (Lokono)* for golden objects, chiefly in the form of 'plates', 'croissants' or 'half-moons' – see Whitehead 1990a.

13 This practice, called *jeruma* (Cariban Kapon), is still prevalent among the native peoples of the Guiana uplands, and the Pemon still believe that there is a spirit-master, *esak,* for diamonds, as they do for all species and natural resources; though the name of the *esak* for gold is currently unrecorded. However, a reference to the spirit-master of gold occurs in the quotation from Keymis (see below), where he appears as a 'dragon', possibly alluding to a type of snake or lizard which haunts the kinds of rocks and soils which bear gold (Colson 1956 and personal communication).

14 The native use of silver is not dealt with here, but it was significant. Putijma, controller of Topiawari's Orocoa mine, showed Dudley's men some 'bracelets of silver' (see text) and the name of one of his villages, *Chiparepare [93 sic/83],* is orthographically equivalent to the native word for silver given by Dudley, *Chipperarey* (1899: 65) who also reported native silver-mines on the Paria peninsula. However, the corruption, by the natives, of the Spanish term *plata* into *perota* was widespread, leading modern commentators to argue incorrectly that no native term existed (Roth 1924: 128, Schomburgk 1848: 100 n. 2). Further south, Carvajal (1934: 223) mentions that the 'great overlord' of the lower Amazon north bank, Arripuna (*Carepuna* in Ralegh [22]), who controlled a silver mine and was not ' familiar' with gold.

15 However, it would be unwise to try and sustain this interpretation solely through the possible orthographic equivalence of the terms '*epuremei*' and '*taruma*'. Consistent with current native naming practices, the *Epuremei* could also be understood as simply 'those of Parima'. Spanish sources use the term *Piriamuy*, which seems to support this view of the term.

16 Although the Taruma were widely held to have become extinct by the beginning of this century, a recent filmed encounter between FUNAI (Brazilian Indian Bureau) agents and two individuals claiming to be Taruma (*Auasé*), as well as Wai-Wai reports of contacts with them (George Mentore, personal communication), suggests that this is not so. Although the film is brief it is apparent that their language is not Cariban or Arawakan and that their appearance, especially their wearing of headgear or hats, conforms in at least one critical way with the *Epuremei*'s distinctiveness from the *Guianians*, as Ralegh [63] describes it. References to head shape or position, as with the *Acephali*, may also have meaning in the context of observed Taruma practices of cranial deformation. This practice in itself marks them off from the rest of the Guiana peoples and links them to the Omagua of the upper Amazon. Again we have the possibility then of substituting the idea of a specifically Incan invasion for this link with another powerful polity to the west.

17 Fox (1987) has shown exactly this to be the case for the formation of successive political kingships in the Mayan region, and it was a key aspect of the emergence of Norman power, at about the same time in Europe – see Douglas (1969).

18 It is thus interesting to note that Sampaio (quoted in Edmundson 1906: 245) found the Arequenas of the upper Vaupés/Icana rivers using the *quipu* for writing 'after the manner of the [. . .] ancient Peruvians', and it was also reported that llamas were being kept amongst Río Negro groups. Indeed Edmundson (1906) plausibly argues that the Arequenas were in contact with Dutch traders by the early seventeenth century, again reinforcing the notion that native and European knowledge of the interior at this time was far better than the professional geographers of the nineteenth and twentieth centuries have allowed.

19 There are also further connections between the 'Amazons' of that river and *Calamahala* to the 'south of Orinoco', which, like *Matinino*, was a site for the exchange of women, body-paints and probably *guanin* and *takua*. Sparry (in Purchas 1906: XVI, 307) writes of his visit to this place: 'In this Faire, which is called *Calamahala* [. . .] I bought eight young Women [. . .] away to certaine Salvages which were my friends, at the request of Warituc, the Kings Daughter of Murrequito.' This may also have been the market from which the trading party that Ralegh [47] encountered was returning.

20 For references to a wide variety of monstrous beings see Humboldt 1907: II, 318, Penard and Penard 1907, Roth 1915: 170-2, 363-6. The account given by Lourens Lourenszoon is in Nicholas Wassenaer, *Twaelfde deel of 't vervolgh van het Historisch Verhael aller gedenckwaerdiger geschiedeniss die in Europa [. . .] America [. . .] voorgevallen zijn.* (Amsterdam, 1627). Clearly this text needs a longer exercise in interpretation than can be carried out here, but thanks are due to Steffen Baetsen for his assistance in making this translation.

21 This political tension is alluded to by Berrio (AGI Consejo – Escriviania de Camera Pleitos, años 1597 à1599, Legajo 1011 1 January 1593, BL Add. MS 36315, *f*.186) who travelled from *Amapaia,* where he had stayed with the *Anebas* (also *Discoverie* 25-6), downstream to the Caroni in the company of *caribes* from the Barima river who told him of their uneasy peace with the *Guayanos* (Orinoqueponi) and of wider conflicts with other *caribes,* as in the Caura river – see Whitehead 1988.

22 Recent archaeological research by Janine Kimble in the Russian steppes also demonstrates that there were empirical referents for the original Greek tale as well. Investigation of the ancient Saramacian culture indicates the presence of female warriors who were interred in full battle regalia. The presence of bone traumas in these remains consistent with combat, such as an arrow-point lodged in the skull, are persuasive indications that this was not a purely symbolic role. Herodotus reported women warriors in this region and historical ethnography suggests that the *epata* or 'man-killers', were a cohort of young women who could marry only after success in battle. References to breast-mutilation may therefore be a mistranslation of Herodotus's term 'amazon', since it may refer to the fact they did not, yet, breast-feed infants, rather than to a physical deformation of the breast. In the hands of the patriarchical Roman Strabo (1917-33: Book II), the tale Herodotus (1942) originally told of such 'masculinised' women became so distorted that it then appeared fantastical. Similar cultural processes were at work in the colonial rendering of native practices in America.

23 It is important to note that Tupian women played a very active role in the ritual cannibalism of captured men, marrying them and even bearing their children for a period before their sacrifice. The women were also very prominent in the anthropophagic ceremony itself (see Combès 1992, Viveiros de Castro 1992). Ralegh's [24] observation seems to support this as a native element in *Amazon* practice.

24 Gaspar de Carvajal (1934: 25) describes one of the altars where this was done as being: 'a hewn tree trunk ten feet in girth, there being represented and carved in relief a walled city with its enclosure and with a gate. At this gate were two towers, very tall and having windows, and each tower had a door, the two facing each other, and at each door were two columns, and this entire structure that I am telling about rested upon two very fierce lions, which turned their glances backwards as though suspicious of each other, holding between their forepaws and claws the entire structure, in the middle of which there was a round open space [. . .] through which they offered [. . .] *chicha* [maize libation] for the Sun.'

25 An apparent decline in the vitality of the Marajó culture, just prior to the encounter with the Europeans, may coincide with the 'retreat' of these women from the Amazon mouth and their 'seclusion' on the Trombetas. This was possibly under pressure from the male-orientated warrior and shamanic cults of the Tupinamba, who may have begun their occupation of the Amazon river in the thirteenth or early fourteenth century (Metraux 1948).

26 However, his status as a colonial icon of British imperialism in South America, although briefly seen in the seventeenth century, does not really emerge until the nineteenth century, in a curious, but most relevant conjunction with that of other empire heroes, such as Captain Cook.

27 Schomburgk's edition of the *Discoverie* reprints the following list (1848: 228) extracted from a letter from Thomas Naunton, Secretary of State, to Thomas Wilson being an 'inventory of such things as were found on the body of Sir Walter Rawleigh, Knight, the 15th day of August 1618', which was made after his arrest on the Thames as he attempted to flee to France, just prior to his execution:

A Guiana idol of Gold.

A Spleenstone (*left with him for his own use*).
One wedge of fine gold at 22 carratts.
Another stob of coarser gold.
Item one plott of Guiana and Nova (R—) and another of the river of Orenoque.
The description of the river Orenoque.
A tryal of Guianan ore with a description thereof. [my emphasis]

Such a choice of items must indicate that Ralegh remained a *doradista* to the last.

28 As well as economic consumers, for Ralegh's association with the introduction of tobacco and potatoes gives him a folkloric quality, distinct from the high myth of ideology, and so poor Sir Walter still brings the wonders and marvels of America to his Queen:

'When Sir Walter Raleigh brought the potato back to England, little did he know that the British diet would never be the same again. The chip was born. And today, chips of a very different kind have changed the way we live forever. Introducing the "Gateway 2000 Liberty". From the land where potatoes were found comes Gateway 2000's amazing new portable PC [. . .] Arise Sir Walter, this Liberty is grand!' (Advertising copy for computer manufacturer Gateway 2000).

Part 2

The *Discoverie*

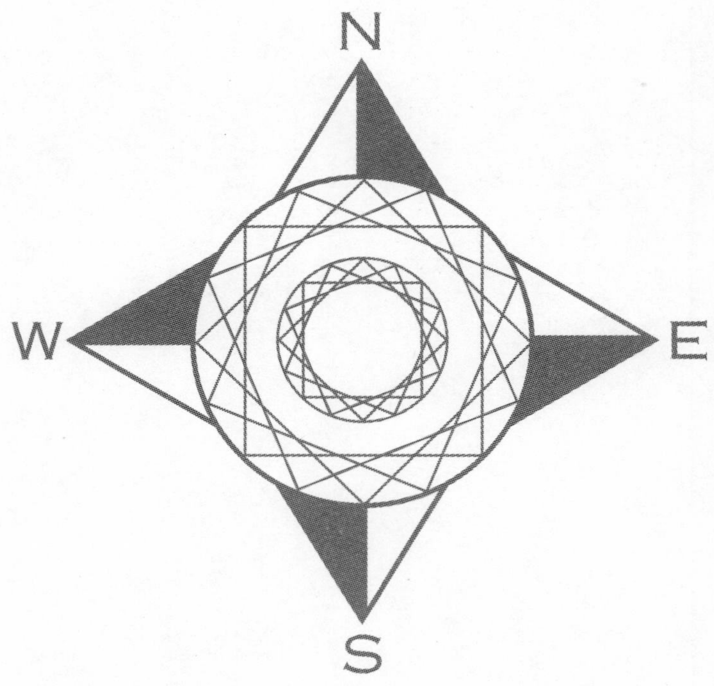

THE DISCOVERIE OF THE LARGE, RICH, AND BEWTIFUL EMPYRE OF GUIANA, WITH

a relation of the great and Golden Citie of Manoa *(which the Spanyards call* El *Dorado)* And of the Provinces of *Emeria, Arromaia, Amapaia,* and other Countries, with their rivers, adjoyning.

Performed in the yeare 1 5 9 5. by Sir *W. Ralegh* Knight, Captaine of her *Majesties Guard, Lo.* Warden* of the Stanneries, and her Highnesse Lieutenant generall of the Countie of Cornewall.

Imprinted at London by Robert Robinson.

1 5 9 6.

*Denotes words which appear in the glossary

[*The Epistle Dedicatorie* A2]

TO THE RIGHT HONORABLE MY *singuler good Lord and kinsman, Charles Howard,* knight of the Gar-*ter, Barron, and Counceller, and of the Ad-mirals of England the most renow-*ned: And to the Right Honorable S[r] *Robert Cecyll* Knight, Councel-ler in her Highnes privie Councels.

F*OR your Honors many Honorable and friendlie parts, I have hitherto onely returned promises, and nowe for answeare of both your adventures, I have sent you a bundle of papers which I have devided betwen your Lo. &* S[r] Robert Cecyl[1] *in these two respects chiefly: First for that it is reason, that wastful factors**, *when they have consumed such stockes as they had in trust, doe yeeld some cullor for the same in their account, secondly for that I am assured, that whatsoever shalbe done, or written by me, shall neede*

[*The Epistle Dedicatorie* A2 verso]

a double protection and defence. The triall that I had of both your loves, when I was left of all, but of malice and revenge, makes me still presume that you will be pleased (knowing what little power I had to performe ought, and the great advantage of forewarned enemies) to answeare that out of knowledge, which others shall but object out of malice. In my more happy times as I did especially honour you both, so I found that your loves sought me out in the darkest shadow of adversitie, and that the same affection which accompanied my better fortune,

[1] In fact both men intrigued against Ralegh for the favour of James I (Stuart).

sored not away from me in my manie miseries: all which though I cannot requite, yet I shal ever acknowledge: and the great debt which I have no power to pay, I can doe no more for a time but confesse to be due. It is true that as my errors were great, so they have yeelded very grievous effects, and if ought might have beene deserved in former times to have counterpoysed anie part of offences, the fruite thereof (as it seemeth) was long before fallen from the tree, and the dead stocke onely remained. I did therefore even in the winter of my life, undertake these travels, fitter for bodies lesse blasted with misfortunes, for men of greater abilitie, and for mindes of better incouragement, that thereby if it were possible I might recover but the moderation of excesse, and the least tast of the

[***The Epistle Dedicatorie*** **A3**]

greatest plentie formerly possessed. If I had knowen other way to win, if I had imagined how greater adventures might have regained, if I coulde conceive what farther meanes I might yet use, but even to appease so powrefull a displeasure, I would not doubt but for one yeare more to hold fast my soule in my teeth, till it were performed. Of that little remaine I had, I have wasted in effect all herein, I have undergone many constructions, I have beene accompanied with many sorrows, with labor, hunger, heat, sicknes, & perill: It appeareth notwithstanding that I made no other bravado of going to the sea, then was meant, and that I was neither hidden in Cornewall, or elsewhere, as was supposed. They have grosly belied me, that forejudged that I would rather become a servant to the Spanish king, then return, & the rest were much mistaken, who would have perswaded, that I was too easeful and sensuall to undertake a jorney of so great travel. But, if what I have done, receive the gracious construction of a paineful pilgrimage, and purchase the least remission, I shal thinke all too little, and that there were wanting to the rest, many miseries: But if both the times past, the present, and what may be in the future, doe all by one graine of gall continue in an eternall distast, I doe not then knowe whether I should bewaile my selfe either for my too much travel

[***The Epistle Dedicatorie*** **A3 verso**]

and expence, or condemne my selfe for doing lesse then that, which can deserve nothing. From my selfe I have deserved no thankes, for I am returned a begger, and withered, but that I might have bettred my poore estate, it shall appeare by the following discourse, if I had not onely respected her Majesties future Honor, and riches. It became not the former fortune in which I once lived, to goe journeys of picorie,[2] *and it had sorted ill with the offices of Honor, which by her Majesties grace, I hold this day in England, to run from Cape to Cape, & from place to place, for the pillage of ordinarie prizes. Many yeares since, I had*

[2] Apparently derived from the Spanish *picaro*, 'villainous', and so implying pillage and plunder.

knowledge by relation, of that mighty, rich, and beawtifull Empire of Guiana, *and of that great and Golden City, which the Spanyards call* El Dorado, *and the naturals* Manoa, *which Citie was conquered, reedified, and inlarged by a yonger sonne of* Guainacapa *Emperor of* Peru, *at such time as* Francisco Pazaro *and others conquered the saide Empire, from his two elder brethren* Guascar, *and* Atabalipa, *both then contending for the same, the one being favoured by the* Oreiones *of* Cuzco, *the other by the people of* Caximalca. I *sent my servant* Jacob Whiddon *the yeare before, to get knowledge of the passages, and I had some light from Captaine* Parker *sometime my servant, and nowe attending*

[*The Epistle Dedicatorie* A4]

on your Lo. that such a place there was to the southward of the great bay of Charuas, *or* Guanipa: *but I found that it was* 600. *miles farther off, then they supposed, and manie other impediments to them unknowen and unheard. After I had displanted* Don Anthonio de Berreo, *who was upon the same enterprize, leaving my ships at* Trinedado, *at the port called* Curiapan, I *wandred* 400. *miles, into the said countrey by land and river: the particulars I will leave to the following discourse. The countrey hath more quantity of Gold by manifolde, then the best partes of the* Indies, *or* Peru: *All the most of the kings of the borders are already become her Majesties vassals: & seeme to desire nothing more then her Majesties protection, and the returne of the English nation. It hath another grounde and assurance of riches and glory, then the voiages of the west* Indies, *& an easier way to invade the best parts therof, then by the common course. The king of* Spaine *is not so impoverished by taking 3 or 4 port townes in* America *as we suppose, neyther are the riches of* Peru, or Nueva Espania *so left by the sea side, as it can be easily washt away, with a great flood, or spring tide, or left drie upon the sandes on a lowe ebbe. The port townes are few and poore in respect of the rest within the land, and are of little defence,*[3] *and are onely rich*

[*The Epistle Dedicatorie* A4 verso]

when the fleets are to receive the treasure for Spaine: And we might thinke the Spanyards verie simple, having so many horses and slaves, that if they could not upon two daies warning, carrie all the Golde they have into the land, and farre enough from the reach of our footmen especiallie the* Indies *beeing (as it is for the most part) so mounteynous, so full of woods, rivers, and marishes.* In the port townes of the province of* Vensuello, *as* Cumana, Coro, *and S.* Iago

[3] This assumption was valid until Philip II commissioned the Italian military architect, Antonelli, to improve the defences of the Spanish Caribbean in the late 1580s. Ralegh's failed attack on Cumaná and Francis Drake's defeat at San Juan del Puerto Rico in 1595 were symptomatic of this change - see Parry 1966: 252-5.

(whereof Coro *and S.* Iago *were taken by Captaine* Preston *and* Cumana *and S.* Josephus *by us) we found not the value of one riall of plate in either: but the Cities of* Barquasimeta, Valentia, S. Sebastian, Cororo, S. Lucia, Alleguna, Marecabo, *and* Truxillo, *are not so easelie invaded: neither doth the burning of those on the coast impoverish the king of Spayne anie one Ducket, and if we sacke the river of* Hache, S. Marta, *and* Cartagena, *which are the portes of* Nuevo reyno *and* Popayan. *There are besides within the land which are indeed rich and populous, the townes and Cities of* Merida, Lagrita, S. Christophero, *the great Cities of* Pampelone, S. Fe de Bogota, Tunja *and* Mozo *where the* Esmeralds *are founde, the townes and Cities of* Morequito, velis, la villa de Leva, Palma, unda, Angustura, *the greate Citie*

[The Epistle Dedicatorie ¶]

of Timana, Tocaima, S. Aguila, Pasto, Juago, *the great citie of* Popaian *it selfe,* Los Remedios, *and the rest. If we take the ports and villages within the bay of* Uraba *in the kingdom or rivers of* Dariena, *and* Caribana, *the cities and townes of* S. Juan de Roydas, *of* Cassaris, *of* Antiocha, Carramanta, Cali, *and* Auserma *have golde enough to pay the King part, and are not easily invaded by the way of the* Ocean, *or if* Nombre de Dios *and* Panama *be taken in the province* of Castillo de oro, *and the villages upon the rivers of* Cenu *and* Chagre. Peru *hath besides those and besides the magnificent cities of* Quito *and* Lima *so many Ilands, portes, Cities, and mines, as if I should name them with the rest, it would seeme incredible to the reader: of all which because I have written a particuler treatise of the west* Indies,[4] I *will omit their repetition at this time, seing that in the saide treatise I have anatomized the rest of the sea townes as well of* Nicaragna, Jucata, Nueva Espanna, *and the Ilands, as those of the Inland, and by what meanes they may be beste invaded, as farre as any meane Judgement can comprehend. But I hope it shall appeare that there is a way found to answere every mans longing, a better Indies for her majestie then the King of Spaine hath any, which if it shall please her highnes to undertake,*

[The Epistle Dedicatorie ¶ verso]

I shall most willingly end the rest of my daies in following the same: If it be left to the spoyle and sackage of common persons, if the love and service of so many nations be despised, so great riches, and so mightie an Empyre refused, I hope her Majestie will yet take my humble desire and my labour therein in gracious part, which if it had not beene in respect of her highnes future honor & riches, I could have laid hands and ransomed many of the kings & Cassiqui *of the Country, & have had a reasonable proportion of gold for their redemption: But I have chosen*

[4] This is now lost and was never published - see Lefranc 1968.

rather to beare the burthen of poverty, then reproch, & rather to endure a second travel & the chaunces therof, then to have defaced an enterprise of so great assurance, untill I knew whether it pleased God to put a disposition in her princely and royall heart eyther to follow or foreslow the same: I will therefore leave it to his ordinance that hath onely power in al things, and do humbly pray that your honors wil excuse such errors, as without the defence of art, overrunne in every part, the following discourse, in which I have neither studied phrase, forme, nor fashion, and that you will be pleased to esteeme me as your owne (though over dearly bought) and I shall ever remaine ready to doe you all honour and service.*

W: R.

[*To the Reader* 2]

To the Reader

BEcause there have been divers opinions conceived of the golde oare brought from *Guiana*, and for that an Alderman of London and an officer of her majesties minte, hath given out that the same is of no price, I have thought good by the addition of these lines to give aunswere as well to the said malicious slaunder, as to other objections. It is true that while we abode at the Iland of *Trinedado*, I was informed by an Indian, that not farre from the Port, where we ancored, there were founde certaine minerall stones which they esteemed to be gold, and were thereunto perswaded the rather for that they had seen both English, and French men gather,[5] and imbarque some quantities therof: uppon this liklyhoode I sent 40 men and gave order that each one should bring a stone of that myne, to make triall of the goodnesse, which being performed, I assured them at their returne that the same was *Marcasite*, and of no riches or value: Notwithstanding divers trusting more to their owne sence, then to my opinion, kept of the saide *Marcasite*, and have tried thereof, since my returne, in divers places. In *Guiana* it selfe I never sawe *Marcasite*, but all the rocks, mountaines, all stones in the plaines, in woodes, and by the rivers sides are in effect thorow shining, and appeare marveylous rich, which being tried to be no *Marcasite*, are the trew signes of rich mineralles, but are no other then *El madre del oro* (as the Spanyards terme them) which is the mother of golde, or as it is saide by others the scum of gold: of divers sortes of these manie of my companie brought also into England, everie one taking the fayrest for the best, which is not generall. For mine owne partte, I did not countermand any mans desire, or opinion, & I could have aforded

[*To the Reader* ¶ 2 verso]

them little if I shoulde have denied them the pleasing of their owne fancies therein: But I was resolved that golde must be found either in graines separate from the stone (as it is in most of al the rivers in *Guiana*) or else in a kinde of hard stone, which we call the white Sparre, of which I saw divers hils, and in sundrie places, but had neither tyme, nor men, nor instruments fitte to labour. Neere unto one of the rivers I founde of the saide white Sparre or flint a very great ledge, or banke, which I endevored to breake by al the meanes I coulde, because there appeared on the out side some small graines of gold, but finding no meane to worke the same uppon the upper part, seeking the sides and circuite of the sayd rock, I founde a clift in the

[5] The landings made by Jean Retud in 1587 (BL Add. MS363155, f.104) and Robert Dudley in 1595.

same, from whence with daggers, and with the heade of an ax, we gotte out some small quantitie thereof, of which kinde of white stone (wherein golde is engendred) we sawe divers hils and rocks in everie part of *Guiana,* wherein we travelled. Of this there hath been made manie trialls, and in London, it was first assaide by Master *Westwood* a refiner dwelling in wood-street, and it helde after the rate of 12000 or 13000 pounds a tunne. Another sort was afterward tried by Master *Bulmar* and Master *Dimoke* assay master, and it held after the rate of 23000 pounds a tunne. There was some of it againe tried by Master *Palmer* comptroller of the minte, and Master *Dimoke* in golde smiths hall, and it helde after 26900 pounds a tunne. There was also at the same time, and by the same persons a triall made of the dust of the said myne which held 8. pound 6. ounces weight of gold, in the hundred: there was likewise at the same time a triall made of an Image of Copper made in *Guiana,* which helde a third part gold,[6] besides divers trialls made in the countrey, and by others in London. But because there came of ill with the good, and belike the said Alderman was not presented with the best, it hath pleased him therefore to scandall all the rest, and to deface the enterprize as much as in him lyeth. It hath also been concluded by divers, that if there had been anie such oare in *Guiana,* and the same discovered, that

[*To the Reader* ¶ 3]

I woulde have brought home a greater quantitie thereof: first I was not bound to satisfie anie man of the quantitie, but such onely as adventured, if any store had been returned thereof: but it is verie true that had all their mountaynes beene of massie gold, it was impossible for us to have made anie longer staye to have wrought the same: and whosoever hath seene with what strength of stone, the best golde oare is invironned, hee will not thinke it easie to be had out in heaps, and especiallie by us who had neither men, instrumentes, nor time (as it is saide before) to performe the same: There were on this discoverie, no lesse than 100 personnes, who can all witnesse, that when we past any braunch of the river to vewe the land within, and staid from our boats but six houres, wee were driven to wade to the eyes, at our returne: and if we attempted the same the day following, it was impossible either to forde it, or to swim it, both by reason of the swiftnesse, and also for that the borders were so pestred with fast woods, as neither bote nor man could finde place, either to land, or to imbarque: for in June, July, August, and September, it is impossible to navigate any of those rivers,[7] for

[6] This accords with the typical composition of native *guanin.*

[7] This is the season of most intense rains in the lower Orinoco and Ralegh's protestations are credible enough in the context of these yearly floods.

such is the furie of the *Current,* and there are so many trees and woods overflowne, as if anie boate but touch uppon anie tree or stake, it is impossible to save any one person therein: and ere we departed the land, it ran with that swiftnesse, as we drave downe most commonly against the winde, little lesse then one hundred miles a day: Besides our vessels were no other than wherries, one little barge, a small cockboate, and a bad Galiota,* which wee framed in hast for that purpose at *Trinedado,* and those little boates had nyne or ten men apeece, with all their victuals, and armes. It is further true, that we were about 400. miles from our shippes, and had bene a moneth from them, which also we left weakely mande in an open roade, and had promised our return in 15 dayes. Others have devised that the same oare was had from Barbery, and that we caried it with us into *Guiana:* surely

[*To the Reader* **¶ 3 verso**]

the singularitie of that device, I do not well comprehend, for mine owne parte, I am not so much in love with these long voiages, as to devise, thereby to cozen my selfe, to lie hard, to fare worse, to be subjected to perils, to diseases, to ill savours, to be parched and withered, and withall to sustaine the care and labour of such an enterprize, excepte the same had more comfort, then the fetching of *Marcasite* in *Guiana,* or bying of gold oare in Barbery. But I hope the better sort will judge me by themselves, & that the way of deceipt, is not the way of honor or good opinion: I have herein consumed much time, & many crowns, and I had no other respecte or desire then to serve her majesty and my Country thereby. If the spanishe nation had beene of like beleefe to these detractors, we should litle have feared or doubted their attempts, wherewith we now are daily threatned. But if we now consider of the actions both of *Charles* the fifte, who had the Maydenhead of *Peru,* & the aboundant treasures of *Atabalipa,* together with the affaires of the Spanish king now living, what territories he hath purchased, what he hath added to the actes of his predecessors, how many kingdoms he hath indangered, how many armies, garrisons, and navies, he hath & doth maintaine, the greate losses which he hath repayred, as in 88 above 100 sayle of greate shippes with their artillery[8], and that no yere is lesse unfortunate but that many vessels, treasures, and people are devoured, & yet notwithstanding he beginneth againe like a storme to threaten shipwracke to us all, we shall finde that these abilities rise not from the trades of sackes, and Civil* Orenges, norfrom ought else that either Spaine, Portugal, or any of his other provinces produce: It is his Indian Golde that indaungereth and disturbeth all the nations of Europe, it purchaseth intelligence, creepeth into

[8] A reference to the Spanish *armada* sent to conquer England in 1588.

Councels, and setteth bound loyalty at libertie, in the greatest Monarchies of Europe. If the Spanish king can keepe us from forraine enterprizes, and from the impeachment of his trades, eyther by offer of invasion, or by beseiging us in Britayne, Ireland, or else where, he hath then brought the worke of our perill in greate forwardnes.

[*To the Reader* ¶4]

Those princes which abound in treasure have greate advantages over the rest, if they once constraine them to a defensive warre, where they are driven once a yeare or oftner to cast lots for their own garments, & from such shal al trades, & entercourse, be taken away, to the general losse & impoverishment of the kingdom, & common weale so reduced: besides when men are constrained to fight, it hath not the same hope as when they are prest & incouraged by the desire of spoyle & riches. Farther it is to be doubted how those that in time of victorie seeme to affect their neighbour nations, will remaine after the first view of misfortunes, or ill successe; to trust also to the doubtfulnes of a battel, is but a fearefull and uncertaine adventure, seeing therein fortune is as likely to prevaile, as vertue. It shall not be necessary to alleage all that might be said, and therefore I will thus conclude, that whatsoever kingdome shalbe inforced to defend it selfe, may be compared to a body daungerouslie diseased, which for a season may be preserved with vulgar medicines, but in a short time, and by little and little, the same must needs fall to the ground, and be dissolved. I have therefore laboured all my life, both according to my small power, & perswasion, to advance al those attempts, that might eyther promise return of profit to our selves, or at last be a lett & impeachment to the quiet course, & plentiful trades of the Spanish nation, who in my weake judgement by such a warre were as easily indaungered and brought from his powerfulnes, as any prince in Europe, if it be considered from how many kingdomes and nations his revenewes are gathered, and those so weake in their owne beings, and so farre severed from mutuall succor. But because such a preparation and resolution is not be hoped for in hast, and that the time which our enemies embrace, can not be had againe to advantage, I will hope that these provinces, and that Empyre now by me discovered shall suffice to inable her Majesty, and the whole kingdome, with no lesse quantities of treasure, then the king of Spayne hath in all the Indies, east and west, which he possesseth, which if the same be considered and followed, ere the Spanyards enforce the same, and

[*To the Reader* **¶4 verso**]

if her Majesty will undertake it, I wilbe contented to lose her highnes favour and good opinion for ever, and my life withall, if the same be not found rather to exceed, then to equall whatsoever is in this discourse promised or declared. I will nowe referre the reader to the following discourse with the hope that the perilous and chargeable labors and indevours of such as thereby seeke the profit and honor of her Majesty, and the English nation, shall by men of qualitie and vertue receive such construction, and good acceptance, as them selves would looke to be rewarded withall in the like.

W: R.

THE DISCOVERIE OF GUIANA

ON Thursday the 6. of Februarie in the yeare 1595. we departed *England*, and the sunday following had sight of the North cape of *Spayne*, the winde for the most part continuing prosperous: wee passed in sight of the *Burlings* and the rocke,[9] and so onwardes for the *Canaries*, and fell with *Fuerte ventura* the 17. of the same moneth, where we spent two or three daies, and relieved our companies with some fresh meate. From thence wee coasted by the *Gran Canaria*, and so to *Tenerife*, and staied there for the Lyons whelp your Lordships ship, and for captaine *Amys Preston* and the rest: But when after 7. or 8. daies we found them not, wee departed and directed our course for *Trinedado* with mine owne shippe, and a small barke of Captaine *Crosses* onely (for we had before lost sight of a small Gallego on the coast of *Spayne*, which came with us from *Plymmouth*.) wee arrived at *Trinedado* the 22. of March, casting ancour at point *Curiapan*, which the Spanyards call *punto de Gallo*, which is situate in 8. degrees[10] or there abouts: we abode there 4. or 5. daies, and in all that time we came not to the

[2]

speach of anie Indian or Spaniard: on the coast we saw a fire, as we sailed from the point *Carao* towards *Curiapan*, but for feare of the Spaniards, none durst come to speake with us. I my selfe coasted it in my barge close abord the shore and landed in every Cove, the better to know the Iland, while the ships kept the chanell. From *Curiapan* after a fewe daies we turned up Northeast to recover that place which the Spaniards cal *puerto de los Hispanioles*, and the inhabitants *Conquerabia*, and as before (revictualing my barge) I left the shippes and kept by the shore, the better to come to speach with some of the inhabitantes, and also to understand the rivers,

[9] Cape Roca, Portugal.

[10] In fact 10° 2′ 30″- all of Ralegh's reckonings are 2° too far south.

watring places and portes of the Iland which (as it is rudely done) my purpose is to send your Lordship after a few daies. From *Curiapan* I came to a port & seat of Indians called *Parico*[11] where we found a fresh-water river, but sawe no people. From thence I rowed to another port, called by the naturals *Piche*, and by the Spaniardes *Tierra de Brea*:[12] In the way betweene both were divers little brooks of fresh water, & one salt river that had store of oisters upon the branches of the trees, & were very salt & wel tasted. Al their oisters grow upon those boughs and spraies, and not on the ground: the like is commonlie seene in the West Indies and else where. This tree is described by *Andrewe Thevet* in his french *Antartique*, and the forme figured in his booke as a plante verye straunge, and by *Plinie* in his XII. booke of his naturall historie. But in this Ilande, as also in *Guiana* there are verie manie of them.[13]

At this point called *Tierra de Brea* or *Piche* there is

[3]

that abundance of stone pitch, that all the ships of the world may be therewith loden from thence, and wee made triall of it in trimming our ships to be most excellent good, and melteth not with the sunne as the pitch of *Norway*, and therefore for ships trading the south partes very profitable. From thence we went to the mountaine foote called *Annaperima* ,[14] and so passing the river *Carone* on which the Spanish Citie was seated, we met with our ships at *puerto de los Hispanioles* or *Conquerabia*.

This Iland of *Trinedado* hath the forme of a sheep-hook, and is but narrow, the north part is very mounteynous, the soile is very excellent and wil beare sugar, ginger, or any other commodity that the Indies yeeld. It hath store of deare, wyld porks, fruits, fish & fowle: It hath also for bread sufficient *Mais, Cassavi*,[15] and of those roots and fruits which are common every where in the west *Indies*. It hath divers beasts, which the *Indies* have not: the spaniards confessed that they found grains of gold in some of the rivers, but they having a purpose to enter *Guiana* (the *Magazin* of all rich

[11] Ralegh exactly follows Dudley's itinerary of a month earlier. Dudley reported (1899: 21-37) a marcasite mine east of Curiapan and encountered Spaniards at *Parico* (from the Arawakan *bara* 'sea', *koan* 'to be there'). Dudley's native guide to Orinoco, Baltizar, was 'threatened unto death' to secure his services, and Ralegh is similarly tempted below [46-7].

[12] A natural source of pitch often used by incoming vessels of the colonial powers to careen their ships' hulls.

[13] Taken as a 'marvel' by contemporaries. Three species are known to attach to mangrove roots in this way - *mytilus, ostrea folium* and *ostrea rhizophorae*.

[14] This mountain (192 m) is known to the Warao of the delta as the home of the Northern God *Na'barima*, 'father of the waves', who anchors their world-disk as it floats on the sea. The mountain is also the source of magic white crystals.

[15] These are the basic crops of native tropical agriculture, *zea mays* and *manihot utilissima*.

mettels) cared not to spend time in the search therof any farther. This Iland is called by the people therof *Cairi*,[16] and in it are divers nations: those about *Parico* are called *Jaio;* those at *Punto Carao* are of the *Arwacas,* and betweene *Carao* and *Curiapan* they are called *Salvaios,* betweene *Carao* and *punto Galera* are the *Nepoios,* and those about the Spanish Citie tearme themselves *Carinepagotos*:[17] Of the rest of the nations, and of other portes and rivers I leave to speake heere, beeing impertinent to my purpose, and meane to describe them as they are situate in the particular plot and description

[4]

of the Iland, three partes whereof I coasted with my barge, that I might the better discribe it.

Meeting with the ships at *puerto de los Hispanioles,* we found at the landing place a company of Spanyardes who kept a guard at the descent, and they offering a signe of peace I sent Captaine *Whiddon* to speake with them, whome afterward to my great griefe I left buried in the said Iland after my returne from *Guiana,* beeing a man most honest and valiant. The Spanyards semed to be desirous to trade with us, and to enter into tearms of peace, more for doubt of their own strength then for ought else, and in the end upon pledge, some of them came abord: the same evening there stale also abord us in a small *Canoa* two Indians, the one of them being a *Casique* or Lord of people called *Cantyman,* who had the yeare before beene with Captaine *Whiddon,* and was of his acquaintance. By this *Cantyman* wee understood what strength the Spaniardes had, how farre it was to their Citie, and of *Don Anthonio de Berreo* the governour, who was said to be slaine in his second attempt of *Guiana,* but was not.

While we remained at *puerto de los Hispanioles* some Spaniardes came abord us to buy lynnen of the company, and such other thinges as they wanted, and also to view our shippes and company, all which I entertained kindly and feasted after our manner: by meanes whereof I learned of one and another as much of the estate of *Guiana* as I could, or as they knew, for those poore souldiers having beene many yeares without wine, a fewe

[16] From the Arawakan *cai,* 'island'. The occurrence of this term, and the Cariban for a body of water, *tona,* in a number of the place names for the 'provinces' mentioned by Ralegh may also imply a political domain and not just an ecological feature - appropriately enough in view of the fluvial orientation of native society - see Chapter 2 (i).

[17] These 'nations' are actually either ethno-linguistic or political units. The political designations *arwacas* and *carinepagotos* ('those-who-live-at-*carinepa*') signal alliance and proximity to the Spanish, while the *Yao, Suppoyo* and *Salvaios* were native ethnic identities already extant within the region.

draughtes made them merry, in which moode they vaunted of *Guiana* and of the riches therof, and all what they knew of the waies and passages, my

[5]

selfe seeming to purpose nothing lesse then the enterance or discoverie thereof, but bred in them an opinion that I was bound onely for the reliefe of those english, which I had planted in *Virginia,* whereof the brute* was come among them, which I had performed in my returne if extremity of weather had not forst me from the said coast.

I found occasions of staying in this place for two causes: the one was to be revenged of *Berreo,* who the yeare before betraied 8. of Captaine *Whiddons* men, and toke them while he departed from them to seeke the *E. Bonaventure,* which arrived at *Trinedado* the day before from the East *Indies:* in whose absence *Berreo* sent a *Canoa* abord the pinnace onely with *Indians* and dogs inviting the company to goe with them into the wods to kil a deare, who like wise men in the absence of their Captaine followed the *Indians,* but were no sooner one harquebush* shot from the shore, but *Berreos* souldiers lying in ambush had them all, notwithstanding that he had given his worde to Captaine *Whiddon* that they should take water and wood safelie: the other cause of my stay was, for that by discourse with the *Spaniards* I daily learned more and more of *Guiana,* of the rivers and passages, and of the enterprize of *Berreo,* by what meanes or fault he failed, and how he meant to prosecute the same.

While we thus spent the time I was assured by another *Casique* of the north side of the Iland, that *Berreo* had sent to *Marguerita* & to *Cumana* for souldiers, meaning to have given me a *Cassado* at parting, if it had bin possible. For although he had given order through all the Iland that no *Indian* should come aborde to trade

[6]

with me upon paine of hanging and quartering, (having executed two of them for the same which I afterwardes founde) yet every night there came some with most lamentable complaints of his cruelty, how he had devided the Iland & given to every soldier a part, that he made the ancient *Casiqui* which were Lordes of the country to be their slaves, that he kept them in chains, & dropped their naked bodies with burning bacon, & such other torments, which I found afterwards to be true: for in the city after I entred the same, there were 5. of the Lords or litle kings (which they cal *Casiqui* in the west Indies) in one chaine almost dead of famine, and wasted with torments: these are called in their own language *Acarewana,* and now of late since English, French, & Spanish are come among them, they cal themselves

Capitaynes, because they perceive that the chiefest of every ship is called by that name. Those five *Capitaynes* in the chaine were called *Wannawanare, Carroaori, Maquarima, Tarroopanama,* & *Aterima.* So as both to be revenged of the former wrong, as also considering that to enter *Guiana* by small boats, to depart 400. or 500. miles from my ships, and to leave a garison in my backe interessed in the same enterprize, who also daily expected [s]upplies out of Spaine, I should have savoured very much of the Asse: and therfore taking a time of most advantage, I set upon the *Corp du guard* in the evening, and having put them to the sword, sente Captaine *Calfeild* onwards with 60. soldiers, & my self followed with 40. more & so toke their new city which they called *S. Joseph,* by breake of day: they abode not any fight after a few shot, & al being dismissed but onely *Berreo* and his companion, I brought them with me abord,

[7]

and at the instance of the Indians I set their new city of *S. Josephs* on fire.

The same day arrived Captaine *George Gifford* with your Lordships ship, & Captaine *Keymis* whom I lost on the coast of Spaine, with the *Gallego,* and in them divers Gent. and others, which to our little army was a great comfort and supply.

We then hastened away towards our purposed discovery, and first I called all the Captaines of the Iland together that were enemies to the Spaniards, for there were some which *Berreo* had brought out of other countries, & planted there to eat out & wast those that were natural of the place, & by my Indian interpreter, which I caried out of England, I made them understand that I was the servant of a Queene, who was the great *Casique* of the north, and a virgin, and had more *Casiqui* under her then there were trees in their Iland: that she was an enemy to the Castellani[18] in respect of their tyrannie and oppression, and that she delivered all such nations about her, as were by them oppressed, and having freed all the coast of the northern world from their servitude had sent me to free them also, and with al to defend the countrey of *Guiana* from their invasion and conquest. I shewed them her majesties picture which they so admired and honored, as it had beene easie to have brought them Idolatrous thereof.

The like & a more large discourse I made to the rest of the nations both in my passing to *Guiana,* & to those of the borders, so as in that part of the world her majesty is very famous and admirable, whom they now call *Ezrabeta Cassipuna Aquerewana,* which is as much as *Elizabeth,* the great princesse or greatest commaunder.[19]

[18] *Parana-kiri* ('spirits from the sea') was the native term for Europeans but the politics of colonial rivalry soon tutored native leaders in the subtleties of various European identities.

[19] See discussion of this phrase in Chapter 2 (i).

[8]

This done wee left *puerto de los Hispanioles,* and returned to *Curiapan,* and having *Berreo* my prisonour I gathered from him as much of *Guiana* as he knewe.

This *Berreo is* a gent. well descended, and had long served the Spanish king in *Millain, Naples,* the lowe Countries and else where, very valiant and liberall, and a Gent. of great assurednes, and of a great heart: I used him according to his estate and worth in all things I could, according to the small meanes I had.

I sent Captaine *Whiddon* the yeare before to get what knowledge he could of *Guiana,* and the end of my jorney at this time was to discover and enter the same, but my intelligence was farre from trueth, for the country is situate above 600. English miles further from the sea,[20] then I was made beleeve it had beene, which afterward understanding to be true by *Berreo,* I kept it from the knowledge of my companie, who else woulde never have beene brought to attempt the same: of which 600. miles I passed 400.[21] leaving my shippes so farre from me at ancor in the sea, which was more of desire to performe that discovery, then of reason, especially having such poore & weake vessels to transport our selves in;[22] for in the bottom of an old *Gallego* which I caused to be fashioned like a Galley, and in one barge, two wherries, and a ship bote of the Lyons whelpe, we caried 100 persons and their victuals for a moneth in the same, being al driven to lie in the raine and wether, in the open aire, in the burning sunne, & upon the hard bords, and to dresse our meat, and to carry al manner of furniture in them, wherewith they were so pestred and unsavery, that what with victuals being most fish,

[9]

with the weete clothes of so many men thrust together and the heate of the sunne, I will undertake there was never any prison in England, that coulde be founde more unsavory and lothsome, especially to my selfe, who had for many yeares before beene dieted and cared for in a sort farre differing.

If Captaine *Preston* had not beene perswaded that he should have come too late to *Trinedado* to have found us there (for the moneth was expired which I promised to tarry for him there ere he could recover the coast of Spaine) but that it had pleased God he might have joyned with us, and that wee had entred the countrey but some ten daies sooner ere the rivers were

[20] This estimate would place 'the Empyre of Guiana' in the savannas of the upper Caroni and Essequibo and Rupununi.

[21] At most it is only 250 miles from Point Curiapan to the mouth of the Caroni river.

[22] See Plate VII.

overflowen, we had adventured either to have gone to the great City of *Manoa,* or at least taken so many of the other Cities and townes neerer at hand, as would have made a royall returne: But it pleased not God so much to favour me at this time: if it shalbe my lot to prosecute the same, I shall willingly spend my life therein, and if any else shalbe enabled thereunto, and conquere the same, I assure him thus much, he shall performe more then ever was done in *Mexico* by *Cortez,* or in *Peru* by *Pacaro,* whereof the one conquered the Empire of *Mutezuma,* the other of *Guascar,* and *Atabalipa,* and whatsoever Prince shall possesse it, that Prince shalbe Lorde of more Gold, and of a more beautifull Empire, and of more Cities and people, then eyther the king of Spayne, or the great Turke.

But because there may arise many doubtes, and how this Empire of *Guiana* is become so populous, and adorned with so manie greate Cities, Townes, Temples, and threasures, I thought good to make it

[10]

knowen, that the Emperour now raigning is discended from those magnificent Princes of *Peru* of whose large territories, of whose pollicies, conquests, edifices, and riches *Pedro de Cieza, Francisco Lopez,*[23] and others have written large discourses: for when *Francisco Pacaro, Diego Almagro* and others conquered the said Empire of *Peru,* and had put to death *Atabalipa* sonne to *Guaynacapa,* which *Atabalipa* had formerly caused his eldest brother *Guascar* to be slaine, one of the younger sonnes of *Guaynacapa* fled out of *Peru,* and tooke with him many thousandes of those souldiers of the Empyre called *Oreiones,*[24] and with those and many others which followed him, he vanquished al that tract and valley of *America* which is situate betweene the great rivers of *Amazones* and *Baraquan,* otherwise called *Orenoke* and *Maranion.*

The Empyre of *Guiana* is directly east from *Peru* towards the sea, and lieth under the Equinoctial line, and it hath more abundance of Golde then any part of *Peru,* and as many or more great Cities then ever *Peru* had when it florished most: it is governed by the same lawes, and the Emperour and people observe the same religion, and the same forme and pollicies in government as was used in *Peru,* not differing in any part: and as I have beene assured by such of the *Spanyardes* as have seene *Manoa* the emperiall Citie of *Guiana,* which the *Spanyardes* cal *el Dorado,* that for the greatnes, for the riches, and for the excellent seate, it farre exceedeth any of the world, at least

[23] In Cieza de Léon's *Cronica del Peru* (Seville, 1553) and Lopez de Gomara's *Historia de la conquista de Nueva España* (Seville, 1552).

[24] Called *pakoyoc* in Quechua, but so called by the Spanish because the wearing of large ear ornamentation was a sign of élite status.

of so much of the world as is knowen to the Spanish nation: it is founded upon a lake of salt water[25] of 200. leagues long like unto *mare caspium.** And if we compare it to that of *Peru,* & but

[11]

reade the report of *Francisco Lopez* & others, it wil seeme more then credible, and because we may judge of the one by the other, I thought good to insert part of the 120. chapter of *Lopez* in his generall historie of the *Indies,* wherein he discribeth the court and magnificence of *Guaynacapa,* auncestor to the Emperour of *Guiana,* whose very words are these. *Todo el servicio de su casa, mesa, y cozina era de oro, y de plata, y quando menos de plata, y cobre por mas rezio. Tenia en su recamara estatuas huecas de oro que parecian gigantes, y las figuras al propio, y tamano de quantos animales, aves, arboles, y yervas produze la tierra, y de quantos peces cria la mar y aguas de sus reynos. Tenia assi mesmo sogas, costales, cestas, y troxes de oro y plata, rimeros de palos de oro, que pareciessen lenna raiada para quemar. En fin no avia cosa en su tierra, que no la tuviesse de oro contrahecha: y aun dizen, que tenian los Ingas un vergel en una Isla cerca de la Puna, donde se yvan a holgar, quando querian mar, que tenia la ortaliza, las flores, y arboles de oro y plata, invencion y grandeza hasta entonces nunca vista. Allende de todo esto tenia infinitissima cantidad de plata, y oro por labrar en el Cuzco, que se perdio por la muerte de Guascar, ca los Indios lo escondieron, viendo que los espanioles se lo tomavan, y embiavan a Espania.* That is, All the vessels of his house, table, and kitchin were of Gold and Silver, and the meanest of silver and copper for strength and hardnes of the mettal. He had in his wardroppe hollow statues of golde which seemed giants, and the figures in proportion and bignes of all the beastes, birdes, trees and hearbes, that the earth bringeth forth: and of all the fishes that the sea or waters of his kingdome breedeth. Hee had also ropes, budgets,* chestes and troughs of golde and silver, heapes of billets of golde that seemed woode,

[12]

marked out to burne. Finally there was nothing in his countrey, whereof hee had not the counterfeat in gold: Yea and they say, The *Ingas* had a garden of pleasure in an Iland neere *Puna,* where they went to recreate themselves, when they would take the ayre of the sea, which had all kind of garden hearbes, flowers and trees of Gold and Silver, an invention, & magnificence til then never seene: Besides all this, he had an infinite quantitie of silver

[25] The annual flooding of the Rupununi savannas were suggestive of a lake, and native geophagy of local soils (still practised today) may have been understood as 'salt' eating.

and gold unwrought in *Cuzco* which was lost by the death of *Guascar,* for the Indians hid it, seeing that the Spaniards tooke it, and sent it into Spayne.

And in the 117. Chapter *Francisco Picarro* caused the Golde and Silver of *Atabalipa* to bee weyed, after hee had taken it, which *Lopez* setteth downe in these wordes following.

Hallaron cinquenta y dos mil marcos de buena plata, y un millon y trezientos y veinte y seys mil, y quinientos pesos de oro, which is: They founde fiftie and two thousand markes of good silver, and one million, and three hundred twentie and sixe thousand and five hundred pesoes of golde.

Nowe although these reportes may seeme straunge, yet if wee consider the many millions which are daily brought out of *Peru* into Spaine, wee may easely beleeve the same, for wee finde that by the abundant treasure of that countrey, the Spanish King vexeth all the Princes of Europe, and is become in a fewe yeares from a poore king of *Castile* the greatest monarke of this part of the worlde, and likelie every day to increase, if other Princes forsloe* the good occasions offered, and suffer him to adde this Empire to

[13]

the rest, which by farre exceedeth all the rest: if his golde now indaunger us, hee will then be unresistable. Such of the Spaniards as afterwarde endevoured the conquest thereof (whereof there have beene many as shall bee declared heereafter) thought that this *Inga* (of whome this Emperor now living is descended) tooke his way by the river of *Amazones,* by that braunch which is called *Papamene,* for by that way followed Oreliano[26] (by the commaundement of the Marquis *Pacarro* in the yeare 1542.) whose name the river also beareth this day, which is also by others called *Maragnon,* althogh *Andrew Thevet* doth affirm that between *Maragnon* and *Amazones* there are 120 leagues: but sure it is that those rivers have one head & beginning, and that *Maragnon* which *Thevet* describeth is but a braunch of *Amazones* or *Oreliano,* of which I wil speake more in an other place. It was also attempted by *Diego Ordace,* but whether before *Oreliano* or after I knowe not: but it is now little lesse than 70. yeares since that *Ordace* a knight of the order of *Saint Iago* attempted the same: and it was in the yeare 1542. that *Oreliano* discovered the river of *Amazones;* but the first that ever sawe *Manoa* was *Johannes Martines* master of the munition to *Ordace.* At a porte called *Morequito* in *Guiana* there lyeth at this daie a great ancor of *Ordaces* shippe, and this port is some 300. miles within the lande, upon the greate river of *Orenoque.*

[26] See Chapter 2 (ii).

I rested at this port fowre daies: twentie daies after I left the shippes at *Curiapan.* The relation of this *Martynes* (who was the first that discovered *Manoa)* his successe & end is to be seene in the Chauncery of *Saint Juan de puerto rico,* whereof *Berreo* had a coppie, which

[14]

appeared to be the greatest incouragement as well to *Berreo* as to others that formerly attempted the discovery and conquest. *Oreliano* after he failed of the discoverie of *Guiana* by the said river of *Amazones,* passed into Spaine, and there obtained a patent of the king for the invasion and conquest, but died by sea about the Ilands, and his fleet beeing severed by tempest, the action for that time proceeded not. *Diego Ordace* followed the enterprize, and departed Spaine with 600. soldiers and 30. horse, who arriving on the coast of *Guiana* was slaine in a muteny with the most part of such as favoured him, as also of the rebellious part, in so much as his ships perished, and few or none returned, neither was it certainely knowen what became of the said *Ordace,* untill *Berreo* found the ancor of his ship in the river of *Orenoque;* but it was supposed, and so it is written by *Lopez* that he perished on the seas, and of other writers diversly conceived & reported.[27] And heereof it came that *Martynes* entred so farre within the lande and arrived at that Citie of *Inga* the Emperor, for it chaunced that while *Ordace* with his armie rested at the port of *Morequito* (who was either the first or second that attempted *Guiana*) by some negligence, the whol store of powder provided for the service was set on fire, & *Martines* having the chief charge was condemned by the generall *Ordace* to be executed forthwith: *Martines* being much favored by the soldiers had al the meane possible procured for his life, but it could not be obtained in other sort then this: That he shuld be set into a *Canoa* alone without any victual, onely with his armes, and so turnd loosse into the great river: but it pleased God that the *Canoa* was carried

[15]

downe the streame, & that certain of the *Guianians* met it the same evening, & having not at any time sene any Christian, nor any man of that colour, they caried *Martynes* into the land to be wondred at, and so from towne to towne, untill he came to the great Citie of *Manoa,* the seate and

[27] See Ojer 1966: 87-173. This incident became a part of Venezuelan folklore as reports of the 'lost expedition' of Ordaz continued to surface during the sixteenth century. However, Ojer persuasively argues that survivors were present among the *aruacas* in the uplands of Guiana and that this was of material importance in the emergence of an alliance with the Spanish - see also commentary on the map attributed to Ralegh in Chapter 2 (iv).

residence of *Inga* the Emperor. The Emperor after he had beheld him, knew him to be a Christian (for it was not long before that his brethren *Guascar* and *Atabalipa* were vanquished by the Spaniards in *Peru)* and caused him to be lodged in his pallace, and well entertained: hee lived 7. moneths in *Manoa,* but not suffered to wander into the countrey any where: hee was also brought thither all the waie blindfield, led by the Indians, untill he came to the entrance of *Manoa* it selfe, and was 14. or 15. daies in the passage: he avowed at his death that he entred the City at *Noon,* & then they uncovered his face, and that he travelled al that daie til night thorow the Citie, and the next day from sun rising to sun setting, ere he came to the pallace of *Inga.* After that *Martynes* had lived 7. moneths in *Manoa,* and began to understand the language of the country, *Inga* asked him whether he desired to returne into his own countrey, or would willingly abide with him: but *Martynes* not desirous to stay, obtained the favour of *Inga* to depart, with whom he sent divers *Guianians* to conduct him to the river of *Orenoque* all loden with as much gold as they could carrie, which he gave to *Martines* at his departure: but when he was arrived neere the rivers side, the borderers which are called *Orenoqueponi*[28] robbed him and his *Guianians* of all the treasure[29] (the borderers beeing at that time at warres which [*sic*] *Inga,* and not conquered) save onely of

[16]

two great bottels of gords, which were filled with beads of gold curiously wrought, which those *Orenoqueponi* thought had ben no other thing then his drink or meate or grain for foode with which *Martynes* had libertie to passe, and so in *Canoas* he fell down by the river of *Orenoque* to *Trinedado,* and from thence to *Marguerita,* and so to *Saint Juan de puerto rico,* where remaining a long tyme for passage into *Spayne* he died. In the time of his extreme sicknesse, and when he was without hope of life, receaving the *Sacrament* at the handes of his Confessor, he delivered these thinges, with the relation of his travels, and also called for his *Calabaza* or gords of the gold beades which he gave to the Church & friers to be praied for. This *Martynes* was he that christned the citie of *Manoa,* by the name of *El Dorado,* and as *Berreo* informed me upon this occasion.[30] Those *Guianians*

[28] An econym, designating no more than 'those living on Orinoco'. Despite the Macuxi form of the term, as Schomburgk noted, many Cariban languages would also express such a designation in an orthographically similar form so it does not license Schomburgk's inference that the *Orinoqueponi* were a branch of the upland Macuxi.

[29] See commentary for Plate IV, Chapter 2 (iv) and below [32].

[30] This is a crucial identification of the wider *El Dorado* legend with that of the *Manoa* in Guiana, '*Manoa*' being the ethnonym of the famed gold-traders from Río Negro. Their

and also the borderers, and all others in that tract which I have seen are marveylons [*sic*] great drunkardes, in which vice I think no nation can compare with them and at the times of their solemne feasts when the Emperor carowseth with his Captayns, tributories, & governours, the manner is thus. All those that pledge him are first stripped naked, & their bodies annoynted al over with a kinde of white *Balsamum* (by them called *Curcai*[31]) of which there is great plenty and yet very deare amongst them, and it is of all other the most pretious, wherof we have had good experience: when they are annointed all over, certaine servants of the Emperor having prepared gold made into fine powder blow it thorow hollow canes upon their naked bodies, untill they be al shining from the foote to the head,[32] & in this sort they sit drinking by twenties and hundreds & continue

[17]

in drunkennes somtimes sixe or seven daies togither: the same is also confirmed by a letter written into *Spaine* which was intercepted, which master *Robert Dudley* told me he had seen. Upon this sight, and for the abundance of gold which he saw in the citie, the Images of gold in their Temples, the plates, armors, and shields of gold which they use in the wars, he called it *El Dorado.*[33] After *Oreliano* who was emploied by *Pacaro* afterwards *Marques Pacaro* conqueror and governor of *Peru,* and the death of *Ordace* and *Martynes,* one *Pedro de Osua,* a knight of *Navarre* attempted *Guiana,* taking his way from *Peru,* and built his brigandines upon a river called *Oia,* which riseth to the southward of *Quito,* and is very great: this river falleth into *Amazones,* by which *Osua* with his companies descended, and came out of that Province which is called *Mutylones:* and it seemeth to me that this Empire is reserved for her Majestie and the *English* nation, by reason of the hard successe which all these & other *Spaniards* found in attempting the

power in the Guiana highlands was still very evident to the Dutch and Brazilians of the late seventeenth century through the activities of the war-chief *Ajuricaba,* whose statue may be seen today in Manaos on the central Amazon - see Whitehead 1988: 168-9.

31 *Copaifera officinalis, copaiba* or *curucai.* It is mixed with annatto to make a body-paint or used as an anointment for skin and hair. It became an important item of trade with the Dutch - see Whitehead 1988.

32 See Plate II. As Humboldt also noted: 'On the banks of the Caura, and in other wild parts of Guiana, where painting the body is used instead of tattooing, the nations anoint themselves with turtle-fat, and stick spangles of mica with a metallic lustre, white as silver and red as copper, on their skin, so that at a distance they seem to wear lace clothes. The fable of "the gilded man" is, perhaps, founded on a similar custom' (Humboldt 1907: III, 46).

33 This was not, therefore, a confused geographical identification but a claim as to cultural analogy between known native custom and the recently encountered cultural practice of the Manoa.

same, wherof I will speake brieflie, though impertinent in some sort to my purpose. This *Pedro de Osua* had among his troupes a *Biscayn* called *Agiri,* a man meanlie borne, & bare no other office than a Surgeant or *Alferez:* but after certaine months, when the soldiers were grieved with travels and consumed with famine, and that no entrance could be found by the branches or body of *Amazones,* this *Agiri* raised a muteny,[34] of which hee made himselfe the head, and so prevailed as he put *Osua* to the sword, and all his followers, taking on him the whole charge and commandement with a purpose not onely to make himselfe Emperor of *Guiana,*

[18]

but also of *Peru,* and of al that side of the *West Indies:* he had of his partie seven hundred soldiers, and of those many promised to draw in other captains and companies to deliver up towns and forts in *Peru,* but neither finding by the saide river any passage into *Guiana,* nor any possibilitie to returne towards *Peru* by the same *Amazones* by reason that the descent of the river made so great a currant, he was inforced to desemboque at the mouth of the said *Amazones,*[35] which cannot be lesse than a thousand leagues from the place where they imbarqued: from thence he coasted the land till he arrived at *Marguerita* to the North of *Mompatar,* which is at this daie called *Puerto de Tyranno,* for that he there slue *Don Juan de villa Andreda,* governor of *Marguerita,* who was father to *Don Juan Sermiento* governor of *Marguerita* when Sir *John Burgh* landed there, and attempted the *Iland. Agiri* put to the sword all others in the Iland that refused to be of his partie, and tooke with him certaine *Cemerones,* and other desperate companions: From thence he went to *Cumana,* and there slew the *Governor,* and dealt in all as at *Marguerita:* he spoiled* all the coast of *Caracas,* and the province of *Vensuello,* and of *Rio de hache,* and as I remember it was the same yeer that Sir *John Hawkins* sailed to Saint *Juan de Lua* in the *Jesus* of *Lubeck,* for himselfe told me that he met with such a one upon the coast that rebelled, and had sailed downe all the river of *Amazones. Agiri* from hence landed about *Sancta Marta,* and sacked it also, putting to death so many as refused to be his followers, purposing to invade *Nuevo reyno de Granada,* & to sack *Pampelone, Merida, Lagrita, Tunja,* & the rest of the cities of *Nuevo reygno,* and from

[34] A notorious incident in the history of colonial Latin America, which was the subject of a film by Werner Herzog, *Aguirre: Wrath of God.*

[35] However, there is also a long historiographical tradition beginning with Fray Pedro Simón's *Noticias Historiales* (Cuenca, 1627, chapters 30-9, translated in Markham 1861) of interpreting the accounts of Aguirre's journey as indicating a route up the Río Negro and then down Orinoco to the Atlantic.

[19]

thence againe to enter *Peru:* but in a fight in the said *Nuevo reygno* he was overthrowne, & finding no way to escape, he first put to the sword his own children, foretelling them that they should not live to be defamed or opbraid by the *Spaniards* after his death, who would have tearmed them the children of a *Traytor* or *Tyrant,* and that sithence* he could not make them Princes, he woulde yet deliver them from shame and reproch: These were the ends and tragedies of *Oreliano, Ordace, Osua, Martynes,* and *Agiri.*

After these followed *Jeronimo Ortal de Saragosa* with 130. soldiers, who failing his entrance by sea was cast with the currant on the coast of *Paria,* and peopled about S. *Miguell de Neveri.* It was then attempted by *Don Pedro de sylva* a *Portugues* of the familie of *Rigomes de sylva,* and by the favour which *Rigomes* had with the king, he was set out, but he also shot wide of the mark, for being departed from *Spaine* with his fleete, he entred by *Maragnon* or *Amazones,* where by the nations of the river, and by the *Amazones* he was utterly overthrowen, and himselfe and all his armie defeated, onely seven escaped, and of those but two returned.

After him came *Pedro Hernandez de Serpa,* and landed at *Cumana* in the *West Indies,* taking his journey by land towards *Orenoque,* which may bee some 120. leagues, but ere he came to the borders of the said river, he was set upon by a nation of Indians called *Wikiri,*[36] and overthrowen in sort, that of 300. soldiers, horsemen, many Indians, and *Negros,* there returned but 18: others affirm that he was defeated in the very entrance of *Guiana,* at the first civill towne of the Empire called *Macureguarai.*[37] Captaine *Preston* in taking

[20]

S. Iago de Leon (which was by him and his companies very resolutely performed, being a great towne, and far within the land) held a gentleman prisoner who died in his ship, that was one of the companie of *Hernandez de Serpa,* and saved among those that escaped, who witnessed what opinion is held among the *Spaniards* thereabouts of the great riches of *Guiana,* and *El Dorado* the citie of *Inga.* Another *Spaniard* was brought aboord me by captaine *Preston,* who told me in the hearing of himselfe and divers other gentlemen, that he met with *Berreos* Campmaster at *Caracas,* when he came from the borders of *Guiana,* and that he saw with him fortie of most pure plates of golde curiously wrought, and swords of *Guiana* decked and inlaid

[36] Guayqueries - see Whitehead 1988: 73-5.

[37] Schomburgk (1848: 78) made the suggestion that this could be a compound word to indicate *macuwari* ('sword' or 'club'), *guarai* ('like'), although, as with his other derivations for the place names *Orocotona, Iconuri, Wanuretona* and *Arowacai,* the Cariban orthography does not necessarily indicate a uniquely Macuxi etymology for such terms.

with golde, feathers garnished with golde, and divers rarities which he carried to the *Spanish* king.[38]

After *Hernandez de Serpa* it was undertaken by the *Adelantado, Don Gonzales Cemenes de Casada,* who was one of the chiefest in the conquest of *Nuevo reygno,* whose daughter & heire *Don Anthonio de Berreo* maried: *Gonzales* sought the passage also by the river called *Papamene,* which riseth by *Quito* in *Peru,* & runneth southeast 100. leagues, & then falleth into *Amazones,* but he also failing the entrance, returned with the losse of much labour and cost: I tooke one captaine *George* a *Spaniard* that followed *Gonzales* in this enterprise. *Gonzales* gave his daughter to *Berreo* taking his oth and honor to follow the enterprise to the last of his substance and life, who since as he hath sworne to me hath spent 300000. ducates in the same, and yet never could enter so far into the land as my selfe with that poore troupe or rather a handfull of men, being in all about

[21]

100. gentlemen, soldiers, rowers, bote-keepers, boies,[*] and of all sorts: neither could any of the forepassed undertakers, nor *Berreo* himselfe discover the country, till now lately by conference with an ancient king called *Carapana*[39] he got the true light thereof: for *Berreo* came above 1500. miles, ere he understood ought, or could finde any passage or entrance into any part thereof, yet he had experience of all these forenamed, and divers others, and was perswaded of their errors and mistakings. *Berreo* sought it by the river *Cassanar,* which falleth into a great river called *Pato, Pato* falleth into *Meta,* and *Meta* into *Baraquan,* which is also called *Orenoque.*

He tooke his journey from *Nuevo reygno de granada* where he dwelt, having the inheritance of *Gonzales Cemenes* in those parts: he was followed with 700. horse, he drave with him 1000. head of cattell, he had also many women, Indians, and slaves. How all these rivers crosse and encounter, how the countrie lieth and is bordred, the passage of *Cemenes,* and of *Berreo,* mine owne discoverie, and the way that I entred, with all the rest of the nations and rivers, your Lordship shall receive in a large Chart or Map, which I have not yet finished,[40] and which I shall most humbly pray your Lo. to secret, and not to suffer it to passe your own hands; for by a draught thereof all may bee prevented by other nations. For I know it is this very yeere

[38] Domingo de Vera raised, with Philip II's financial support, a huge colonising expedition on the strength of these precious proofs, which both underlines the extent of already plundered gold and confirms claims as to the prevalence of gold work amongst Guiana's native cultures, see also Schomburgk (1848: 17) and below [34].

[39] That is 'The Mosquito'.

[40] See commentary in Chapter 2 (iv), as well as Map II and Plate VIII.

sought by the French, although by the way that they now take, I feare it not much. It was also told me ere I departed England, that *Villiers* the Admirall was in preparation for the planting of *Amazones,* to which river the French have made divers voiages, and returned

[22]

much gold and other rarities. I spake with a captaine of a French ship that came from thence, his ship riding in *Falmouth,* the same yeere that my ships came first from *Virginia.*

There was another this yeere in *Helford* that also came from thence, and had been 14. moneths at an ancor in *Amazones,* which were both very rich. Although as I am perswaded, *Guiana* cannot be entred that way, yet no doubt the trade of gold from thence passeth by branches of rivers into the river of *Amazones,* and so it doth on every hand farre from the countrey it selfe, for those Indians of *Trenedado* have plates of gold from *Guiana,* those *Canibals of Dominica*[41] which dwell in the Ilands by which our ships passe yeerly to the *West Indies,* also the Indians of *Paria,* those Indians called *Tucaris, Chochi, Apotomios, Cumanagotos,* and all those other nations inhabiting nere about the mountaines that run from *Paria* thorow the Province of *Vensuello,* and in *Maracapana,* and the Canibals[42] of *Guanipa,* the Indians called *Assawai, Coaca, Aiai,* and the rest (all which shall be described in my description as they are situate) have plates of gold of *Guiana.* And upon the river of *Amazones Thevet* writeth that the people weare *Croissants* of gold, for of that form the *Guianians* most commonly make them: So as from *Dominica* to *Amazones* which is above 250. leagues, all the chiefe Indians in al parts weare of those plates of *Guiana.* Undoubtedly those that trade *Amazones* returne much gold, which (as is aforesaid) commeth by trade from *Guiana,* by some branch of a river that falleth from the countrey into *Amazones,* and either it is by the river which passeth by the nations called *Tisnados,* or by *Carepuna.*[43]

[23]

I made inquirie amongst the most ancient and best traveled of the *Orenoqueponi,* & I had knowledge of all the rivers between *Orenoque* and

[41] The war-chiefs of Dominica continued to raid the Lokono (*aruacas*) of the Atlantic coast for these items, well into the sixteenth century - see Chapter 2, n. 2.

[42] As with the preceding instance, the political nature of an ascription of 'cannibalism' is obvious from this usage, the term *caribe* doing similar work in Spanish colonial discourse - see Chapter 1 (iv) and Hulme and Whitehead 1992.

[43] *Tisnados* from the Spanish 'painted', indicating the use of the indigo stain derived from *genipa americana*; *Carepuna* is related to the term *Cassipuna* - see Chapter 2 (i).

Amazones, and was very desirous to understand the truth of those warlike women, bicause of some it is beleeved, of others not: And though I digresse from my purpose, yet I will set downe what hath been delivered me for truth of those women, and I spake with a *Casique* or Lord of people that told me he had been in the river, and beyond it also. The nations of these women are on the south side of the river in the Provinces of *Topago*,[44] and their chiefest strengths and retraicts are in the Ilands scituate on the south side of the entrance, some 60. leagues within the mouth of the said river. The memories of the like women are very ancient as well in *Africa* as in *Asia:* In *Africa* those that had *Medusa* for *Queene*: others in *Scithia* neere the rivers of *Tanais* and *Thermadon*: we find also that *Lampedo* and *Marthesia* were *Queens* of the *Amazones:* in many histories they are verified to have been, and in divers ages and Provinces: But they which are not far from *Guiana* do accompanie* with men but once in a yeere, and for the time of one moneth, which I gather by their relation to be in Aprill. At that time all the Kings of the borders assemble, and the Queenes of the *Amazones,* and after the Queens have chosen, the rest cast lots for their *Valentines.* This one moneth, they feast, daunce, & drinke of their wines in abundance, & the Moone being done, they all depart to their owne Provinces. If they conceive, and be delivered of a sonne, they returne him to the father, if of a daughter they nourish it, and reteine it, and as many as have daughters send

[24]

unto the begetters a Present, all being desirous to increase their owne sex and kinde, but that the cut of the right dug of the brest I do not finde to be true. It was farther told me, that if in the wars they tooke any prisoners that they used to accompany with those also at what time soever, but in the end for certaine they put them to death: for they are said to be very cruell and bloodthirsty,[45] especially to such as offer to invade their territories. These *Amazones* have likewise great store of these plates of golde, which they recover by exchange chiefly for a kinde of greene stones, which the Spaniards call *Piedras Hijadas,* and we use for spleene stones, and for the disease of the stone we also esteeme them: of these I saw divers in *Guiana,* and commonly every king or *Casique* hath one, which their wives for the most part weare, and they esteeme them as great jewels.[46]

But to returne to the enterprise of *Berreo,* who (as I have said) departed

[44] Río Tapajos, a mid-Amazon tributary.

[45] This recalls Tupian sacrificial rituals - see Chapter 2, n. 23.

[46] There was a congruence of native and colonial ideas as to the power of crystals - see Chapter 1, n. 20 - and the gendered basis for their display seems apposite in the light of their native symbolism.

from *Nuevo reygno* with 700. horse, besides the provisions above rehearsed; he descended by the river called *Cassanar,* which riseth in *Nuevo reygno* out of the mountaines by the citie of *Tuuja* [*sic*], from which mountaine also springeth *Pato,* both which fall into the great river of *Meta,* and *Meta* riseth from a mountaine joining to *Pampelone* in the same *Nuevo reygno de Granada:* these as also *Guaiare,* which issueth out of the mountains by *Timana,* fall all into *Baraquan,* and are but of his heads, for at their comming togither they lose their names, and *Baraquan* farther down is also rebaptized by the name of *Orenoque.* On the other side of the citie and hils of *Timana* riseth *rio grande,* which falleth into the sea by *Sancta Marta.* By *Cassonar*

[25]

first, and so into *Meta Berreo* passed, keeping his horsemen on the banks, where the countrie served them for to march, and where otherwise he was driven to embarque them in botes which he builded for the purpose, & so came with the currant down the river of *Meta,* and so into *Baraquan.* After he entred that great and mightie river, he began dailie to loose of his companies both men and horse, for it is in many places violentlie swift, and hath forcible eddies, many sands, and divers Ilands sharpe pointed with rocks: But after one whole yeere, journeying for the most part by river, and the rest by land, he grew dailie to fewer numbers, for both by sicknes, and by encountring with the people of those regions, through which he travelled, his companies were much wasted, especially by divers incounters with the *Amapaiens:* And in all this time he never could learne of any passage into *Guiana,* nor any newes or fame thereof, untill he came to the farther border of the said *Amapaia,* eight daies journey from the river *Caroli,* which was the farthest river that we entred. Among those of *Amapaia, Guiana* was famous, but few of these people accosted *Berreo,* or woulde trade with him the first three months of the six which he sojourned there. This *Amapaia is* also marvellous rich in gold (as both *Berreo* confessed, and those of *Guiana* with whom I had most conference) and is situate upon *Orenoke* also. In this countrey *Berreo* lost 60. of his best soldiers, and most of all his horse that remained of his former yeeres travell: but in the end after divers encounters with those nations they grew to peace, and they presented *Berreo* with 10. Images of fine gold among divers other plates

[26]

and *Croissants,* which as he sware to me and divers other gentlemen were so curiouslie wrought, as he had not seene the like either in *Italy, Spaine,* or the *Lowe Cuntries:* and he was resolved that when they came to the hands of the

Spanish king, to whom he had sent them by his Campmaster, they would appeer very admirable, especially being wrought by such a nation as had no Iron instrument at all, nor anie of those helps which our goldsmiths have to worke withall. The particular name of the people in *Amapaia* which gave him these peeces are called *Anebas*,[47] and the river of *Orenoque* at that place is above 12. *English* miles brode, which may be from his outfall into the sea 700. or 800. miles.

This Province of *Amapaia* is a verie low and a marish ground neere the river, and by reason of the red water which issueth out in small branches thorow the fenny and boggie ground, there breed divers poysonfull wormes and serpents, and the Spaniards not suspecting, nor in anie sort foreknowing the danger were infected with a greevous kind of flux by drinking therof, and even the very horses poisoned therewith: In so much as at the end of the six months that they abode there, of all there troups, there were not left above 120. soldiers, and neither horse nor cattle. For *Berreo* hoped to have found *Guiana* by 1000. miles neerer than it fell out to be in the end, by means wherof they susteined much want and much hunger, oppressed with greevous diseases, and all the miseries that could be imagined. I demanded of those in *Guiana* that had travelled *Amapaia* how they lived with that tawnie or red water when they travelled thither, and they told

[27]

me that after the *Sun* was neere the middle of the skie, they used to fill their pots and pitchers with that water, but either before that time, or towards the setting of the *Sun* it was dangerous to drinke of, and in the night strong poison. I learned also of divers other rivers of that nature among them which were also (while the *Sun* was in the *Meridian)* verie safe to drink, and in the morning, evening, and night, woonderfull dangerous and infective. From this Province *Berreo* hasted away assoone as the *Spring* and beginning of *Summer* appeered, and sought his entrance on the borders of *Orenoque* on the south side, but there ran a ledge of so high & impassable mountaines, as he was not able by any means to march over them, continuing from the east sea into which *Orenoque* falleth, even to *Quito in Peru:* neither had he means to carrie victuall or munition over those craggie, high, and fast hils, being all wooddy, and those so thicke and spiny, and so full of prickles, thorns, and briers, as it is impossible to creepe thorow them: he had also neither friendship among the people, nor any interpreter to perswade or treate with them, and more, to his disadvantage, the *Casiqui* and kings of

[47] Perhaps the *Baniva*, now located further south on the Río Negro. The name *Amapaiens*, occurring earlier on, is an econym referring to the *llanos* of the Casanare.

Amapaia had given knowledge of his purpose to the *Guianians,* and that he sought to sacke and conquer the Empire, for the hope of their so great abundance and quantities of gold: he passed by the mouths of many great rivers, which fell into *Orenoque* both from the north and south, which I forbeare to name for tediousnes, and bicause they are more pleasing in describing than reading.

Berreo affirmed that there fell an hundred rivers into *Orenoque* from the north and south, whereof the

[28]

lest was as big as *Rio grande,* that passeth between *Popayan* and *Nuevo reyno de granada (Rio grande* being esteemed one of the renowned rivers in al the west Indies, & numbred among the great rivers of the world:) But he knew not the names of any of these, but *Caroli* only, neither from what nations they descended, neither to what Provinces they led, for he had no meanes to discourse with the inhabitants at any time: neither was he curious in these things, being utterlie unlearned, & not knowing the east from the west.[48] But of al these I got som knowledge, & of manie more, partly by mine own travel, & the rest by conference: of som one I lerned one, of others the rest, having with me an Indian that spake many languages, & that of *Guiana* naturally. I sought out al the aged men, & such as were greatest travelers, and by the one & the other I came to understand the situations, the rivers, the kingdoms from the east sea to the borders of *Peru,*[49] & from *Orenoque* southward as far as *Amazones or Maragnon,* and the regions of *Maria Tamball,*[50] and of all the kings of Provinces and captains of townes and villages, how they stood in tearms of peace or war, and which were friends or enimies the one with the other, without which there can be neither entrance nor conquest in those parts, nor els where: For by the dissension betweene *Guascar* and *Atabalipa, Paçaro* conquered *Peru,* and by the hatred that the *Traxcallians* bare to *Mutezuma, Cortez* was victorious over *Mexico,* without which both the one and the other had failed of their enterprize, and of the great honor and riches, which they attained unto.

[48] This seems disingenuous in view of the information he garnered from Spanish sources, including Berrio, though they may have been reason on both sides to conceal the extent to which Berrio had informed Ralegh - see Chapter 1.

[49] Particularly Martyn the *Arwacan*– see [53]. The possession of a continent-wide geography by the Lokono ('arawaks') is amply confirmed by the records of the Moravian missionaries in Surinam (see Staehelin 1913: II-2, 174-5).

[50] As Schomburgk (1848: 34) also noted, Pedro Mártir (1530: I, chapter 9) records this as the name of 'fortunate and fruitful' islands proximate to the Paria Gulf, inhabited by meek and pliant natives but possessing no gold or riches; perhaps the isles of Los Roques, off the Venezuelan coast.

Now *Berreo* began to grow into despaire, and looked for no other successe than his predecessors in this

[29]

enterprize, untill such time as he arrived at the Province of *Emeria* towards the east sea and mouth of the river, where he found a nation of people very favorable, and the countrey full of all maner of victuall. The king of this land is called *Carapana,* a man very wise, subtill, and of great experience, being little lesse than 100. yeeres old: In his youth he was sent by his father into the Iland of *Trinedado,* by reason of civill warre among themselves, and was bred at a village, in that Iland, called *Parico:* at that place in his youth he had seene many Christians both French and Spanish, and went divers times with the Indians of *Trinedado* to *Marguerita* and *Cumana* in the west Indies, (for both those places have ever been releeved with victuall from *Trinedado)* by reason whereof he grew of more understanding, and noted the difference of the nations, comparing the strength and armes of his country with those of the Christians, and ever after temporized so, as whosoever els did amisse, or was wasted by contention, *Carapana* kept himselfe and his country in quiet and plentie: he also held peace with *Caribas* or *Canibals* his neighbors, and had free trade with all nations whosoever els had war.

Berreo sojourned and rested his weake troupe in the towne of *Carapana* six weeks, and from him learnd the way and passage to *Guiana,* and the riches & magnificence thereof: but being then utterly disable to proceed, he determined to trie his fortune another yeere, when he had renewed his provisions, and regathered more force, which he hoped for as wel out of Spain, as from *Nuevo reyno,* where he had left his son *Don Anthonio Xemenes* to second him upon the first notice given of his

[30]

entrance, & so for the present embarqued himselfe in *Canoas,* & by the branches of *Orenoque* arrived at *Trinedado,* having from *Carapana* sufficient Pilots to conduct him. From *Trinedado* he coasted *Paria,* and so recovered *Marguerita:* and having made relation to *Don Juan Sermiento* the governour of his proceeding, and perswaded him of the riches of *Guiana,* he obtained from thence 50. soldiers, promising presentlie to returne to *Carapana,* and so into *Guiana.* But *Berreo* meant nothing lesse at that time, for he wanted manie provisions necessarie for such an enterprize, and therfore departing from *Marguerita* seated himselfe in *Trinedado,* and from thence sent his Campmaster, and his Sargeant major back to the borders to discover the neerest passage, into the Empire, as also to treat with the borderers, and to drawe them to his partie and love, without which, he knew he could neither passe safelie, nor in anie sort be releeved with victuall or ought els. *Carapana* directed this companie to a king called *Morequito,* assuring them that no man could deliver so much of *Guiana* as *Morequito* could, and that his dwelling was but five daies journey from *Macureguarai* the first civill towne of *Guiana.*

Now your Lordship shall understand that this *Morequito,* one of the greatest Lords or Kings of the borders of *Guiana,* had two or three yeeres before beene at *Cumana,* and at *Marguerita* in the west Indies, with great store of plates of gold, which he carried to exchange for such other things as he wanted in his owne countrey, and was dailie feasted, and presented by the governors of those places, and

[31]

held amongst them some two moneths, in which time one *Vides* governor of *Cumana* wan him to be his conductor into *Guiana,* being allured by those *Croissants* and Images of gold which he brought with him to trade, as also by the ancient fame and magnificence of *El Dorado:* whereupon *Vides* sent into Spaine for a Patent to discover and conquer *Guiana,* not knowing of the precedence of *Berreos* patent, which as *Berreo* affirmeth was signed before that of *Vides:* so as when *Vides* understood of *Berreo,* and that he had made entrance into that territorie, and foregone his desire and hope, it was verilie thought that *Vides* practised with *Morequito* to hinder and disturbe *Berreo* in all he could, and not to suffer him to enter through his *Seignory,* nor anie of his companies, neither to victuall, nor guide them in anie sort; for *Vides* governor of *Cumana,* and *Berreo* were become mortall enimies, as well for that *Berreo* had gotten *Trinedado* into his Patent with *Guiana,* as also in that he was by *Berreo* prevented in the journey of *Guiana* it selfe: howsoever it was I know not, but *Morequito* for a time dissembled his disposition, suffered Spaniards, and a Frier (which *Berreo* had sent to discover *Manoa)* to travell through his countrey, gave them a guide for *Macureguarai* the first towne of civill and apparelled people, from whence they had other guides to bring them to *Manoa* the great citie of *Inga:* and being furnished with those things, which they had learned of *Carapana,* were of most price in *Guiana,* went onward, and in eleven daies arrived at *Manoa,* as *Berreo* affirmeth for certain: although I could not be assured therof by the Lord which now governeth the Province of

[32]

Morequito, for he told me that they got all the gold they had, in other townes on this side *Manoa,* there being many very great and rich, and (as he said) built like the townes of Christians, with many roomes.

When these ten Spaniards were returned, and readie to put out of the border of *Arromaia,* the people of *Morequito* set upon them,[51] & slew them all but one that swam the river, and tooke from them to the value of 40000. pesoes of golde, and as it is written in the storie of *Job,* one onelie lived to bring the newes to *Berreo,* that both his nine soldiers and holie father were benighted in the saide Province. I my selfe spake with the Captaines of *Morequito* that slew them, and was at the place where it was executed. *Berreo* inraged heerewithall sent all the strength he could make into *Arromaia,* to be revenged of him, his people, and countrey: but *Morequito* suspecting the same fled over *Orenoque,* and thorow the territories of the *Saima,* and *Wikiri,* recovered *Cumana,* where he thought himselfe very safe with *Vides* the governor: But *Berreo* sending for him in the kings name, and his messengers finding him in the house of one *Fashardo* on the sudden ere it was suspected, so as he could not then be conveied away, *Vides* durst not deny him, as well to avoide the suspition of the practise, as also for that an holy father was slaine by him and his people. *Morequito* offred *Fashardo* the weight of three quintals[52] in gold, to let him escape, but the poore *Guianian* betraid of all sides was delivered to the Campmaster of Berreo, and was presently executed.

After the death of this *Morequito,* the soldiers of *Berreo* spoiled his territorie, & tooke divers prisoners,

[33]

among others they tooke the unckle of *Morequito* called *Topiawari,* who is now king of *Arromaia,* (whose sonne I brought with me into *England)* and is a man of great understanding and pollicie: he is above 100. yeeres old, and yet of a very able bodie: the *Spanyards* led him in a chain 17. daies, and made him their guide from place to place betweene his countrey & *Emeria* the province of *Carapana* aforesaid, and was at last redeemed for 100. plates of gold, and divers stones called *Piedras Hijadas,* or *Spleen* stones. Now *Berreo* for executing of *Morequito* and other cruelties, spoiles, and slaughters done in *Arromaia* hath lost the love of the *Orenoqueponi,* and of all the borderers, and dare not send any of his soldiers any farther into the land than to *Carapana,* which he calleth the port of *Guiana:* but from thence by the helpe of *Carapana* he had trade farther into the countrey, and alwaies appointed 10. *Spaniards* to reside in *Carapanas* towne; by whose favor and by being conducted by his people, those ten searched the countrey thereabouts as well for mines, as for other trades and commodities.

They have also gotten a nephew of *Morequito,* whom they have Christened and named *Don Juan,* of whom they have great hope, endevoring

[51] See Plate V.

[52] Approximately 300–36 lb.

by all means to establish him in the said province. Among manie other trades those *Spaniards* used in *Canoas* to passe to the rivers of *Barema, Pawroma,* and *Dissequebe,* which are on the south side of the mouth of *Orenoque,* and there buie women and children from the *Canibals,* which are of that barbarous nature, as they will for 3. or 4. hatchets sell the sonnes and daughters of their owne brethren and sisters, and for somewhat more

[34]

even their own daughters: heerof the Spaniards make great profit, for buying a maid of 12. or 13. yeeres for three or fower hatchets, they sell them againe at *Marguerita* in the west Indies for 50. and 100. pesoes, which is so many crownes.[53]

The master of my ship *Jo. Douglas* tooke one of the *Canoas* which came loden from thence with people to be sold, and the most of them escaped, yet of those hee brought, there was one as well favored, and as well shaped as ever I saw anie in England, and afterward I sawe many of them, which but for their tawnie colour may bee compared to anie of *Europe.* They also trade in those rivers for bread of *Cassavi,* of which they buy an hundred pound weight for a knife, and sell it at *Marguerita* for ten pesoes.[54] They also recover great store of cotten, brasill wood, and those beds which they call *Hamacas* or brasill beds, wherein in hot countries all the Spaniards use to lie commonlie, and in no other, neither did we our selves while we were there: By means of which trades, for ransom of divers of the *Guianians,* and for exchange of hatchets and knives, *Berreo* recovered some store of gold plates, eagles of gold, and Images of men and divers birds, and dispatched his Campmaster for Spaine with all that he had gathered, therewith to levy soldiers, and by the shew therof to draw others to the love of the enterprize: and having sent divers Images as well of men as beasts, birds and fishes so curiouslie wrought in gold, doubted not but to perswade the king to yeeld to him some further helpe, especiallie for that this land hath never been sacked, the mines never wrought, and in the

[53] *Caribe* (or 'cannibal') 'slaving' was a highly complex phenomenon implying reciprocal obligations rather than just a transfer of ownership in persons. This evidence of early Spanish involvement in developing the trade contrasts with their later condemnation as it undermined eighteenth-century missionary attempts to control the native population and was blamed on the growth of the Dutch Guiana colonies - see also fn. 93.

[54] As with the early slave trade in Orinoco, the commerce of the *aruacas* with the Spanish at Margarita was critical not just for the establishment of the Spanish colony but also for the place of the *aruacas* within the wider native regional polity. The intimacy of this relationship is thought to be reflected both in the name 'aru-aca' (*aru* = cassava flour) and in the name of the principal river from which this supply derived, 'Pomeroon', a corruption of the Lokono word for a ball of such flour, *baurooma* - see Bennett 1989, Ojer 1966.

[35]

Indies their works were well spent, and the gold drawn out with great labor and charge: he also dispatched messengers to his son in *Nuevo reyno* to levy all the forces he could, and to come down the river of *Orenoque* to *Emeria,* the province of *Carapana,* to meet him: he had also sent to *Sant Iago de Leon* on the coast of the *Caracas* to buy horses and mules.

After I had thus learned of his proceedings past & purposed: I told him that I had resolved to see *Guiana,* and that it was the end of my journey, & the cause of my comming to *Trinedado,* as it was indeed, (& for that purpose I sent *Ja. Whiddon* the yeere before to get intelligence, with whom *Berreo* himselfe had speech at that time, and remembred how inquisitive *Ja. Whiddon* was of his proceedings, and of the countrey of *Guiana,*) *Berreo* was striken into a great melancholie and sadnes, and used all the arguments he could to disswade me, and also assured the gentlemen of my company that it would be labor lost: and that they should suffer many miseries if they proceeded: And first he delivered that I could not enter anie of the rivers with any barke or pinace, nor hardly with anie ships bote, it was so low, sandie, and full of flats, and that his companies were daily grounded in their *Canoas* which drew but twelve inches water: he further saide that none of the countrey would come to speake with us, but would all flie, and if we followed them to their dwellings, they would burne their owne townes, and besides that the way was long, the winter at hand, and that the rivers beginning once to swel, it was impossible to stem the currant, and that we could not in those smal botes by any means carry victuall

[36]

for halfe the time, and that (which indeed most discouraged my company) the Kings and Lords of all the borders and of *Guiana* had decreed, that none of them should trade with any Christians for gold, bicause the same would be their owne overthrow, and that for the love of gold the Christians meant to conquer and dispossesse them of all together.

Many and the most of these I found to be true, but yet I resolving to make trial of all whatsoever hapned, directed Captaine *George Gifford* my Vice-admirall to take the *Lions whelpe,* and Captaine *Calfield* his barke to turne to the eastward, against the brize what they could possible, to recover the mouth of a river called *Capuri,* whose entrance I had before sent Captaine *Whiddon* and *Jo. Douglas* the master, to discover, who founde some nine foote water or better upon the flood, and five at lowe water, to whom I had given instructions that they shoulde ancor at the edge of the shold,* and upon the best of the flood to thrust over, which shold *John Douglas* boyed and bekonned* for them before: but they laboured in vain, for neither could they turne it up altogither so farre to the east, neither did the flood continue so long, but the water fell ere they coulde have passed the sands, as we after founde by a second experience: so as now we must either give over our enterprize, or leaving our ships at adventure 400. mile behind us, to run up in our ships botes, one barge, and two wherries, but being doubtfull how to carrie victuals for so long a time in such bables,* or anie strength of men, especiallie for that *Berreo* assured us that his sonne must be by that time come downe with manie soldiers,

[37]

I sent away one *King* maister of the *Lions whelp* with his ships bote to trie another branch of a river in the bottome of the bay of *Guanipa,* which was called *Amana,* to proove if there were water to be found for either of the small ships to enter: But when he came to the mouth of *Amana,* he found it as the rest, but staied not to discover it throughlie, bicause he was assured by an Indian his guide that the *Canibals* of *Guanipa*[55] would assaile them with many *Canoas,* and that they shot poisonned arrowes, so as if he hasted not backe they should all be lost.

In the mean time fearing the worst I caused all the Carpenters we had to cut down a *Gallego* bote, which we meant to cast off, and to fit her with banks to row on, and in all things to prepare her the best they could, so as she might be brought to drawe but five foote, for so much we had on the bar of *Capuri* at lowe water: And doubting of *Kings* return I sent *Jo. Douglas* againe in my long barge, as well to releeve him as also to make a perfect search in the bottom of that baie: For it hath beene held for infallible that whatsoever ship or bote shall fall therein, can never dessemboque againe, by reason of the violent currant which setteth into the said bay, as also for that the brize and easterlie wind bloweth directlie into the same, of which opinion I have heard *John Hampton* of *Plimmouth* one of the greatest experience of *England,* & divers others besides that have traded *Trinedado.*

I sent with *John Douglas* an old *Cassique* of *Trinedado* for a Pilot, who tolde us that we could not returne again by the bay or gulfe, but that he knew a by branch which ran within the land to the Eastward, and that

[38]

he thought by it we might fall into *Capuri,* and so returne in fower daies: *John Dowglas* searched those rivers, and found fower goodly entrances, whereof the least was as bigge as the *Thames* at *Wolwich,* but in the baie

[55] The *caribes* (Karinya) of the Guanipa river resisted Spanish encroachment until the Franciscan missionary campaigns of the 1720s - see Whitehead 1988: 109-11.

thitherward it was shole and but six foote water, so as we were now without hope of any ship or barke to passe over, and therefore resolved to go on with the botes, and the bottome of the *Gallego,* in which we thrust 60. men: In the *Lions whelps* bote and wherrie we carried 20. Captaine *Calfeild* in his wherrie carried ten more, and in my barge other ten, which made up a hundred: we had no other meanes but to carrie victuall for a moneth in the same, and also to lodge therein as we could, and to boile and dresse our meat. Captaine *Gifford* had with him Master *Edw. Porter,* captaine *Eynos,* and eight more in his wherrie with all their victuall, weapons, and provisions: Captaine *Calfield* had with him my cosen *Butshead Gorges* and eight more. In the galley, of gent. and officers[56] my selfe had captaine *Thyn,* my cosen *John Greenvile,* my nephew *John Gilbert,* captaine *Whiddon,* captaine *Keymis, Edw. Hancocke,* captaine *Clarke,* lieutenant *Hewes, Tho. Upton,* captaine *Facy, Jerome Ferrar, Antho. Wells, Will. Connock,* and about 50. more. We could not learne of *Berreo* any other waie to enter but in branches, so farre to the windeward, as it was impossible for us to recover: for we had as much sea to crosse over in our wherries as betweene *Dover* and *Callys,* and in a great billow, the winde and currant being both very strong, so as we were driven to go in those small botes directly before the winde into the bottome of the baie of *Guanipa,* and from thence to enter the mouth of some

[39]

one of those rivers, which *Jo. Dowglas* had last discovered, and had with us for Pilote an *Indian* of *Barema,* a river to the south of *Orenoque,* betweene that and *Amazones,* whose *Canoas* we had formerlie taken as he was going from the said *Barema,* laden with *Cassavi* bread to sell at *Marguerita:* this *Arwacan* promised to bring me into the great river of *Orenoque,* but indeed of that which we entred he was utterly ignorant, for he had not seene it in twelve yeeres before, at which time he was very yoong, and of no judgement, and if God had not sent us another helpe, we might have wandred a whole yeere in that laborinth of rivers, ere we had found any way, either out or in, especiallie after we were past the ebbing and flowing, which was in fower daies: for I know all the earth doth not yeeld the like confluence of streames and branches, the one crossing the other so many times, and all so faire and large, and so like one to another, as no man can tell which to take: and if we went by the Sun or compasse hoping thereby to go directly one way or other, yet that waie we were also caried in a circle amongst multitudes of Ilands, and every Iland so bordered with high trees, as no man could see any further than the bredth of the river, or length of the breach:

[56] See Plate VII.

But this it chanced that entring into a river, (which bicause it had no name we called the river of the *Red crosse,* our selves being the first *Christians* that ever came therein:)[57] the 22. of *May* as we were rowing up the same, we espied a smal *Canoa* with three *Indians,* which (by the swiftnes of my barge, rowing with eight oares) I overtooke ere they could crosse the river, the rest of the people on the banks shadowed under the

[40]

thicke wood gazed on with a doubtfull conceit what might befall those three which we had taken: But when they perceived that we offred* them no violence, neither entred their *Canoa* with any of ours, nor tooke out of the *Canoa* any of theirs, they then began to shew themselves on the banks side, and offred to traffique with us for such things as they had, and as we drewe neere they all staide, and we came with our barge to the mouth of a little creeke which came from their towne into the great river.

As we abode there a while, our Indian Pilot called *Ferdinando* would needs go ashore to their village to fetch some fruites, and to drinke of their artificiall* wines, and also to see the place, and to know the Lord of it against another time, and tooke with him a brother of his which he had with him in the journey: when they came to the village of these people, the Lord of the Iland offred to lay hands on them, purposing to have slaine them both, yeelding for reason that this Indian of ours had brought a strange nation into their territorie to spoyle and destroy them:[58] But the Pilot being quicke and of a disposed body slipt their fingers, and ran into the woods, and his brother being the better footman* of the two, recovered the creekes mouth, where we staied in our barge, crying out that his brother was slaine, with that we set hands on one of them that was next us, a very old man, and brought him into the barge, assuring him that if we had not our Pilot againe, we would presently cut off his head. This old man being resolved that he should paie the losse of the other, cried out to those in the woods to save *Ferdinando* our Pilot, but they followed him notwithstanding,

[41]

and hunted after him upon the foote with their Deere dogs, and with so maine a crie that all the woods eckoed with the shoute they made, but at last this poore chased Indian recovered the river side, and got upon a tree, and as we were coasting, leaped down and swam to the barge halfe dead

[57] This is simply not true, as is shown by the extensive prior Spanish activity all across the delta and lower Orinoco.

[58] The *aruacas* had indeed done just this for the Spanish in both the Orinoco and Barima rivers - see Chapter 1 (iv), and Chapter 2 (iii), also comments of Ralegh above [7].

with feare; but our good hap was, that we kept the other old Indian, which we handfasted* to redeeme our Pilot withall, for being naturall of those rivers, we assured our selves he knew the way better than any stranger could, and indeed, but for this chance I thinke we had never founde the way either to *Guiana,* or backe to our ships: for *Ferdinando* after a few daies knew nothing at all, nor which way to turne, yea and many times the old man himselfe was in great doubt which river to take. Those people which dwell in these broken Ilands & drowned lands are generally called *Tivitivas,* there are of them two sorts, the one called *Ciawani,* and the other *Waraweete.* [59]

The great river of *Orenoque* or *Baraquan* hath nine branches which fall out on the north side of his owne maine mouth: on the south side it hath seven other fallings into the sea, so it disemboketh by 16. armes in al, betweene Ilands and broken ground, but the Ilands are verie great, manie of them as bigge as the Isle of *Wight* and bigger, and many lesse: from the first branch on the north to the last of the south it is at lest 100. leagues, so as the rivers mouth is no lesse than 300. miles wide at his entrance into the sea, which I take to be farre bigger than that of *Amazones:* al those that inhabite in the mouth of this river upon the severall north branches are these *Tivitivas,* of which there

[42]

are two chiefe Lords which have continuall warres one with the other: the Ilands which lie on the right hand are called *Pallamos,* and the land on the left *Hororotomaka,*[60] and the river by which *John Dowglas* returned within the land from *Amana* to *Capuri,* they call *Macuri.*

These *Tivitivas* are a verie goodlie people and verie valiant, and have the most manlie speech and most deliberate that ever I heard of what nation soever. In the summer they have houses on the ground as in other places: In the winter they dwell upon the trees, where they build very artificiall townes and villages,[61] as it is written in the Spanish storie of the *West Indies,* that those

[59] Ralegh accurately names the *Siawani* and *Waraowitu* ('true Warao'), related groups together comprising the Warao or *Tivitivas.* A minor controversy rages over this term, some preferring derivation from an onomatopoeic term for sandpipers, *tigüe-tigüe,* others noting the Lokono term for 'mollusc', *tibitibe* (Dudley 1899: 78), reflecting their delta habitat.

[60] As with the designations of the Warao sub-groups, Ralegh's information accurately reflects what is known from subsequent ethnography, in this case the sacred geography which divides the Warao homeland into various mystical and ecological domains - see Wilbert 1993.

[61] See commentary for Plate VI in Chapter 2 (iv). The stilt houses of the Warao are iconic in their ethnological representation, but Ralegh's characterization of them as 'manlie', apart from its significance for this text (fn. 73), is unusual since the Warao tend otherwise to be very negatively represented as 'dirty', 'cowardly' and 'treacherous' in colonial ethnology, possibly due to their early decimation by the Spanish - see fn. 64, 73.

people do in the low lands neere the gulfe of *Uraba:* for betweene *May* and *September* the river of *Orenoke* riseth thirtie foote upright, and then are those Ilands overflowen twentie foote high above the levell of the ground, saving some few raised grounds in the middle of them: and for this cause they are enforced to live in this maner. They never eate of anie thing that is set or sowen, and as at home they use neither planting nor other manurance, so when they com abroad they refuse to feede of ought, but of that which nature without labor bringeth foorth. They use the tops of *Palmitos*[62] for bread, and kil Deere, fish and porks for the rest of their sustenance, they have also manie sorts of fruits that grow in the woods, and great varietie of birds and foule.

And if to speake of them were not tedious and vulgare, surely we sawe in those passages of very rare colours & forms, not else where to be found, for as much as I have either seen or read. Of these people those that

[43]

dwell upon the branches of *Orenoque* called *Capuri* and *Macureo,* are for the most part Carpenters of *Canoas,* for they make the most and fairest houses, and sell them into *Guiana* for gold, and into *Trinedado* for *Tobacco,* in the excessive taking whereof, they exceede all nations, and notwithstanding the moistnes of the aire in which they live, the hardnes of their diet, and the great labors they suffer to hunt, fish, and foule for their living, in all my life either in the Indies or in Europe did I never behold a more goodlie or better favoured people, or a more manlie.[63] They were woont to make warre upon all nations, and especiallie on the *Canibals,* so as none durst without a good strength trade by those rivers, but of late they are at peace with their neighbors, all holding the *Spaniards* for a common enimie.[64] When their commanders die, they use great lamentation, and when they thinke the flesh of their bodies is putrified, and fallen from the bones, then they take up the carcase againe, and hang it in the *Casiquies* house that died, and decke his skull with feathers of all colours, and hang all his gold plates about the bones of his armes, thighes, and legges. Those nations which are called *Arwacas* which dwell on the south of *Orenoque,* (of which place and nation

[62] That is, the *Ita* palm (*Mauritia flexuosa*), in contrast to the usual native staples of manioc and/or maize.

[63] These observations of the importance of Warao carpentry, the use of tobacco in shamanic practice and their ecological adaptations are strongly borne out by subsequent ethnography - see Wilbert (1987, 1993). On their 'manlie' character see fn. 61, 73.

[64] Warao folklore reflects this antipathy to the emergence of the *caribes* (see Whitehead 1988: 69), but earlier vicious confrontations with Spanish expeditionaries, such as the destruction of the Warao town of Baratubaro by Diego de Ordaz in July 1532 (Oviedo 1959: 393), meant there was also a real possibility for wider native alliances.

our Indian Pilot was) are dispersed in manie other places, and do use to beate the bones of their Lords into powder,[65] and their wives and friends drinke it all in their severall sorts of drinks.

After we departed from the port of these *Ciawani,* we passed up the river with the flood, and ancored the ebbe, and in this sort we went onward. The third daie

[44]

that we entred the river our *Calley* came on ground, and stuck so fast, as we thought that even there our discovery had ended, and that we must have left 60. of our men to have inhabited like rookes upon trees with those nations: but the next morning, after we had cast out all her ballast, with tugging and hawling to and fro, we got her afloate, and went on: At fower daies ende wee fell into as goodlie a river as ever I beheld, which was called the great *Amana,* which ran more directlie without windings and turnings than the other. But soone after the flood of the sea left us, and we enforced either by maine strength to row against a violent currant, or to returne as wise as we went out, we had then no shift but to perswade the companies that it was but two or three daies worke, and therfore desired them to take paines, every gentleman and others taking their turns to row, and to spell one the other at the howers end. Everie daie we passed by goodlie branches of rivers, some falling from the west, others from the east into *Amana,* but those I leave to the description in the *Chart* of discoverie, where everie one shall be named with his rising and descent. When three daies more were overgone, our companies began to despaire, the weather being extreame hot, the river bordered with verie high trees that kept away the aire, and the currant against us every daie stronger than other: But we evermore commanded our Pilots to promise an end the next daie, and used it so long as we were driven to assure them from fower reaches of the river to three, and so to two, and so to the next reach: but so long we laboured as many daies were spent, and so driven to

[45]

draw our selves to harder allowance, our bread even at the last, and no drinke at all: and our men and our selves so wearied and scorched, and doubtfull withall whether we should ever performe it or no, the heat encreasing as we drew towards the line; for wee were now in five degrees.[66]

[65] Both these funerary customs have been repeatedly observed over subsequent centuries. They point to different eschatologies however, the former emphasising a symbolic association of gold and élite ancestral authority (see Chapter 2 (ii) and Plate VI), the latter a quotidian collective participation in the genesis and nemesis of chiefly authority.

The farther we went on (our victuall decreasing and the aire breeding great faintnes) we grew weaker and weaker when we had most need of strength and abilitie, for howerlie the river ran more violently than other against us, and the barge, wherries, and ships bote of Captaine *Gifford* and Captaine *Calfield,* had spent all their provisions, so as wee were brought into despaire and discomfort, had we not perswaded all the companie that it was but onlie one daies worke more to attaine the lande where we should be releeved of all we wanted, and if we returned that we were sure to starve by the way, and that the worlde would also laugh us to scorne. On the banks of these rivers were divers sorts of fruits good to eate, flowers and trees of that varietie as were sufficient to make ten volumes of herbals, we releeved our selves manie times with the fruits of the countrey, and somtimes with foule and fish: we sawe birds of all colours, some carnation, some crimson, orenge tawny, purple, greene, watched,* and of all other sorts both simple and mixt, as it was unto us a great good passing of the time to beholde them, besides the reliefe we found by killing some store of them with our fouling peeces* without which, having little or no bread and lesse drink, but onely the thick and troubled water of the river, we had been in a very hard case.

[46]

Our old Pilot of the *Ciawani* (whom, as I said before, we tooke to redeeme *Ferdinando,*) told us, that if we would enter a branch of a river on the right hand with our barge and wherries, and leave the *Galley* at ancor the while in the great river, he would bring us to a towne of the *Arwacas* where we should find store of bread, hens, fish, and of the countrey wine, and perswaded us that departing from the *Galley* at noone, we might returne ere night: I was very glad to heare this speech, and presently tooke my barge, with eight musketiers, Captain *Giffords* wherrie, with himselfe & foure musketiers, & Captaine *Calfield* whith his wherrie and as manie, and so we entred the mouth of this river, and bicause we were perswaded that it was so neere, we tooke no victuall with us at all: when we had rowed three howres, we marvelled we sawe no signe of any dwelling, and asked the Pilot where the town was, he told us a litle farther: after three howers more the *Sun* being almost set, we began to suspect that he led us that waie to betraie us, for he confessed that those Spaniards which fled from *Trinedado,* and also those that remained with *Carapana* in *Emeria,* were joyned togither in some village upon that river. But when it grew towardes night, and we demaunding where the place was, he tolde us but fower reaches more: when we had

[66] As Schomburgk (1848: 54) drily noted; 'This was a great mistake of Ralegh, and does not argue much for the astronomical skills of his observers and sailing-master'. In fact they were about 9° north of the equator.

rowed fower and fower, we saw no signe, and our poore water men even hart broken, and tired, were ready to give up the ghost;[67] for we had now come from the *Galley* neer forty miles.

At the last we determined to hang the Pilot, and if we had well knowen the way backe againe by night,

[47]

he had surely gone, but our owne necessities pleaded sufficiently for his safetie: for it was as darke as pitch, and the river began so to narrow it selfe, and the trees to hang over from side to side, as we were driven with arming swordes to cut a passage thorow those branches that covered the water. We were very desirous to finde this towne hoping of a feast, bicause we made but a short breakfast aboord the *Galley* in the morning, and it was now eight a clock at night, and our stomacks began to gnaw apace: but whether it was best to returne or go on, we began to doubt, suspecting treason in the Pilot more and more: but the poore olde Indian ever assured us that it was but a little farther, and but this one turning, and that turning, and at last about one a clocke after midnight we saw a light, and rowing towards it, we heard the dogs of the village. When wee landed we found few people, for the Lord of that place was gone with divers *Canoas* above 400. miles of, upon a journey towards the head of *Orenoque* to trade for gold, and to buy women of the *Canibals*,[68] who afterward unfortunatly passed by us as we rode at an ancor in the port of *Morequito* in the dark of night, and yet came so neer us, as his *Canoas* grated against our barges: he left one of his companie at the port of *Morequito,* by whom we understood that he had brought thirty yoong woomen, divers plates of gold, and had great store of fine peeces of cotton cloth, and cotton beds. In his house we had good store of bread, fish, hens, and Indian drinke, and so rested that night, and in the morning after we had traded with such of his people as came down, we returned

[48]

towards our *Galley,* and brought with us some quantity of bread, fish, and hens.

On both sides of this river, we passed the most beautifull countrie that ever mine eies beheld:[69] and whereas all that we had seen before was nothing

[67] This cultural gulf in the perception of distances and time is certainly familiar to this author, and to any who have travelled extensively with native people, as did Schomburgk, who makes a similar note (1848: 56)

[68] Ralegh here intersects that regional system of trade and élite exchanges described in Chapter 2, sections (ii) and (iii).

[69] See Plate VII.

but woods, prickles, bushes, and thornes, heere we beheld plaines of twenty miles in length, the grasse short and greene, and in divers parts groves of trees by themselves, as if they had been by all the art and labour in the world so made of purpose: and stil as we rowed, the Deere came downe feeding by the waters side, as if they had beene used to a keepers call.[70] Upon this river there were great store of fowle, and of many sorts: we saw in it divers sorts of strange fishes, & of marvellous bignes, but for *Lagartos* it exceeded, for there were thousands of those uglie serpents, and the people call it for the abundance of them the river of *Lagartos,* in their language. I had a *Negro* a very proper yoong fellow, that leaping out of the *Galley* to swim in the mouth of this river, was in all our sights taken and devoured with one of those *Lagartos.*[71] In the mean while our companies in the *Galley* thought we had beene all lost, (for we promised to returne before night) & sent the *Lions Whelps* ships bote with Captaine *Whiddon* to follow us up the river, but the next day after we had rowed up and downe some fower score miles, we returned, and went on our way, up the great river, and when we were even at the last cast for want of victuals, Captaine *Gifford* being before the *Galley,* and the rest of the botes, seeking out some place to land upon the banks to make fire espied fower *Canoas* comming downe the river, & with no small joy caused his men to trie the uttermost of their

[49]

strengths, and after a while two of the 4. gave over, and ran themselves ashore, every man betaking himselfe to the fastnes of the woods, the two other lesser got away, while he landed to lay hold on these, and so turned into some by-creeke, we knew not whither: those *Canoas* that were taken were loden with bread, & were bound for *Marguerita* in the west Indies, which those Indians (called *Arwacas)* purposed to carrie thither for exchange: But in the lesser, there were three Spaniards, who having heard of the defeat of their governour in *Trinedado,* and that we purposed to enter *Guiana,* came away in those *Canoas:* one of them was a *Cavallero,* as the Captaine of the *Arwacas* after told us, another a soldier, and the third a refiner.

In the meane time, nothing on the earth could have been more welcome

[70] Landscape features in Amazonia are often far from 'natural', being a result of the conscious ecological management of flora and fauna by the indigenous population over many centuries. Such copses as Ralegh mentions, called *apêtê,* have been studied by Anderson and Posey (1989) among the Brazilian Kayapó. Native ecologies often explicitly recognise a shamanic keeper or 'master-of-animals' who controls the fortunes of the hunter through the selective release of game in response to his 'keepers call', in this case a shamanic chant.

[71] This incident appears entirely spurious as no record of a 'Negro' amongst Ralegh's crew can be found; see commentary for Plate VII in Chapter 2 (iv).

to us next unto gold, then the great store of very excellent bread which we found in these *Canoas,* for now our men cried, let us go on, we care not how farre. After that Captaine *Gifford* had brought the two *Canoas* to the *Galley,* I tooke my barge, and went to the banks side with a dozen shot, where the *Canoas* first ran themselves ashore, and landed there, sending out Captaine *Gifford* and Captaine *Thyn* on the one hand, and Captaine *Calfield* on the other, to follow those that were fled into the woods, and as I was creeping thorow the bushes, I saw an Indian basket hidden, which was the refiners basket, for I found in it, his quicksiluer, saltpeter, and divers things for the triall of mettals, and also the dust of such ore as he had refined, but in those *Canoas* which escaped there was a good quantity of ore and gold. I then landed more men, and offered 500. pound to what soldier soever

[50]

could take one of those 3. Spaniards that we thought were landed. But our labours were in vaine in that behalfe, for they put themselves into one of the small *Canoas:* and so while the greater *Canoas* were in taking, they escaped: but seeking after the Spaniards, we found the *Arwacas* hidden in the woods which were pilots for the Spaniards, and rowed their *Canoas:* of which I kept the chiefest for a Pilot, and carried him with me to *Guiana,* by whom I understood, where and in what countries the Spaniards had labored for gold, though I made not the same knowen to all: for when the springs began to breake, and the rivers to raise themselves so suddenly as by no meanes we could abide the digging of anie mine, especially for that the richest are defended with rocks of hard stone, which we call the *White Spar,* and that it required both time, men, and instruments fit for such a worke, I thought it best not to hover thereabouts, least if the same had been perceived by the company, there would have bin by this time many barks & ships set out, & perchance other nations would also have gotten of ours for Pilots, so as both our selves might have been prevented, & all our care taken for good usage of the people been utterly lost, by those that onely respect present profit, and such violence or insolence offered, as the nations which are borderers would have changed their desire of our love and defence, into hatred and violence. And for any longer stay to have brought a more quantity (which I heare hath bin often objected) whosoever had seene or prooved the fury of that river after it began to arise, and had been a moneth and od daies as we were from hearing ought from our ships, leaving

[51]

them meanly mand, above 400. miles off, would perchance have turned somewhat sooner than we did, if all the mountaines had been gold, or rich stones: And to say the truth all the branches and small rivers which fell into *Orenoque* were raised with such speed, as if wee waded them over the shooes in the morning outward, we were covered to the shoulders homewarde the very same daie: and to stay to dig out gold with our nailes, had been *Opus laboris,* but not *Ingenii*:* such a quantitie as would have served our turnes we could not have had, but a discovery of the mines to our infinite disadvantage we had made, and that could have been the best profit of farther search or stay; for those mines are not easily broken, nor opened in haste, and I could have returned a good quantity of gold readie cast, if I had not shot at another marke, than present profit.

This *Arwacan* Pilot with the rest, feared that we would have eaten them, or otherwise have put them to some cruell death, for the Spaniards to the end that none of the people in the passage towards *Guiana* or in *Guiana* it selfe might come to speech with us, perswaded all the nations, that we were men eaters, and *Canibals:* but when the poore men & women had seen us, and that we gave them meate, and to everie one some thing or other, which was rare and strange to them, they began to conceive the deceit and purpose of the *Spaniards,* who indeed (as they confessed) tooke from them both their wives, and daughters daily, and used them for the satisfying of their owne lusts,[72] especially such as they tooke in this maner by strength. But I protest before the majestie of the living God, that I

[52]

neither know nor beleeve, that any of our companie one or other, by violence or otherwise, ever knew* any of their women, and yet we saw many hundreds, and had many in our power, and of those very yoong, and excellently favored which came among us without deceit, starke naked.[73]

Nothing got us more love among them then this usage, for I suffred not anie man to take from anie of the nations so much as a *Pina,* or a *Potato* roote, without giving them contentment, nor any man so much as to offer to touch any of their wives or daughters: which course, so contrarie to the Spaniards (who tyrannize over them in all things) drew them to admire hir Majestie, whose commandement I told them it was, and also woonderfully to honour our nation. But I confesse it was a very impatient worke to keepe the meaner sort from spoile and stealing, when we came to their houses, which bicause in all I could not prevent, I caused my Indian interpreter at

[72] It would therefore be wrong to characterise the *aruacas* as simply native appeasers of the Europeans. Keymis (1596: 11) was careful to note that not all *aruacas* 'serve the Spaniards'.

[73] The figurative opposition of continent English to incontinent Spanish, and clothed manly Europe to naked, feminine America bursts through Ralegh's protestation at this point, and gives further significance to his earlier description of the Warao as 'manlie' - see fn. 61.

every place when we departed, to know of the losse or wrong done, and if ought were stolen or taken by violence, either the same was restored, and the party punished in their sight, or els it was paid for to their uttermost demand. They also much woondred at us, after they heard that we had slain the Spaniards at *Trinedado*[74], for they were before resolved, that no nation of *Christians* durst abide their presence, and they woondred more when I had made them know of the great overthrow that hir Majesties army and fleete had given them of late yeers in their owne countries.

After we had taken in this supplie of bread, with divers baskets of rootes which were excellent meate, I

[53]

gave one of the *Canoas* to the *Arwacas,* which belonged to the Spaniards that were escaped, and when I had dismissed all but the Captaine (who by the *Spaniards* was christened *Martin*) I sent backe in the same *Canoa* the old *Ciawan,* and *Ferdinando* my first Pilot, and gave them both such things as they desired, with sufficient victuall to carie them back, and by them wrote a letter to the ships, which they promised to deliver, and performed it, and then I went on with my new hired Pilot *Martyn* the *Arwacan*:[75] but the next or second day after, we came aground againe with our galley, and were like to cast hir away, with all our victuall and provision, and so lay on the sand one whole night, and were farre more in despaire at this time to free hir then before, bicause we had no tide of flood to helpe us, and therfore feared that all our hopes would have ended in mishaps: but we fastened an ankor upon the land, and with maine strength drew hir off: and so the 15. day we discovered a farre off the mountaines of *Guiana* to our great joy, and towards the evening had a slent* of a northerly winde that blew very strong, which brought us in sight of the great river of *Orenoque,* out of which this river descended wherein we were: we descried a farre off three other *Canoas* as far as we could discerne them, after whom we hastened with our barge and wherries, but two of them passed out of sight, and the third entred up the great river, on the right hand to the westward, & there staied out of sight, thinking that we meant to take the way eastward towards the province

[74] This attitude, and the capture of San José, did impress native opinion as Ralegh supposed, since Ferdinando, their *Arwacan* pilot at this point, subsequently joined with a Yao *acarewana,* Wareo, at the head of the Essequibo. This caused Wareo, on report of Ralegh's return in 1596, to seek him out earnestly (Keymis 1596: 4) - see Chapter 1 (iv).

[75] Ralegh's dependence on the *aruacas,* just as for the Spanish, shows that this was a political disposition, not ethnic sentiment, with regard to the European presence generally. This is also demonstrated by the pattern of *aruaca* alliances elsewhere, such as in Surinam (Whitehead 1990b, 1996c).

of *Carapana,* for that way the Spaniards keepe, not daring to go upwards to *Guiana,* the people in those parts being all their

[54]

enimies, and those in the *Canoas* thought us to have beene those Spaniards that were fled from *Trinedado,* and had escaped killing: and when we came so farre downe as the opening of that branch into which they slipped, being neere them with our barge and wherries, we made after them, and ere they could land, came within call, and by our interpreter tolde them what we were, wherewith they came backe willingly aboord us: and of such fish and *Tortugas* egges[76] as they had gathered, they gave us, and promised in the morning to bring the Lord of that part with them, and to do us all other services they could.

That night we came to an ankor at the parting of three goodlie rivers (the one was the river of *Amana* by which we came from the north, and ran athwart towards the south, the other two were of *Orenoque* which crossed from the west and ran to the sea towards the east) and landed upon a faire sand, where we found thousands of *Tortugas* egges, which are very wholsome meat, and greatly restoring, so as our men were now well filled and highlie contented both with the fare, and neerenes of the land of *Guiana* which appeered in sight. In the morning there came downe according to promise the Lord of that border called *Toparimaca,*[77] with some thirtie or fortie followers, and brought us divers sorts of fruits, & of his wine, bread, fish, and flesh, whom we also feasted as we could, at least he dranke good Spanish wine (whereof we had a small quantitie in bottels) which above all things they love. I conferred with this *Toparimaca* of the next way to *Guiana,* who conducted our galley and botes to his owne port, and carried us from thence some

[55]

mile and a halfe to his towne, where some of our captaines garoused of his wine till they were reasonable pleasant, for it is very strong with pepper, & the juice of divers herbs, and fruits digested and purged, they keepe it in

[76] Nearly all writers who treat of the Orinoco make mention of the immense numbers of freshwater turtle nests on the sand bars of the river, which seasonally formed an significant supply of food, oil for trade, and the occasion for market-fairs of regional importance.

[77] Schomburgk chose to derive many such personal and place names from Macuxi, but, given the variety of ethno-linguistic affiliations among the people that Ralegh describes, there seems no good reason to follow this lead. For example, Toparimaca and Carapana were Nepoyo, and Topiawari an Orinoqueponi, yet none of them led ethnically homogenous settlements, or appeared to have made alliances with only their co-ethnics.

great earthen pots of ten or twelve gallons very cleane and sweete, and are themselves at their meetings and feasts the greatest garousers and drunkards of the world: when we came to his towne we found two *Cassiques,* whereof one of them was a stranger that had beene up the river in trade, and his boates, people, and wife incamped at the port where we ankored, and the other was of that countrey a follower of *Toparimaca:* they laie each of them in a cotton *Hamaca,* which we call brasill beds, & two women attending them with six cups and a litle ladle to fill them, out of an earthen pitcher of wine, and so they dranke ech of them three of those cups at a time, one to the other, and in this sort they drinke drunke at their feasts and meetings.

That *Cassique* that was a stranger had his wife staying at the port where we ankored, and in all my life I have seldome seene a better favored woman: She was of good stature, with blacke eies, fat of body, of an excellent countenance, hir haire almost as long as hir selfe, tied up againe in pretie knots, and it seemed she stood not in that aw of hir husband, as the rest, for she spake and discourst, and dranke among the gentlemen and captaines, and was very pleasant, knowing hir owne comelines, and taking great pride therein. I have seene a Lady in England so like hir, as but for the difference of colour I would have sworne might have beene the same.

[56]

The seate of this towne of *Toparimaca* was very pleasant, standing on a little hill, in an excellent prospect, with goodly gardens a mile compasse round about it, and two very faire and large ponds of excellent fish adjoyning. This towne is called *Arowacai*: the people are of the nation called *Nepoios,* and are followers of *Carapana.*[78] In that place I sawe very aged people, that we might perceive all their sinewes and veines without any flesh, and but even as a case covered onely with skin. The Lord of this place gave me an old man for Pilot, who was of great experience and travell, and knew the river most perfectly both by day and night, and it shall be requisite for any man that passeth it to have such a Pilot, for it is fower, five, and six miles over in many places, and twentie miles in other places, with woonderfull eddies, and strong currants, many great Ilands and divers sholds, and many dangerous rocks, and besides upon any increase of winde so great a billow, as we

[78] *Arua-cai* ('jaguar-island') was a centre for the dispersion of the ancient Barrancoid pottery, and so an indication of the possible antiquity of the settlement. It was closely described by Oviedo (1959: 435-6) who says that it was earlier ruled by *aruacas,* in the 1530s. This underlines the political nature of native affiliations and the instability, even irrelevance, of ethnicity, since the Nepoyo here may have been *aruaca* at this time, only later to accept the leadership of their co-ethnic, Carapana. The consonance of the terms *arowacaii* and *arowak* may therefore seem significant but could easily be fortuitous.

were sometimes in great perill of drowning in the galley, for the small botes durst not come from the shore, but when it was very faire.

The next day we hasted thence, and having an easterly wind to helpe us, we spared our arms from rowing: for after we entred *Orenoque,* the river lieth for the most part east and west, even from the sea unto *Quito* in *Peru.*[79] This river is navigable with ships little lesse than 1000. miles, and from the place where we entred it may be sailed up in small pinaces to many of the best parts of *Nuevo reyno de granada,* and of *Popayan:* and from no place may the cities of these parts of the Indies be so easily taken and invaded as from hence.

[57]

All that day we sailed up a branch of that river, having on the left hand a great Iland, which they cal *Assapana,*[80] which may containe some five and twentie miles in length, & 6. miles in bredth, the great body of the river running on the other side of this Iland: Beyond that middle branch there is also another Iland in the river, called *Iwana,* which is twise as big as the Isle of *Wight,* and beyond it, and betweene it and the maine of *Guiana,* runneth a third branch of *Orenoque* called *Arraroopana:* all three are goodly branches, and all navigable for great ships. I judge the river in this place to be at least thirtie miles brode, reckoning the Ilands which divide the branches in it, for afterwards I sought also both the other branches.

After we reached to the head of this Iland, called *Assapana,* a little to the westward on the right hand there opened a river which came from the north, called *Europa,* and fell into the great river, & beyond it, on the same side, we ankored for that night, by another Iland six miles long and two miles brode, which they call *Ocaywita:* From hence in the morning we landed two *Guianians,* which we found in the towne of *Toparimaca,* that came with us, who went to give notice of our comming to the Lord of that countrey called *Putyma,* a follower of *Topiawari,* chiefe Lord of *Arromaia,* who succeeded *Morequito,* whom (as you have heard before) *Berreo* put to death, but his towne being farre within the land, he came not unto us that day, so as we ankored againe that night neere the banks of another Iland, of bignes much like the other, which they call *Putapayma* on the maine lande, over against which Iland was a very high mountaine called *Oecope*:

[79] This is not true of course, but Berrio's descent from Bogotá (see Introduction) made this statement at least plausible. This constant iteration of such geographical information serves to remind the reader of Ralegh's own preparedness for 'Discoverie' - see below [72-3].

[80] All such suffixes, *-pana, -pona, -tona, -tuna,* indicate water, sea, river, etc. in Cariban languages.

[58]

we coveted to ankor rather by these Ilands in the river, than by the maine, because of the *Tortugas* egges, which our people found on them in great abundance, & also because the ground served better for us to cast our nets for fish, the maine banks being for the most part stonie and high, and the rocks of a blew metalline colour, like unto the best steele ore, which I assuredly take it to be: of the same blew stone are also divers great mountaines, which border this river in many places.

The next morning towards nine of the clocke, we weied ankor, & the brize encreasing, we sailed alwaies west up the river, and after a while opening the lande on the right side, the countrey appeered to be champaine,* and the banks shewed very perfect red: I therefore sent two of the little barges with captaine *Gifford,* and with him captaine *Thyn,* captaine *Calfield,* my cosen *Greenvile,* my nephew *Jo. Gilbert,* captaine *Eynus,* master *Edw. Porter,* and my cosen *Butshead Gorges,* with some fewe soldiers, to march over the banks of that red land, and to discover what maner of countrey it was on the other side, who at their returne found it all a plaine levell, as farre as they went or could discerne, from the highest tree they could get upon: And my old Pilot, a man of great travell brother to the *Cassique Toparimaca* told me, that those were called the plaines of the *Sayma,* and that the same levell reached to *Cumana,* and *Carracas* in the west Indies, which are 120. leagues to the north, and that there inhabited fower principall nations. The first were the *Sayma,* the next *Assawai,* the third and greatest the *Wikiri,* by whom *Pedro Hernandez de Serpa* before mentioned was overthrowen,

[59]

as he passed with three hundred horse from *Cumana* towards *Orenoque,* in his enterprize of *Guiana,* the fourth are called *Aroras,*[81] and are as blacke as *Negros,* but have smooth haire, and these are very valiant, or rather desperate people, and have the most strong poison on their arrowes, and most dangerous of all nations, of which poison I will speake somwhat being a digression not unnecessary.

There was nothing whereof I was more curious, than to finde out the true remedies of these poisoned arrowes, for besides the mortalitie of the wound they make, the partie shot indureth the most insufferable torment in the world, and abideth a most uglie and lamentable death, somtimes dying starke mad, somtimes their bowels breaking out of their bellies, and are

[81] Mentioned here are the historically or ethnographically known Chayma, Assawanú (Karinya), Guayqueri and Yaruro. The 'blackness' of the *Aroras* refers to *genipa* body-paint.

presently discolored, as blacke as pitch, and so unsavery, as no man can endure to cure, or to attend them. [82] And it is more strange to know, that in all this time there was never Spaniard, either by gift or torment that could attaine to the true knowledge of the cure, although they have martyred and put to invented torture I know not how many of them. But every one of these Indians know it not, no not one among thousands, but their southsaiers and priests, who do conceale it, and onely teach it but from the father to the sonne.[83]

Those medicines which are vulgar, and serve for the ordinarie poison, are made of the juice of a roote called *Tupara:* the same also quencheth marvellously the heate of burning feavers, and healeth inward wounds, and broken veines, that bleed within the body.[84] But I was more beholding to the *Guianians* than any other,

[60]

for *Anthonio de Berreo* told me that he could never attaine to the knowledge therof, & yet they taught me the best way of healing as wel therof, as of al other poisons. Some of the Spaniards have been cured in ordinary wounds, of the common poisoned arrowes with the juice of garlike: but this is a generall rule for all men that shall heerafter travell the Indies where poisoned arrowes are used, that they must abstaine from drinke, for if they take any licor into their body, as they shall be marvellously provoked therunto by drought, I say, if they drink before the wound be dressed, or soone upon it, there is no way with them but present death.[85]

And so I wil returne again to our journey which for this third day we finished, and cast ankor againe neere the continent, on the left hand betweene two mountaines, the one called *Aroami,* and the other *Aio*: I made no stay heere but till midnight, for I feared howerly least any raine should fall, and then it had beene impossible to have gone any further up, notwithstanding that there is every day a very strong brize, and easterly winde. I deferred the search of the countrie on *Guiana* side, till my returne downe the river. The next day we sailed by a great Iland, in the middle of the river, called

[82] This knowledge was presumably derived, and certainly reinforced, after the abortive attack on Cumaná, following Ralegh's departure from Trinidad.

[83] For a discussion of native poisons and the transmission of knowledge about them see Chapter 1, n. 17 and in text.

[84] Although no equivalent for the term *Tupara* is recorded in the ethnological literature, the description of the action of the poison seems to indicate that it was curare, or *ourari* (after Keymis 1596).

[85] This and preceding passages obviously link to Ralegh's particular interest in 'chymistry' and pharmacology - see Chapter 1, n. 20. Urine was also considered a partially effective antidote, but it depended on the strength of the poison.

Manoripano, and as wee walked a while on the Iland, while the *Galley* got a head of us, there came after us from the maine, a small *Canoa* with seven or eight *Guianians,* to invite us to ankor at their port, but I deferred it till my returne; It was that *Cassique* to whom those *Nepoios* went, which came with us from the towne of *Toparimaca:* and so the fift day we reached as high up as the Province of *Arromaia* the countrey of *Morequito* whom *Berreo*

[61]

executed, and ankored to the west of an Iland called *Murrecotima,* ten miles long and five brode: and that night the *Cassique Aramiari,* (to whose towne we made our long and hungry voiage out of the river of *Amana)* passed by us.

The next day we arrived at the port of *Morequito,* and ankored there, sending away one of our Pilots to seeke the king of *Aromaia,* uncle to *Morequito,* slaine by *Berreo* as aforesaide. The next day following, before noone he came to us on foote from his house, which was 14 English miles, (himself being 110. yeers old) & returned on foote the same daie, & with him many of the borderers, with many women & children, that came to woonder at our nation, and to bring us down victuall, which they did in great plenty, as venison, porke, hens, chickens, foule, fish, with divers sorts of excellent fruits, and rootes, & great abundance of *Pinas,* the princesse of fruits, that grow under the *Sun,* especially those of *Guiana.* They brought us also store of bread, and of their wine, and a sort of *Paraquitos,* no bigger than wrens, and of all other sorts both small and great: one of them gave me a beast called by the Spaniards *Armadilla,* which they call *Cassacam,* which seemeth to be all barred over with small plates somewhat like to a *Renocero,* with a white horne growing in his hinder parts, as big as a great hunting horn, which they use to winde in steed of a trumpet.[86] *Monardus* writeth that a little of the powder of that horne put into the eare, cureth deafnes.

After this old king had rested a while in a little tent, that I caused to be set up, I began by my interpretor to discourse with him of the death of *Morequito*

[62]

his predecessor, and afterward of the Spaniards, and ere I went anie farther I made him know the cause of my comming thither, whose servant I was, and that the Queenes pleasure was, I should undertake the voiage for their defence, and to deliver them from the tyrannie of the Spaniards, dilating at

[86] The armadillo's tail is also used as part of the *kanaima* assassin's ritual equipment, in this case being applied to the anal rather than facial orifice - see Chapter 1, n. 18 and text. Ralegh's inversion of tail and horn in his description thus seems oddly apposite.

large (as I had done before to those of *Trinedado)* her Majesties greatnes, her justice, her charitie to all oppressed nations, with as manie of the rest of her beauties and vertues, as either I coulde expresse, or they conceive, all which being with great admiration attentively heard, and marvellously admired, I began to sound the olde man as touching *Guiana,* and the state thereof, what sort of common wealth it was, how governed, of what strength and pollicy, how farre it extended, and what nations were friends or enimies adjoining, and finally of the distance, and way to enter the same: he told me that himselfe and his people with all those downe the river towards the sea, as farre as *Emeria,* the Province of *Carapana,* were of *Guiana,* but that they called themselves *Orenoqueponi,* bicause they bordered the great river of *Orenoque,* and that all the nations betweene the river and those mountaines in sight called *Wacarima,* were of the same cast and appellation: and that on the other side of those mountaines of *Wacarima* there was a large plaine (which after I discovered in my returne) called the valley of *Amariocapana,* in all that valley the people were also of the ancient *Guianians.*[87] I asked what nations those were which inhabited on the further side of those mountaines, beyond the valley of

[63]

Amariocapana, he answered with a great sigh (as a man which had inward feeling of the losse of his conntrey and liberty, especially for that his eldest sonne was slain in a battel on that side of the mountaines, whom he most entirely loved,) that he remembred in his fathers life time when he was very old, and himselfe a yoong man that there came down into that large valley of *Guiana,* a nation from so far off as the *Sun* slept, (for such were his own words,) with so great a multitude as they could not be numbred nor resisted, & that they wore large coats, and hats of crimson colour, which colour he expressed, by shewing a peece of red wood, wherewith my tent was supported, and that they were called *Oreiones,* and *Epuremei,* those that had slaine and rooted out so many of the ancient people as there were leaves in the wood upon all the trees, and had now made themselves Lords of all, even to that mountaine foote called *Curaa,* saving onely of two nations, the one called *Iwarawaqueri,* and the other *Cassipagotos,* and that in the last battell fought betweene the *Epuremei,* and the *Iwarawaqueri,* his eldest son was

[87] Ralegh here identifies the Sierra Imataca as *Wacarima,* but Topiawari also refers to a location *beyond* the valley of *Amariocapana* (Yururari–Cuyuni basin), presumably the Pakaraimas. The Imataca range does not display those geological features of eroded granitic blocks (*tepuii*) that suggested the figurative native name, from *pakara* ('basket'). Beyond this range the savannas of the Rupununi, Ireng and Branco rivers extend some 14,400 sqare miles towards the Amazon basin - see also discussion in Chapter 2 (i) and fn. 91 below.

chosen to carry to the aide of the *Iwarawaqueri,* a great troupe of the *Orenoqueponi,* and was there slaine, with al his people & freinds, and that he had now remaining but one sonne: and farther told me that those *Epuremei* had built a great town called *Macureguarai,* at the said mountaine foote, at the beginning of the great plaines of *Guiana,* which have no end: and that their houses have many roomes, one over the other, and that therein the great king of the *Oreiones* and *Epuremei* kept three thousand men to defend the borders against them, and withall daily to invade and slaie

[64]

them: but that of late yeeres since the Christians offred to invade his territories, and those frontires, they were all at peace, and traded one with another, saving onely the *Iwarawaqueri,* and those other nations upon the head of the river of *Caroli,* called *Cassipagotos,*[88] which we afterwards discovered, each one holding the *Spaniard* for a common enimie.

After he had answered thus far, he desired leave to depart, saying that he had far to go, that he was old, & weake, and was every day called for by death, which was also his owne phrase: I desired him to rest with us that night, but I could not intreat him, but he told me that at my returne from the countrie above, he would againe come to us, and in the meane time provide for us the best he could, of all that his countrie yeelded: the same night hee returned to *Orocotona* his owne towne, so as he went that day 28. miles, the weather being very hot, the countrie being situate betweene 4. and 5. degrees of the *Equinoctiall.* This *Topiawari* is held for the proudest, and wisest of al the *Orenoqueponi,* and so he behaved himselfe towards me in all his answers at my returne, as I marvelled to finde a man of that gravity and judgement, and of so good discourse, that had no helpe of learning nor breed.

The next morning we also left the port, and sailed westward up the river, to view the famous river called *Caroli,* as well bicause it was marvellous of it selfe, as also for that I understood it led to the strongest nations of all the frontires, that were enimies to the *Epuremei,* which are subjects to *Inga,* Emperor of *Guiana,* and *Manoa,* and that night we ankored at another Iland called *Caiama,* of some five or sixe miles

[65]

in length, and the next day arrived at the mouth of *Caroli,* when we were short of it as low or further downe as the port of *Morequito* we heard the great rore and fall of the river, but when we came to enter with our barge and wherries

[88] Embedded in these ethnonyms we can recognise the designation *waika, waikeri* ('fierce') associated in this locale with the Akawaio, and the suffix *-goto* ('people of'). Thus Cassipa-goto ('Turtle Lake people'), and Arawa-goto and Epara-goto later in the text.

thinking to have gone up some fortie miles to the nations of the *Cassipagotos,* we were not able with a barge of eight oares to rowe one stones cast in an hower, and yet the river is as broad as the Thames at Wolwich, and we tried both sides, and the middle, and every part of the river, so as we incamped upon the bankes adjoyning, and sent off our *Orenoquepone* (which came with us from *Morequito)* to give knowledge to the nations upon the river of our being there, and that we desired to see the Lords of *Canuria,* which dwelt within the province upon that river, making them know that we were enemies to the Spanyards, (for it was on this rivers side that *Morequito* slew the *Frier,* and those nine Spaniards which came from *Manoa,* the Citie of *Inga,* and tooke from them 40000. pesoes of Golde) so as the next daie there came downe a Lorde or *Cassique* called *Wanuretona*[89] with many people with him, and brought all store of provisions to entertaine us, as the rest had done. And as I had before made my comming knowne to *Topiawari,* so did I acquaint this *Cassique* therewith, and howe I was sent by her Majesty for the purpose aforesaid, and gathered also what I could of him touching the estate of *Guiana,* and I founde that those also of *Caroli* were not onely enemies to the Spaniardes but most of all to the *Epuremei,* which abounde in Gold, and by this *Wanuretona,* I had knowledge that on the heade of this river were three mighty nations,

[66]

which were seated on a great lake, from whence this river descended, and were called *Cassipagotos, Eparagotos,* and *Arawagotos,* and that all those eyther against the Spaniards, or the *Epuremei* would joine with us, and that if wee entred the lande over the mountaines of *Curaa,* wee should satisfie our selves with golde and all other good things: hee told us farther of a nation called *Iwarawaqueri* before spoken off, that held daily warre with the *Epuremei* that inhabited *Macureguarai* the first civill towne of *Guiana,* of the subjectes of *Inga* the Emperor.

Upon this river one Captaine *George,* that I tooke with *Berreo* tolde me there was a greate silver mine, and that it was neere the banckes of the saide river. But by this time as well *Orenoque, Caroli,* as all the rest of the rivers were risen fowre or five foote in height, so as it was not possible by the strength of any men, or with any boate whatsoever to rowe into the river against the streame. I therefore sent Captaine *Thyn,* Captaine *Greenvile,* my nephew *John Gylbert,* my cosen *Butshead Gorges,* Captaine *Clarke,* and some 30 shot more to coast the river by lande, and to goe to a towne some twentie miles over the valley called *Amnatapoi,* and if they found guides there, to

[89] From *wanure,* the Great Heron (*Ardea cinerea*) and the suffix for water. Note that the name of the *cassique* and the name of the village are interchangeable - see Chap. 1, n. 27.

goe farther towardes the mountaine foote to another greate towne, called *Capurepana,* belonging to a *Cassique* called *Haharacoa* (that was a nephew to old *Topiawari* king of *Arromaia* our chiefest friend) because this towne and province of *Capurepana* adjoyned to *Macureguarai,* which was the frontier towne of the Empire: and the meane while my selfe with Captaine *Gifford,* Captaine *Calfield, Edw. Hancocke,* & some halfe a dosen shot

[67]

marched over land to view the strange overfals of the river of *Caroli,* which rored so farre of, & also to see the plaines, adjoyning and the rest of the province of *Canuri:* I sent also captaine *Whiddon, W. Connocke,* and some eight shot with them, to see if they coulde finde any minerall stone alongst the rivers side. When we ronne to the tops of the first hils of the plaines adjoyning to the river, we behelde that wonderfull breach of waters, which ranne downe *Caroli:* and might from that mountaine see the river how it ran in three parts, above twentie miles of, and there appeared some ten or twelve overfals in sight, every one as high over the other as a Church tower, which fell with that fury, that the rebound of waters made it seeme, as if it had beene all covered over with a great shower of rayne: and in some places we tooke it at the first for a smoke that had risen over some great towne.[90] For mine owne part I was well perswaded from thence to have returned, being a very ill footeman, but the rest were all so desirous to goe neere the said straunge thunder of waters, as they drew mee on by little and little, till we came into the next valley, where we might better discerne the same. I never saw a more beawtifull countrey, nor more lively prospectes, hils so raised heere and there over the vallies, the river winding into divers braunches, the plaines adjoyning without bush or stubble, all faire greene grasse, the ground of hard sand easy to march on, eyther for horse or foote, the deare crossing in every path, the birds towardes the evening singing on every tree with a thousand several tunes, cranes & herons of white, crimson, and carnation pearching on the rivers side, the ayre fresh with a gentle

[68]

easterlie wind, and every stone that we stooped to take up, promised eyther golde or silver by his complexion. Your L. shall see of many sortes, and I hope some of them cannot be bettered under the sunne, and yet we had no meanes but with our daggers and fingers to teare them out heere and there, the rockes being most hard of that minerall sparre aforesaid, and is like a flint, and is alto-

[90] This spot is now a civic park for the new town of Ciudad Guayana - see description of this locale in the Introduction.

gether as hard or harder, and besides the veynes lie a fathome or two deepe in the rockes. But we wanted all thinges requisite save onelie our desires, and good will to have performed more if it had pleased God. To be short when both our companies returned, each of them brought also severall sortes of stones that appeared very faire, but were such as they found loose on the ground, and were for the most part but cullored, and had not any gold fixed in them, yet such as had no judgement or experience kept all that glistered, and would not be perswaded but it was rich because of the lustre, and brought of those, and of *Marquesite* with all, from *Trinedado,* and have delivered of those stones to be tried in many places, and have thereby bred an opinion that all the rest is of the same: yet some of these stones I shewed afterward to a Spaniard of the *Caracas* who told me that it was *El Madre deloro,* and that the mine was farther in the grounde. But it shall bee founde a weake pollicie in mee, eyther to betray my selfe, or my Countrey with imaginations, neyther am I so farre in love with that lodging, watching, care, perill, diseases, ill savoures, bad fare, and many other mischiefes that accompany these voyages, as to woo my selfe againe into any of them, were I not assured that the sunne covereth

[69]

not so much riches in any part of the earth. Captaine *Whiddon,* and our Chirurgion *Nich. Millechap* brought me a kinde of stones like *Saphires,* what they may prove I knowe not, I shewed them to some of the *Orenoqueponi,* and they promised to bring me to a mountaine, that had of them verye large peeces growing Diamond wise: whether it be Christall of the mountaine, *Bristoll Diamond,* or *Saphire* I doe not yet knowe, but I hope the best, sure I am that the place is as likely as those from whence all the rich stones are brought, and in the same height or very neare.[91] On the left hand of this river *Caroli* are seated those nations which are called *Iwarawakeri* before remembred, which are enemies to the *Epuremei:* and on the heade of it adjoyning to the greate lake *Cassipa,* are situate those other nations which also resist *Inga,* and the *Epuremei,* called *Cassepagotos, Eparegotos,* and *Arrawagotos.* I farther understood that this lake of *Cassipa* is so large, as it is above one daies journey for one of their *Canoas* to crosse, which may be some 40. miles, and that therein fall divers rivers, and that great store of graines of Golde are found in the summer time when the lake falleth by the banckes, in those braunches. There is also another goodly river beyond *Caroli* which is called *Arui,* which also runneth thorow the lake *Cassipa,* and falleth into *Orenoque* farther west, making all that land betweene *Caroli* and *Arui* an Iland, which is likewise a

[91] The Pakaraima and Imataca ranges are still an abundant source of crystals, including diamonds: this particular source is later mentioned as *Wacarima* [85].

most beawtifull countrey. Next unto *Arui* there are two rivers *Atoica* and *Caora,* and on that braunch which is called *Caora* are a nation of people, whose heades appeare not above their shoulders, which though it may be thought a meere fable, yet for mine

[70]

owne parte I am resolved it is true, because every child in the provinces of *Arromaia* and *Canuri* affirme the same: they are called *Ewaipanoma:* they are reported to have their eyes in their shoulders, and their mouths in the middle of their breasts, & that a long train of haire groweth backward betwen their shoulders. The sonne of *Topiawari,* which I brought with mee into England tolde mee that they are the most mightie men of all the lande,[92] and use bowes, arrowes, and clubs thrice as bigge as any of *Guiana,* or of the *Orenoqueponi,* and that one of the *Iwarawakeri* tooke a prisoner of them the yeare before our arrivall there, and brought him into the borders of *Arromaia* his fathers Countrey: And farther when I seemed to doubt of it, hee tolde me that it was no wonder among them, but that they were as great a nation, and as common, as any other in all the provinces, and had of late yeares slaine manie hundreds of his fathers people, and of other nations their neighbors, but it was not my chaunce to heare of them til I was come away, and if I had but spoken one word of it while I was there, I might have brought one of them with me to put the matter out of doubt. Such a nation was written of by *Maundevile,* whose reportes were held for fables many yeares, and yet since the East *Indies* were discovered, wee finde his relations true of such thinges as heeretofore were held incredible: whether it be true or no the matter is not great, neither can there be any profit in the imagination, for mine owne part I saw them not, but I am resolved that so many people did not all combine, or forethinke to make the report.

When I came to *Cumana* in the west *Indies* afterwards,

[71]

by chaunce I spake with a spanyard dwelling not farre from thence, a man of great travell, and after he knew that I had ben in *Guiana,* and so farre directlie west as *Caroli,* the first question he asked me was whether I had seene anie of the *Ewaipanoma,* which are those without heades: who being esteemed a most honest man of his word, and in all thinges else, told me that he had seen manie of them: I may not name him because it may be for his disadvantage, but he is well known to *Monsier Mucherons* sonne of

[92] Exceptionally tall and heavily muscled male warrior élites are a plausible interpretation for this information since archaeology has noted this kind of di-morphism amongst the skeletal remains of Amazonian populations (Roosevelt 1991: 57-9) - Chapter 2 (iii).

London, and to *Peter Mucheron* marchant of the *Flemish* shipp that was there in trade, who also heard what he avowed to be true of those people. The fourth river to the west of *Caroli* is *Casnero* which falleth into *Orenoque* on this side of *Amapaia,* and that river is greater then *Danubius,* or any of *Europe:* it riseth on the south of *Guiana* from the mountaines which devide *Guiana* from *Amazones,* and I thinke it to be navigable many hundred miles: but we had no time, meanes, nor season of the yeare, to search those rivers for the causes aforesaid, the winter being come uppon us, although the winter & summer as touching cold & heate differ not, neither do the trees ever senciblie* lose their leaves, but have alwaies fruite either ripe or green, and most of them both blossomes, leaves, ripe fruite, & green at one time: But their winter onelie consisteth of terrible raynes, and overflowings of the rivers, with many great stormes and gusts, thunder, and lightnings, of which we had our fill, ere we returned. On the North side, the first river that falleth into *Orenoque* is *Cari,* beyond it on the same side is the river of *Limo,* betweene these two is a great nation of *Canibals,* and their

[72]

chiefe towne beareth the name of the river and is called *Acamacari:* at this towne is a continuall markette of women for 3 or 4 hatchets a peece, they are bought by the *Arwacas,* and by them solde into the west Indies.[93] To the west of *Limo* is the river *Pao,* beyond it *Caturi,* beyond that *Voari* and *Capuri*[94] which falleth out of the great river of *Meta,* by which *Berreo* descended From *Nuevo reyno de granada.* To the westward of *Capuri* is the province of *Amapaia,* where *Berreo* wintered, and had so many of his people poysoned with the tawny water of the marshes of the *Anebas.* Above *Amapaia,* towarde *Nuevo reyno* fall in, *Meta, Pato,* and *Cassanar:* to the west of these towardes the provinces of the *Ashaguas & Catetios* are the rivers of *Beta, Dawney,* and *Ubarro,* and towardes the frontyer of *Peru* are the provinces of *Thomebamba* and *Caximalta:* adjoyning to *Quito* in the North of *Peru* are the rivers of *Guiacar* and *Goavar:*[95] and on the other side of the

[93] Historical ethnography has long suffered from the illusion that the *caribes* (Karinya), stimulated by the Dutch, were entirely responsible for slave-taking in the Orinoco area. Apart from the fact that such Dutch stimulation was minimal (Whitehead 1988), the persistent involvement of both Spanish and Arawaks is clearly evident from this passage, as well as Ralegh's earlier remarks [33-4] - see also fn. 53.

[94] That is, the Manapire, Guarico and Apure rivers.

[95] Ralegh's identifications are largely accurate although some names are unfamiliar and small streams are given a geographical significance equal to that of large waterways. In particular *Papamene* refers to the Caqueta–Japura rivers, *Dawney* to the Tomo river, *Goavar* to the Guaviare river. The *Ashaguas* (Achagua) are accurately located, but the *Catetios* (Caquetio) were much closer to the Caracas region.

saide mountaines the river of *Papamene* which descendeth into *Maragnon or Amazones* passing through the province of *Mutylones* where *Don Pedro de Osua* who was slayne by the traytour *Agiri* before rehearsed, built his *Brigandines,* when he sought *Guiana* by the waie of *Amazones.* Betwene *Dawney* and *Beta* lieth a famous Iland in *Orenoque* now called *Baraquan* (For above *Meta* it is not knowne by the name of *Orenoque)* [96] which is called *Athule,* beyond which, ships of burden cannot passe by reason of a most forcible overfall, and Current of waters: but in the eddy all smaller vesselles may be drawen even to *Peru* it selfe: But to speake of more of these rivers without the description were but tedious, and therefore I will

[73]

leave the rest to the discription. This river of *Orenoque* is navigable for ships little lesse then 1000. miles, & for lesser vessels neere 2000. By it (as aforesaid) *Peru, Nuevo reyno,* & *Popaian,* may be invaded: it also leadeth to that great Empire of *Inga,* and to the provinces of *Amapaia* and *Anebas* which abound in gold: his branches of *Cosnero, Manta, Caora* descend from the middle land and valley, which lyeth betweene the easter province of *Peru* and *Guiana;* and it falles into the sea betweene *Maragnon* and *Trinedado* in two degrees and a half, al which your Honors shal better perceive in the generall description[97] of *Guiana, Peru, Nuevo reyno,* the kingdom of *Popayan,* and *Roidas,* with the province of *Vensuello,* to the bay of *Uraba* behind *Cartagena,* westward: and to *Amazones* southward. While we lay at ancor on the coast of *Canuri,* and had taken knowledge of all the nations upon the head and braunches of this river, and had founde out so many severall people, which were enemies to the *Epuremei,* and the newe Conquerers: I thought it time lost to linger any longer in that place, especially for that the fury of *Orenoque* beganne dailie to threaten us with daungers in our returne, for no halfe day passed, but the river began to rage and overflowe very fearefully, and the raines came downe in terrible showers, and gusts in greate abundance: and withall, our men beganne to cry out for want of shift, for no man had place to bestowe any other apparrell then that which he ware on his backe, and that was throughly washt on his body for the most part ten times in one day: and we had nowe beene well neare a

[96] Various names were given to the Orinoco and sources tend to agree that native usage separately designated the upper and lower reaches, with the Atures rapids as the marker of this divide. Thus *Huyapari* and *Baraguan* were names also given for the lower portion and *Orinoco* for the upper: Ralegh seems to reverse this.

[97] This was apparently never written. As Schomburgk (1848: 90) noted, the observation as to the geographical position of the outflow of the Orinoco contradicts Ralegh's earlier statement that the Caroni was between four and five degrees of latitude [64].

moneth, every day passing to the westwarde, farther & farther from our shippes. Wee

[74]

therefore turned towards the east, and spent the rest of the time in discovering the river towardes the sea, which we had not yet viewed, and which was most materiall. The next day following we left the mouth of *Caroli,* and arrived againe at the port of *Morequito* where we were before (for passing downe the streame we went without labour, and against the winde, little lesse then 100. miles a day): Assoon as I came to ancor I sent away one for old *Topiawari,* with whom I much desired to have farther conference, & also to deal with him for some one of his countrey, to bring with us into England, as well to learne the language, as to conferre withall by the way, (the time being now spent of anie longer stay there) within three howers after my messenger came to him, he arrived also, and with him such a rabble of all sortes of people, and every one loden with somewhat, as if it had beene a great market or faire in England: and our hungrie companies clustered thicke and threefold among their baskets, every one laying hand on what he liked. After he had rested a while in my tent, I shut out all but our selves, and my interpreter, and told him that I knew that both the *Epuremei* and the Spaniards were enemies to him, his countrey, and nations: that the one had conquered *Guiana* alreadie, & that the other sought to regaine the same from them both: And therefore I desired him to instruct me what hee coulde, both of the passage into the golden partes of *Guiana,* and to the civill townes and apparrelled people of *Inga.* Hee gave me an aunswere to this effect: first that hee did not perceive that I meant to goe onwarde towardes the Citie of *Manoa,* for neyther the time of the yeare

[75]

served, neyther could he perceive any sufficient numbers for such an enterprize: and if I did I was sure with all my company to be buried there, for that the Emperour was of that strength, as that many times so many men more were too few: besides he gave me this good counsell and advised me to hold it in minde (as for himselfe he knewe, he coulde not live til my returne) that I shoulde not offer by any meanes heereafter to invade the strong partes of *Guiana* without the helpe of all those nations which were also their enemies: for that it was impossible without those, eyther to be conducted, to be victualled, or to have ought carried with us, our people not being able to indure the march in so great heate, and travell, unlesse the borderers gave them helpe, to carry with them both their meate and furniture: For he remembred that in the plaines of *Macureguarai* 300. Spaniards were overthrowen, who were tired out, and had none of the borderers to their friendes, but meeting their enimies as they passed the frontier, were invironed of all sides, and the people setting the long dry grasse on fire, smothered them so as they had no breath to fight, nor coulde discerne their enemies for the great smoke.[98] He told me farther that fower daies journey from his towne was *Macureguarai,* and that those were the next, and nearest of the subjectes of *Inga,* and of the *Epuremei,* and the first towne of apparrelled and rich people, and that all those plates of Golde which were scattered among the borderers and carried to other nations farre and neare, came from the saide *Macureguarai* and were there made, but that those of the lande within, were farre finer, and were

[76]

fashioned after the Image of men, beastes, birdes, and fishes.[99] I asked him whether he thought that those companies that I had there with me, were sufficient to take that towne or no, he told me that he thought they were. I then asked him whether he woulde assist me with guides, and some companies of his people to joyne with us, he answered that he would go himself with all the borderers, if the rivers did remaine fordable, upon this condition that I woulde leave with him til my returne againe fiftie souldiers, which hee undertooke to victual: I answerd that I had not above fiftie good men in all there, the rest were labourers and rowers, and that I had no provision to leave with them of powder, shot, apparrell, or ought else, and that without those thinges necessarie for their defence, they shoulde be in daunger of the Spaniardes in my absence, who I knew woulde use the same measure towardes mine, that I offered them at *Trinedado:* And although upon the motion Captaine *Calfeide,* Captaine *Greenvile,* my nephewe *John Gilbert* and divers others were desirours to staie, yet I was resolved that they must needs have perished, for *Berreo* expected daily a supply out of Spayne,[100] and looked also howerly for his sonne to come downe from *Nuevo reyno de Granada,* with many horse and foote, and had also in *Valentia* in the *Caracas,* 200. horse readie to march, and I coulde not have spared above fortie, and had not anie store at all of powder, leade, or match to have left with them, nor anie other provision, eyther spade, pickeaxe, or

[98] A description of Berrio's first ascent of the Caroni, also given in Pedro Simón's *Setima Noticia historial de las Conquistas de Tierra Firme* (Seville, 1627). The tactic of firing the savannas was used with success on a number of occasions against Spanish horsemen.

[99] A chest pendant in the form of a shamanic double-headed bird was recovered from the mid-Mazaruni river in 1990 - see Whitehead 1990a.

[100] As a result of Domingo de Vera's journey to Spain bearing examples of the richness of the region, particularly gold objects - see Chapter 2(ii).

ought else to have fortified withall. When I had given him reason that I could not at this time leave him such a company,

[77]

he then desired me to forbeare him, and his countrey for that time, for hee assured me that I shoulde bee no sooner three daies from the coast, but those *Epuremei* woulde invade him, and destroye all the remayne of his people and friendes, if hee shoulde any way eyther guide us, or assist us against them. Hee further alleadged that the Spaniards sought his death, and as they had alreadie murdered his Nephew *Morequito* Lorde of that province, so they had him 17. daies in a chaine before hee was king of the Countrey, and ledde him like a dogge from place to place, untill hee had paide 100. plates of Golde, and divers chaines of spleene stones for his raunsome, and nowe since hee became owner of that province that they had manie times laide waite to take him, and that they woulde be nowe more vehement when they shoulde understand of his conference with the English, and because said hee, they woulde the better displant me, if they cannot lay handes on mee, they have gotten a Nephew of mine called *Eparacano* whome they have christened *Don Juan,* and his sonne *Don Pedro,* whome they have also apparrelled and armed, by whome they seeke to make a partie against mee, in mine owne countrey: hee also hath taken to wife one *Louiana,* of a strong familie, which are my borderers and neighbours: and my selfe beeing nowe olde and in the handes of death, am not able to travell nor to shift, as when I was of younger years: hee therefore prayed us to deferre it till the next yeare, when he would undertake to drawe in all the borderers to serve us, and then also it woulde be more seasonable to travel, for at this time of the yeare, we should not be able to passe

[78]

any river, the waters were and would be so growen ere our returne. Hee farther told me that I could not desire so much to invade *Macureguari,* & the rest of *Guiana* but that the borderers would be more vehement then I, for he yeelded for a chiefe cause that in the wars with the *Epuremei,* they were spoyled of their women, and that their wives and daughters were taken from them, so as for their owne partes they desired nothing of the gold or treasure, for their labors, but onely to recover women from the *Epuremei:* for he farther complayned very sadly (as if it had beene a matter of greate consequence) that whereas they were wont to have ten or twelve wives, they were now inforced to content themselves with three or fower, & that the Lords of the *Epuremei* had 50. or 100. And in truth they warre more for women, then eyther for gold or dominion. For the Lords of countries desire many children of their owne bodies, to encrease their races and kindreds, for in those consist their greatest trust and strength.[101] Divers of his followers afterwardes desired me to make hast againe, that they might sacke the *Epuremei,* and I asked them of what? they answered, of their women for us, and their Golde for you: for the hope of many of those women they more desire the warre, then eyther for Golde, or for the recovery of their ancient territories. For what betweene the subjectes of *Inga,* and the Spaniards, those frontiers are growen thinne of people, and also great numbers are fled to other nations farther off for feare of the Spanyardes.[102] After I received this aunsweare of the olde man, wee fell into consideration, whether it had beene of better aduice to have entered *Macureguarai,*

[79]

and to have begunne a warre upon *Inga* at this time, yea or no, if the time of the yere, and all thinges else had sorted. For mine own part (as we were not able to march it for the rivers, neither had any such strength as was requisite, and durst not abide the coming of the winter, or to tarrie any longer from our ships) I thought it verie evill counsell to have attempted it at that time, although the desire of golde will aunswere many objections: But it woulde have been in mine opinion an utter overthrowe to the enterprize, if the same should be hereafter by her Majestie attempted: for then (whereas now they have heard we were enemies to the Spaniards and were sent by her Majestie to relieve them) they would as good cheape* have joyned with the Spanyards at our returne, as to have yeelded unto us, when they had proved that we came both for one errant, and that both sought but to sacke and spoyle them, but as yet our desier of gold, or our purpose of invasion is not known unto those of the Empire: & it is likely that if her majestie undertake the enterprize, they will rather submit themselves to her obedience then to the Spanyards, of whose cruelty both themselves & the borderers have alreadie tasted: & therfore til I had known her majesties pleasure, I woulde rather have lost the sacke of one or two townes (although they might have been very profitable) then to have defaced or endaungered the

[101] Ralegh's observation underlines a dynastic aspect to Orinocan warfare. Generally native warfare is very much concerned with issues of kinship or genealogy expressed in cyclical and repetitive patterns of military conflict, the capture of females and the killing of offspring. Although Ralegh stresses the extraneous nature of the *Epuremei* to bolster his Incan theory, this passage rather suggests a progressive *incorporation* of the *Epuremei* with the *Guianians* through precisely these exchanges of trade, war and marriage - see [86], fn. 110.

[102] Both direct contacts and the indirect effects of such contacts provoked many such migrations so that it is the specific link with Incan movements, rather than the idea of long-distance migrations, that is problematic in Ralegh's account - see the Yao case in Chapter 2 (i).

future hope of so many millions, and the great good, and rich trade which England maie bee possessed off thereby,[103] I am assured nowe that they will all die even to the last man against the Spanyardes, in hope of our succoure and returne: whereas otherwise if I had

[80]

either laid handes on the borderers, or ransommed the Lordes as *Berreo* did, or invaded the subjects of *Inga,* I knowe all had been lost for hereafter. After that I had resolved *Topiawari* Lorde of *Aromaia* that I could not at this time leave with him the companies he desired, and that I was contented to forbeare the enterprize against the *Epuremei* till the next yeare, he freely gave me his onelie sonne to take with me into England,[104] and hoped, that though he himselfe had but a short tyme to live, yet that by our meanes his sonne shoulde be established after his death: and I left with him one *Frauncis Sparrow,* a servant of captaine *Gifford,* (who was desirous to tarry, and coulde describe a cuntrey with his pen)[105] and a boy of mine called *Hugh Goodwin,* to learne the language. I after asked the manner howe the *Epuremei* wrought those plates of golde, and howe they coulde melt it out of the stone; he tolde me that the most of the gold which they made in plates and images was not severed from the stone, but that on the lake of *Manoa,* and in a multitude of other rivers they gathered it in graines of perfect golde and in peeces as bigg as small stones, and that they put to it a part of copper, otherwise they coulde not worke it, and that they used a great earthen potte with holes round about it, and when they had mingled the gold and copper together, they fastned canes to the holes, and so with the breath of men they increased the fire till the mettell ran, and then they cast it into moulds of stone and clay, and so make those plates and Images.[106] I have sent your Honours, of two sorts such as I coulde by chance recover, more to shew the manner of them, then for the value: For I did not in any sort make my desire of golde

[81]

knowen, because I had neyther time, nor power to have a greater quantitie. I gave among them manye more peeces of Golde then I receaved of the new

[103] Although this passage might be seen as demonstrating an ultimate lack of pragmatic resolution by Ralegh, in view of the significance of gold in both native and colonial calculation this strategy was plausible. As was argued in the introductory chapters, the fact that Ralegh was delayed twenty years in his return, rather than an illusory belief in native support, seems to better explain his failure at that point.

[104] Iwiakanarie Gualtero - for the significance of name exchange see Chapter 1, n. 27.

[105] A description by Sparry is published in Purchas 1906: XIV, 301-8.

[106] See Plate III and commentary in Chapter 2 (iv).

money of 20. shillings with her Majesties picture to weare, with promise that they would become her servants thenceforth.

I have also sent your Honors of the oare, whereof I knowe some is as rich as the earth yeeldeth anie, of which I know there is sufficient, if nothing else were to be hoped for. But besides that we were not able to tarry and search the hils, fo[r] we had neither pioners,* bars, sledges, nor wedges of Iron, to breake the ground, without which there is no working in mynes: but we sawe all the hils with stones of the cullor of Gold and silver, and wee tried them to be no *Marquesite,* and therefore such as the Spaniards call *El Madre del oro,* which is an undoubted assurance of the generall abundance; and my selfe saw the outside of many mines of the white sparre, which I know to be the same that all covet in this worlde, and of those, more then I will speake of.

Having learned what I could in *Canuri* and *Aromaia,* and received a faithful promise of the principallest of those provinces to become servauntes to her Majestie, and to resist the Spanyardes, if they made any attempt in our absence, and that they woulde drawe in the nations about the lake of *Cassipa,* and those *Iwarawaqueri,* I then parted from olde *Topiawari,* and received his sonne for a pledge betweene us, and left with him two of ours as aforesaid: To *Francis Sparrowe* I gave instructions to travell to *Macureguarai,* with such marchaundizes as I left with him,

[92 sic/82]

thereby to learne the place, and if it were possible to go on, to the great City of *Manoa:* which being done, we weyed ancor, and coasted the river on *Guiana* side, because we came up on the north side, by the launes of the *Saima* and *Wikiri.*

There came with us from *Aromaia,* a *Cassique* called *Putijma,* that commaunded the province of *Warapana,* (which *Putijma* slewe the nyne Spaniardes uppon *Caroli* before spoken of,) who desired us to rest at the porte of his Countrey, promising to bring us to a mountaine adjoyning to his towne that had stones of the cullor of Golde, which hee performed: And after wee had rested there one night, I went my selfe in the morning with most of the Gentlemen of my campany, over lande towardes the saide mountaine, marching by a rivers side called *Mana,* leaving on the right hande a towne called *Tuteritona,* standing in the province of *Tarracoa,* of which *Wariaaremagoto* is principall: Beyond it lyeth another towne towardes the south, in the valley of *Amariocapana,* which beareth the name of the saide valley, whose plaines stretch themselves some 60. miles in length, east and west, as fayre grounde, and as beawtifull fieldes, as any man hath ever seene, with divers copses scattered heere and there by the rivers side, and all as full of deare, as any forrest or parke in England, and in every lake and river the like abundance of fish and fowle, of which *Irraparragota* is Lord.

From the river of *Mana,* we crost another river in the said beawtifull valley called *Oiana,* and rested our selves by a cleare lake, which lay in the middle of the said *Oiana,* and one of our guides kindling us fire with

[93 sic/83]

two stickes, we staied a while to dry our shirts, which with the heat hong very weete & heavy on our shoulders. Afterwards we sought the ford to passe over towards the mountain called *Iconuri,* where *Putijma* foretold us of the mine.[107] In this lake we saw one of the great fishes, as big as a wine pipe,* which they call *Manati,* and is most excellent and holsome meate. But after I perceived, that to passe the saide river woulde require halfe a daies march more, I was not able my selfe to indure it, and therefore I sent Captaine *Keymis* with six shotte to goe on, and gave him order not to returne to the port of *Putijma,* which is called *Chiparepare,*[108] but to take leasure, and to march downe the said valley, as farre as a river called *Cumaca,*[109] where I promised to meete him againe, (*Putijma* himselfe promising also to be his guide,) and as they marched, they left the townes of *Emparepana,* and *Capurepana,* on the right hande, and marched from *Putijmas* house, downe the saide valley of *Amariocapana,* & wee returning the same daie to the rivers side, sawe by the way many rockes, like unto Golde oare, and on the left hand, a rounde mountaine which consisted of minerall stone.

From hence we rowed downe the streame, coasting the province of *Parino*: As for the braunches of rivers which I overpasse in this discourse, those shalbe better expressed in the description, with the mountaines of *Aio, Ara,* & the rest, which are situate in the provinces of *Parino* and *Carricurrina.* When wee were come as farre downe as the land called *Arriacoa,* (where *Orenoque* devideth it selfe into three great braunches, each of them beeing most goodly rivers,) I sent away

[84]

Captaine *Henry Thyn,* and Captaine *Greenevile* with the Galley, the nearest way, and tooke with me Captaine *Gifford,* Captaine *Calfeild, Edward Porter,*

[107] Keymis (1596: 17) returned to within fifteen miles of this spot in 1596 and notes that at this time he thought they were being shown where *Curwara* river 'fell' from the mountains.

[108] The native term for 'silver' according to Captain Wyatt's account of Dudley's voyage of 1594-5, where the form given is *chipperarey* (Dudley 1899: 65).

[109] The *kumaka* is the sacred silk-cotton tree (*bombax ceiba*) of the Lokono (*aruacas*). It was underneath such a tree, which towers over others of the coastal forests and so visually 'announces' the presence of Lokono settlement, that the first Lokono sat to create and name their clans.

and Captaine *Eynos* with mine owne barge, and the two wherries, and went downe that braunch of *Orenoque,* which is called *Cararoopana,* which leadeth towards *Emeria* the province of *Carapana,* and towards the east sea, as well to finde out Captaine *Keymis,* whome I had sent over land, as also to acquaint my selfe with *Carapana,* who is one of the greatest of all the Lordes of the *Orenoqueponi:* and when we came to the river of *Cumaca* (to which *Putyma* promised to conduct Captaine *Keymis)* I left Captaine *Eynos* and Master *Porter* in the said river to expect his comming, and the rest of us rowed downe the streame towardes *Emeria.*

In this braunch called *Cararoopana* were also many goodly Ilandes, some of sixe miles long, some of tenne, and some of Twentie, when it grewe towards sunnesett, we entred a braunch of a river that fel into *Orenoque* called *Winicapora,* where I was enformed of the mountaine of Christall, to which in trueth for the length of the way, and the evill season of the yeare, I was not able to march, nor abide any longer upon the journey: we saw it a farre off and it appeared like a white Church towre of an exceeding height: There falleth over it a mightie river which toucheth no pare of the side of the mountaine, but rusheth over the toppe of it, and falleth to the grounde with a terrible noyse and clamor, as if 1000. great belles were knockt one against another. I thinke there is not in the worlde so straunge an overfall, nor so

[85]

wonderfull to beholde: *Berreo* tolde mee that it hath Diamondes and other precious stones on it, and that they shined very farre off: but what it hath I knowe not, neyther durst he or any of his men ascende to the toppe of the saide mountaine, those people adjoyning beeing his enemies (as they were) and the way to it so impassible.

Upon this river of *Winecapora* wee rested a while, and from thence marched into the Countrey to a towne called after the name of the river, whereof the chiefe was one *Timitwara,* who also offered to conduct mee to the toppe of the saide mountaine called *Wacarima:* But when wee came in first to the house of the saide *Timitwara,* beeing uppon one of their feast daies, wee founde them all as drunke as beggers, and the pottes walking from one to another without rest: wee that were weary, and hotte with marching, were glad of the plenty, though a small quantitie satisfied us, their drinke beeing very strong and heady, and so rested our selves a while; after we had fedde, wee drewe our selves backe to our boats, uppon the river, and there came to us all the Lordes of the Countrey, with all such kinde of victuall as the place yeelded, and with their delicate wine of *Pinas,* and with aboundance of hens, and other provisions, and of those stones which wee call Spleene-stones. Wee understoode by these chiefetaines of *Winicapora,* that their Lorde *Carapana* was departed from *Emeria* which was nowe in sight, and that hee was fledde to *Cairamo,* adjoyning to the mountaines of *Guiana,* over the valley called *Amariocapana,* beeing perswaded by those tenne Spanyardes which

[96 *sic*/86]

lay at his house, that we woulde destroy him, and his countrey.

But after these *Cassiqui* of *Winicapora* and *Saporatona* his followers perceived our purpose, and sawe that we came as enemies to the Spanyardes onely, and had not so much as harmed any of those nations, no though wee founde them to bee of the Spanyardes owne servantes, they assured us that *Carapana* woulde bee as readie to serve us, as any of the Lordes of the provinces, which wee had passed; and that hee durst doe no other till this daie but entertaine the Spanyardes, his countrey lying so directly in their waie, and next of all other to any enterance that should bee made in *Guiana* on that side.

And they farther assured us, that it was not for feare of our comming that hee was removed, but to bee acquited of those Spanyardes or any other that shoulde come heereafter. For the province of *Cairoma* is situate at the mountaine foote, which devideth the plaines of *Guiana,* from the countries of the *Orenoqueponi:* by meanes whereof if any shoulde come in our absence into his townes, hee woulde slippe over the mountaines into the plaines of *Guiana* amonge the *Epuremei,*[110] where the Spanyardes durste not followe him without greate force.

But in mine opinion, or rather I assure my selfe, that *Carapana* (beeing a notable wise and subtile fellowe, a man of one hundred yeares of age, and therefore of greate experience) is remooved, to looke on, and if hee finde that wee returne strong,

[97 *sic*/87]

hee will bee ours, if not, hee will excuse his departure to the Spanyards, and say it was for feare of our comming.

We therefore thought it booteles* to rowe so farre downe the streame, or to seeke any farther for this olde fox: and therefore frome the river of *Waricapana* (which lieth at the entrance of *Emeria),* we turned again, and left to the Eastward those 4 rivers which fall from out the mountaines of *Emeria* and *Orenoque,* which are *waracapari, Coirama, Akaniri,* and

[110] This again suggests that the *Epuremei* and *Guianians* were connected in a cycle of exchange involving both persons and artefacts - see also [77] and fn. 101.

Iparoma: belowe those 4. are also these braunches and mouths of *Orenoque,* which fall into the Est sea, whereof the first is *Araturi,* the next *Amacura,* the third *Barima,* the fourth *Wana,* the fift *Morooca,* the sixt *Paroma,* the last *Wijmi:* beyond them, there fall out of the land betweene *Orenoque* and *Amazones* 14. rivers which I forbeare to name, inhabited by the *Arwacas* and *Caniballs.*

It is nowe time to returne towardes the North, and we founde it a wearisome way backe, from the borders of *Emeria,* to recover up againe to the head of the river *Carerapana,* by which we descended, and where we parted from the galley, which I directed to take the next way to the Porte of *Toparimaca,* by which we entred first.

All the night it was stormie and darke, and full of thunder and great showers, so as we were driven to keepe close by the bankes in our small boats, being all heartely afraid both of the billowe, and terrible Current of the river. By the next morning wee recovered the mouth of the river of *Cumaca,* where wee left Captaine *Eynus* and Edward Porter to attend

[88]

the coming of Captaine *keymis* over land: but when we entred the same they had heard no newes of his arivall, which bredde in us a great doubt what might be become of him: I rowed up a league or two farther into the river, shooting off peeces all the way, that he might know of our being there: And the next morning we hearde them answere us also with a peece: we tooke them abord us, and tooke our leave of *Putyma* their guide, who of all others most lamented our departure, and offred to send his sonne with us into England, if we could have staide till he had sent backe to his towne: but our hearts were cold to behold the great rage and increase of *Orenoque,* and therefore departed, and turned towarde the west, till we had recovered the parting of the 3 braunches aforesaide, that we might put downe the streame after the Galley.

The next day we landed on the Iland of *Assapana,* (which devideth the river from that braunch by which we went down to *Emeria)* and there feasted our selves with that beast which is called *Armadilla* presented unto us before at *Winicapora,* and the day following we recovered the galley at ancour at the port of *Toparimaca,* and the same evening departed with verie fowle weather and terrible thunder, and showers, for the winter was come on verie farre: the best was, we went no lesse then 100 miles a day, down the river: but by the way we entred, it was impossible to return, for that the river of *Amana,* being in the bottome of the bay of *Guanipa,* cannot be sayled back by any meanes, both the brize and currente of the sea were so forcible, and therefore we followed a braunch of

[89]

Orenoque called *Capuri,* which entred into the sea eastward of our ships, to the end we might beare with them before the wind, and it was not without neede, for we had by that way as much to crosse of the maine sea, after wee came to the rivers mouth as betweene *Gravelyn* & *Dover,* in such boats as your Ho:* have heard.

To speake of what past homeward were tedious, eyther to describe or name any of the rivers, Ilands, or villages of the *Tivitivas* which dwell on trees, we will leave all those to the generall mappe: And to be short, when we were arrived at the sea side then grew our greatest doubt, and the bitterest of all our journey forepassed, for I protest before God, that wee were in a most desperate estate: for the same night which we ancored in the mouth of the river of *Capuri,* where it falleth into the sea, there arose a mighty storme, and the rivers mouth was at least a league broad, so as we ran before night close under the land with our small boates, and brought the Galley as neere as we could, but she had as much a doe to live as coulde be, and there wanted little of her sinking, and all those in her: for mine own part, I confesse, I was very doubtfull which way to take, eyther to goe over in the pestred Galley, there beeing but sixe foote water over the sands, for two leagues together, and that also in the channell, & she drew five: or to adventure in so great a billow, and in so doubtfull weather, to crosse the seas in my barge. The longer we tarried the worse it was, and therefore I took Captaine *Gifford,* Captaine *Calfeild,* & my cosen *Greenevile,* into my barge, and after it cleared uppe, about midnight wee put our selves to Gods keeping, and thrust out into the sea, leaving the Galley at ancor, who

[90]

durst not adventure but by day light. And so beeing all very sober, and melancholy, one faintly chearing another to shew courage, it pleased God that the next day about nyne of the clocke, we descryed the Iland of *Trinedado,* and stearing for the nearest part of it, wee kept the shore til we came to *Curiapan,* where we found our ships at ancor, then which, there was never to us a more joyfull sight.

Now that it hath pleased God to send us safe to our ships, it is time to leave *Guiana* to the Sunne, whom they worship, and steare away towardes the north: I will therefore in a fewe wordes finish the discovery thereof. Of the severall nations which we found upon this discovery I will once againe make repetition, and how they are affected. At our first entrance into *Amana,* which is one of the outlets of *Orenoque,* we left on the right hand of us in the bottome of the bay, lying directly against *Trinedado,* a nation of inhumaine *Canibals,* which inhabite the rivers of *Guanipa* and *Berbeese;*[111] in the same bay there is also a third river which is called *Areo,* which riseth on *Paria* side towards *Cumana,* and that river is inhabited with the *Wikiri,* whose chiefe towne upon the said river is *Sayma;* In this bay there are no more rivers, but these three before rehearsed, and the fower braunches of *Amana,* all which in the winter thrust so great abundance of water into the sea, as the same is taken up fresh, two or three leagues from the land. In the passages towardes *Guiana,* (that is, in all those landes which the eight branches of *Orenoque* fashione into Ilandes,) there are but one sort of people called *Tivitivas,* but of two castes as they tearme them, the one called *Ciawani,*

[91]

the other *Waraweeti,* and those warre one with the other.

On the hithermost part of *Orenoque,* as at *Toparimaca,* and *Winicapora,* those are of a nation Called *Nepoios,* and are of the followers of *Carapana,* Lorde of *Emeria.* Betweene *Winicapora* and the port of *Morequito* which standeth in *Aromaia,* and all those in the valley of *Amariocapana* are called *Orenoqueponi,* and did obey *Morequito,* and are nowe followers of *Topiawari.* Upon the river of *Caroli,* are the *Canuri,*[112] which are governed by a woman (who is inheritrix of that province) who came farre off to see our nation, and asked mee divers questions of her Majesty, beeing much delighted with the discourse of her Majesties greatnes, and wondring at such reports as we truely made of her highnes many vertues. And upon the head of *Caroli,* and on the lake of *Cassipa,* are the three strong nations of the *Cassipagotos.* Right south into the land are the *Capurepani,* and *Emparepani,* and beyond those adjoyning to *Macureguarai,* (the first Citie of *Inga,*) are the *Iwarawakeri:* all these are professed enemies to the Spanyardes; and to the rich *Epuremei* also. To the west of *Caroli* are divers nations of *Canibals,* and of those *Ewaipanoma* without heades. Directly west are the *Amapaias* and *Anebas,* which are also marveilous rich in gold. The rest towardes *Peru* wee will omit. On the north of *Orenoque,* betweene it and the west Indies are the *Wikiri, Saymi,* and the rest before spoken of, all mortall enemies to

[111] Although it is usual to identify the *canibals* with the Karinya because they too were to become *caribes* in the eyes of the Spanish, the suggestion that this group lived at the mouth of the Guanipa and Berbice rivers indicates that they were probably *Kalinago* from the Antilles. The *Kalinago* were a male warrior and trading association of the Arawakan *Karipuna* ('*Cassipuna*'), known to have settled on the mainland as a result of Spanish military activities on the islands. Keymis (1596) also reported a group on the Malmanoury river, near Cayenne and it should be noted that both Ralegh and Keymis stress a ritual difference from other groups in the practice of anthropophagy - see Sued-Badillo 1978, Whitehead 1995b.

[112] This term is related to *Cuna Ataere* and *Conori,* titles given the 'Queen of the Amazons' (see Chapter 2 (iii)), but Ralegh's allusion here seems gratuitous, if not fictitious, since no other source indicates the lower Caroni as a province of the 'women-without-men'.

the Spanyardes. On the south side of the maine mouth of *Orenoque,* are the *Arwacas:* and beyond them the *Canibals.*

[92]

and to the south of them the *Amazones.*

To make mention of the several beasts, birds, fishes, fruites, flowers, gummes, sweete woodes, and of their severall religions and customes, would for the first require as many volumes as those of *Gesnerus,* and for the rest another bundle of *Decades.*[113] The religion of the *Epuremei* is the same which the *Ingas,* Emperors of *Peru* used, which may be red in *Cieca,* and other Spanish stories, howe they beleeve the immortalitie of the Soule, worship the Sunne, and bury with them alive their best beloved wives and treasure, as they likewise doe in *Pegu* in the east Indies, and other places. The *Orenoqueponi* bury not their wives with them, but their Jewels, hoping to injoy them againe. The *Arwacas* dry the bones of their Lordes, and their wives and friendes drinke them in powder. In the graves of the *Peruvians,* the Spanyards founde their greatest abundance of treasure: The like also is to be found among these people in every province. They have all many wives, and the Lordes five folde to the common sort: their wives never eate with their husbands, nor among the men, but serve their husbandes at meales,[114] and afterwardes feede by themselves. Those that are past their yonger yeares, make all their breade and drinke, and worke their cotten beddes, and doe all else of service and labour, for the men doe nothing but hunte, fish, play, and drinke, when they are out of the wars.[115]

I wil enter no further into discourse of their maners, lawes and customes: and because I have not my selfe seene the cities of *Inga,* I cannot avow on my credit what I have heard, although it be very likely, that the Emperour *Inga* hath built and erected as magnificent pallaces

[93]

in *Guiana,* as his auncestors did in *Peru,* which were for their riches and rarenes most marveilous and exceding al in *Europe,* and I thinke of the world, *China* excepted, which also the Spanyards (which I had) assured me to be of trueth, as also the nations of the borderers, who being but *Salvaios,*[116]

[113] These are references to Conrad Gesner's (1516-65) *Historia Animalium,* Pedro Mártir's (1530) *De Orbe Novo . . . decades . . .,* and in the following line to Cieza de Leon - see also fn. 23.

[114] Polygamy is still a marker of status and gender roles still enjoin this separation.

[115] A division of labour that attracted many laudatory comments from colonial observers over the subsequent centuries.

[116] The Lokono (*aruacas*) use the term *faletti* to similarly describe their Cariban neighbors, see discussion of the interpretation of the term *salvaios* chapter 1 (ii).

to those of the Inland, do cause much treasure to be buried with them, for I was enformed of one of the *Cassiqui* of the valley of *Amariocapana* which had buried with him a little before our arrivall, a chaire of Golde most curiously wrought, which was made eyther in *Macureguarai* adjoyning, or in *Manoa:* But if wee shoulde have grieved them in their religion at the first, before they had beene taught better, and have digged uppe their graves, wee had lost them all:[117] and therefore I helde my first resolution, that her majesty should eyther accept or refuse the enterprise, ere any thing shoulde be done that might in any sort hinder the same. And if *Peru* had so many heapes of Golde, whereof those *Ingas* were Princes, and that they delighted so much therein, no doubt but this which nowe liveth and raigneth in *Manoa,* hath the same humour, and I am assured hath more abundance of Golde, within his territorie, then all *Peru,* and the west Indies.

For the rest, which my selfe have seene I will promise these things that follow and knowe to be true. Those that are desirous to discover and to see many nations, may be satisfied within this river, which bringeth forth so many armes & branches leading to severall countries, & provinces, above 2000. miles east and west, and 800. miles south and north: and of these, the most eyther rich in Gold, or in other marchandizes.

[94]

The common soldier shal here fight for gold, and pay himselfe in steede of pence, with plates of halfe a foote brode, wheras he breaketh his bones in other warres for provant* and penury. Those commanders and Chieftaines, that shoote at honour, and abundance, shal find there more rich and bewtifull cities, more temples adorned with golden Images, more sepulchers filled with treasure, then either *Cortez* found in *Mexico,* or *Pazzarro* in *Peru:* and the shining glorie of this conquest will eclipse all those so farre extended beames of the Spanish nation. There is no countrey which yeeldeth more pleasure to the Inhabitants, either for these common delights of hunting, hawking, fishing, fowling, and the rest, then Guiana doth. It hath so many plaines, cleare rivers, abundance of Phesants, Partridges, Quailes, Rayles, Cranes, Herons, and all

[117] Robert Schomburgk, as with his brother Richard, utterly failed to appreciate the symmetry between their own 'scientific' research on native skeletons and this kind of desecration and theft. Indeed, in his own note to this passage Robert Schomburgk (1848: 110) writes, 'The resting places of the dead are held most sacred and it has cost us the greatest difficulty to procure the few skulls which we were able to collect during our journey. In order to hide our treasures of organic remains we have been obliged to secrete them among our wearing-apparel, and thus they have been unconsciously carried by Indians, whom , if the contents of their burden had been known to them, nothing in the world would have induced to place it upon their shoulders.'

other fowle: Deare of all sortes, Porkes, Hares, Lyons, Tygers, Leopards, and divers other sortes of beastes, eyther for chace, or foode. It hath a kinde of beast called *Cama,* or *Anta,* as bigge as an English beefe, and in greate plenty.[118]

To speake of the severall sortes of every kinde, I feare would be troublesome to the Reader, and therefore I will omitte them, and conclude that both for health, good ayre, pleasure, and riches, I am resolved it cannot bee equalled by any region eyther in the east or west. Moreover the countrey is so healthfull, as 100. persons and more, which lay (without shift most sluttishly, and were every day almost melted with heat in rowing & marching, and suddenly wet againe with great showers, and did eate of all sorts of corrupt fruits, & made meales of fresh fish without seasoning,

[95]

of *Tortugas,* of *Lagartos,* & of al sorts good and bad, without either order or measure, and besides lodged in the open ayre every night) we lost not any one, nor had one ill disposed to my knowledge, nor found anie *Callentura,* or other of those pestilent diseases which dwell in all hote regions, and so nere the Equinoctiall line.

Where there is store of gold, it is in effect nedeles to remember other commodities for trade: but it hath towards the south part of the river, great quantities of Brasill woode, & of divers berries, that die a most perfect crimson and Carnation: And for painting, al *France, Italy,* or the east Indies yeild none such: For the more the skyn is washed, the fayrer the cullour appeareth, and with which, even those brown and tawnie women spot themselves, and cullour their cheekes.[119] All places yeilde abundance of Cotten, of sylke, of *Balsamum,* and of those kindes most excellent, and never known in Europe: of all sortes of gummes, of *Indian* pepper: and what else the countries may afforde within the land wee knowe not, neither had we time to abide the triall, and search. The soile besides is so excellent and so full of rivers, as it will carrie suger, ginger, and all those other commodities, which the west Indies hath.

The navigation is short, for it may bee sayled with an ordinarie wind in six weekes, and in the like time backe againe, and by the way neither lee

[118] Ralegh refers to the tapir (*tapirus americanus*) here. The use of English terms to describe American fauna is often taken to indicate some perceptual or categorical deficiency, as in the description of landscape (see Introduction), but the representation of difference can begin only by analogy to the familiar.

[119] '*Roucou*', or '*annatto*' (*bixa orellana*) used by the Europeans for clothing and food dyes formed a key item of commerce between the Dutch and Karinya (*caribes*) in the Essequibo colony (see Whitehead 1988). Native uses were principally as a body-dye, conditioning and protecting the skin, but wearing it was also understood as a complex sign, with ritual or political significance.

shore, Enimies coast, rocks, nor sandes, all which in the voiages to the West indies, and all other places, wee are subject unto, as the channell of *Bahama*, comming from the West Indies, can not be passed in the Winter, and when it is at the best, it is a

[96]

perillous and a fearefull place: The rest of the Indies for calmes, and diseases very troublesome, and the *Bermudas* a hellish sea for thunder, lightning, and stormes.

This verie yeare there were seventeen sayle of Spanish shipps lost in the channell of *Bahama*, and the great *Phillip* like to have sunke at the *Bermudas* was put back to Saint *Juan de puerto rico*. And so it falleth out in that Navigation every yere for the most parte, which in this voyage are not to be feared: for the time of the yere to leave *England*, is best in July and the Summer in *Guiana* is in October, November, December, Januarie, February, and March, and then the shipps may depart thence in Aprill, and so returne againe into England in June, so as they shall never be subject to Winter weather, eyther comming, going, or staying there, which for my part, I take to be one of the greatest comforts and incouragments that can be thought on, having (as I have done) tasted in this voyage by the west Indies so many Calmes, so much heate, such outragious gustes, fowle weather, and contrarie windes.

To conclude, *Guiana* is a Countrey that hath yet her Maydenhead, never sackt, turned, nor wrought, the face of the earth hath not beene torne, nor the vertue and salt of the soyle spent by manurance, the graves have not beene opened for gold, the mines not broken with sledges, nor their Images puld down out of their temples. It hath never been entred by any armie of strength, and never conquered or possesed by any Christian Prince. It is besides so defensible, that if two fortes be builded in one of the Provinces which I

[97]

have seen, the flood setteth in so neere the banke, where the channell also lyeth, that no shippe can passe up, but within a Pikes length of the Artillerie, first of the one, and afterwardes of the other: Which two Fortes wilbe a sufficient Guard both to the *Empire* of *Inga*, and to an hundred other severall kingdomes, lying within the said River, even to the citie of *Quito in Peru*.[120]

[120] Spanish experience in so fortifying the entrance to Orinoco showed that complex engineering and careful positioning were necessary because of the unpredictability of the annual flooding of the river (see Whitehead 1988: 213).

There is therefore great difference betwene the easines of the conquest of *Guiana,* & the defence of it being conquered, and the West or East Indies: *Guiana* hath but one entraunce by the sea (if it have that) for any vessels of burden, so as whosoever shall first possesse it, it shall bee founde unaccessable for anie Enimie, except he come in Wherries, Barges, or *Canoas,* or els in flatte bottomed boats, and if he do offer to enter it in that manner, the woods are so thicke 200 miles together uppon the rivers of such entraunce, as a mouse cannot sitte in a boate unhit from the banke. By land it is more impossible to approch, for it hath the strongest situation of anie region under the Sunne, and is so environed with impassable mountaynes on everie side, as it is impossible to victuall anye companie in the passage, which hath beene well proved by the Spanish nation, who since the conquest of *Peru* have never left five yeres free from attempting this Empire, or discovering some way into it, and yet of 23 severall gentlemen, knights, and noble men, there was never anie that knewe which way to leade an armie by land, or to conduct shippes by sea, any thing neere the said countrie. *Oreliano,* of which the river

[98]

of *Amazones* taketh name was the first, and *Don Anthonio de Berreo* (whome we displanted) the last: and I doubt much, whether hee himselfe or any of his, yet knowe the best waie into the saide Empyre. It can therefore hardly be regained, if any strength bee formerly set downe, but in one or two places, and but two or three crumsters or galleys buylt, and furnished upon the river within: The west Indies hath many portes, watring places, and landings, and nearer then 300. miles to *Guiana,* no man can harbor a ship, except he know one onely place, which is not learned in hast, and which I will undertake there is not any one of my companies that knoweth, whosoever hearkened most after it.

Besides by keeping one good fort, or building one towne of strength, the whole Empyre is guarded, and whatsoever companies shalbe afterwardes planted within the land, although in twenty severall provinces, those shall bee able all to reunite themselves upon any occasion eyther by the way of one river, or bee able to march by land without eyther wood, bog, or mountaine: whereas in the west Indies there are fewe townes, or provinces that can succour or relieve one the other, eyther by land or sea: By lande the countries are eyther desart, mounteynous, or strong Enemies: By sea, if any man invade to the Eastward, those to the west cannot in many months turne against the brize and easterwind, besides the Spanyardes are therein so dispersed,[121] as

[121] The non-native population of Santo Tomé, the Spanish capital in Orinoco, did not exceed five hundred persons until the mid-eighteenth century (see Whitehead 1988: 27-8).

they are no where strong, but in *Nueva Hispania* onely: the sharpe mountaines, the thornes, & poisoned prickels, the sandy & deepe waies in the vallies, the smothering heate and ayre, and want

[99]

of water in other places, are their onely and best defence, which (because those nations that invade them are not victualled or provided to stay, neyther have any place to friende adjoyning) doe serve them in steede of good armes and great multitudes.

The west Indies were first offered her Majesties Grandfather by *Columbus* a straunger,[122] in whome there might be doubt of deceipt, and besides it was then thought incredible that there were such and so many lands & regions never written of before. This Empire is made knowen to her Majesty by her own vassal, & by him that oweth to her more duty then an ordinary subject, so that it shall ill sort with the many graces and benefites which I have receaved to abuse her highnes, either with fables or imaginations. The countrey is alreadie discovered, many nations won to her Majesties love & obedience, & those Spanyards which have latest and longest labored about the conquest, beaten out, discouraged and disgraced, which amonge these nations were thought invincible. Her majestie may in this enterprize employ all those souldiers and gentlemen that are yonger brethren, and all captaines and Cheiftaines that want employment, and the charge wilbe onely the first setting out in victualling and arming them: for after the first or second yere I doubt not but to see in London a Contratation house of more receipt for *Guiana,* then there is nowe in civil[123] for the West indies.

And I am resolved that if there were but a smal army a foote in *Guiana,* marching towards *Manoa* the chiefe Citie of Inga, he would yeeld her Majesty by composition*

[100]

so many hundred thousand pounds yearely, as should both defende all enemies abroad, and defray all expences at home, and that he woulde besides pay a garrison of 3000. or 4000. soldiers very royally to defend him against other nations: For he cannot but know, how his predecessors, yea how his owne great uncles *Guascar* and *Atibalipa* sonnes to *Cuanacapa* Emperor of *Peru,* were (while they contended for the Empyre) beaten out by the

[122] Henry VII was offered the services of Christopher Columbus through his brother Bartholomew, prior to his first voyage to the West Indies in the service of Isabella of Spain.

[123] That is, the *Casa de Contraccion*, or customs house, in Seville, Spain, which now houses the *Archivo General de Indias.*

Spanyardes, and that both of late yeares, and ever since the said conquest, the Spanyardes have sought the passages and entry of his countrey: and of their cruelties used to the borderers he cannot be ignorant. In which respects no doubt but he wil be brought to tribute with great gladnes, if not, hee hath neyther shotte nor Iron weapon in all his Empyre, and therefore may easely be conquered.

And I farther remember that *Berreo* confessed to me and others (which I protest before the Majesty of God to be true) that there was found among prophecies in *Peru* (at such time as the Empyre was reduced to the Spanish obedience) in their chiefest temples, amongst divers others which foreshewed the losse of the said Empyre, that from *Inglatierra* those *Ingas* shoulde be againe in time to come restored, and delivered from the servitude of the said Conquerors. And I hope, as wee with these fewe handes have displanted the first garrison, and driven them out of the said countrey, so her Majesty will give order for the rest, and eyther defend it, and hold it as tributary, or conquere and keepe it as Empresse of the same. For whatsoever Prince shall possesse it, shall bee greatest, and if the king of

[101]

Spayne enjoy it, he will become unresistable. Her Majesty heereby shall confirme and strengthen the opinions of al nations, as touching her great and princely actions. And where the south border of *Guiana* reacheth to the Dominion and Empire of the *Amazones,*
those women shall heereby heare the name of a
virgin, which is not onely able to defend her
owne territories and her neighbors, but
also to invade and conquere so
great Empyres and so
farre removed.

To speake more at this time, I feare would be but trou-
blesome: I trust in God, this being true, will suf-
fice, and that he which is king of al kings and
Lorde of Lords, will put it into her
hart which is Lady of Ladies to pos-
sesse it, if not, I wil judge those
men worthy to be kings ther-
of, that by her grace and
leave will undertake
it of them-
selves.

[102]

An Abstract taken out of certaine Spanyardes Letters concerning *Guiana* and the Countries lying *upon the great river of* Orenoque: *with* certaine reportes also touching *the same.*

An Advertisement to the Reader.

THOSE letters out of which the abstractes following are taken, were surprised at sea as they were passing for Spayne in the yeare 1594. by Captaine *George Popham:* who the next yeare, and the same that Sir *Walter Ralegh* discovered *Guiana,* as he was in a voyage for the west Indies, learned also the reportes annexed. All which, at his returne, beeing two monthes after Sir *Walter,* as also so long after the writing of the former discourse, hearing also of his discoverie: hee made knowne and delivered to some of her Majesties most honorable privie Councell and

[103]

others. The which seeing they confirme in some parte the substance, I meane, the riches of that Countrey: it hath beene thought fitte that they shoulde be thereunto adjoyned. Wherein the Reader is to be advertised, that although the Spanyards seeme to glorie much of their formall possession taken before *Morequito* then Lord of *Aromaya,* and others there aboutes, which thoroughly understoode them not at that time, whatsoever the Spanyardes otherwise pretende: Yet, according to the former discourse, and as also it is related by *Cayworaco,* the sonne of *Topiawary* nowe chiefe Lorde of the saide *Aromaya,* who was brought into England by Sir *Walter Raleghs,* and was present at the same possession and discoverie of the Spanyardes mentioned in these letters; it appeareth that after they were gone out of their Countrey, the Indians then having farther consideration of the matter, and more then conjecture of their intent, having knowne and hearde of their former cruelties uppon their borderers and others of the Indians elsewhere: At their next comming, there beeing tenne of them sent and imployed for a farther discoverie, they were provided to receive and intertayne them in an other manner of sorte then they had done before; that is to say, they slewe them and buried them in the Countrey, they so much sought. They gave them by that meanes a full and complete possession the which before they had but begunne.[124] And so they are minded to doe, to as many Spanyardes as come after. Other possession they have had none since. Neyther doe the Indians meane as

[104]

they protest, to give them any other. One other thing to bee remembred is that in these letters the Spanyardes seeme to call *Guiana* and other Countries neere it, bordering uppon the river of *Orenoque,* by the name of *Nuevo Dorado,* because of the greate plenty of Golde there, in most places to be founde. Alluding also to the name of *El Dorado* which was given by *Martines* to the greate Citie of *Manoa,* as is in the former treatise specified. This is all I thought good to advertise. As for some other matters, I leave them to the consideration and judgement of the indifferent reader.

W: R.

[124] See Plate V and commentary. The nature of Spanish legalistic possession and its ceremonial features are discussed in Chapter 1, n. 9.

[105]

Letters taken at Sea by Captaine George Popham. 1594.

Allonso *his Letter from the* Gran Canaria *to his brother being commaunder of S.* Lucas, *concerning* El Dorado.

THere have beene certain letters received heere of late, of a land newly discovered called *Nuevo Dorado*, frome the sonnes of certaine Inhabitants of this Citie, who were in the discoverie: they write of wonderful riches to be founde in the said *Dorado,* and that golde there is in great abundance, the course to fall with it is 50. leagues to the windward to the *Marguarita.*

Allonsos letter from thence to certaine Marchants of S. Lucas *concerning the* Dorado.

SIrs, we have no newes worth the writing, saving of a discovery lately made by the Spanyards in a newe land called *Nuevo Dorado,* and is two daies sailing to the windward of the *Marguarita,* there is golde in that abundance, as the like hath not beene heard of. We have it for certaine in letters written from thence by some that were in the discovery, unto their parents heere in the City. I purpose (God willing) to bestow ten or twelve daies in search of the said *Dorado,* as I passe in voyage towards *Carthagena,* hoping there to make some good sale of our commodities, I have sent you therewith part of the information of the saide discovery, that was sent to his Majesty.

Part of the Coppy that was sent to his Majesty of the discovery of Nuevo Dorado.

IN the river of *Pato* otherwise called *Orenoque,* in the principall part thereof called *Warismero,* the 23. of April 1593. *Domingo de vera* Master of the Campe and Generall for *Anth.*

[106]

de Berreo Governour and Captaine generall for our Lord the King, betwixt the rivers of *Pato* and *Papamene* alias *Orenoque,* and *Marannon,* and of the iland of *Trinidado,* in presence of me *Rodrigo de Caranca* register for the sea, commaunded all the soldiers to be drawne together and put in order of battaile, the Captaines and soldiers, and Master of the Campe standing in the middest of them, said unto them; Sirs, Soldiers, and Captaines, you understand long since that our Generall *Anth. de Berreo,* with the travell of 11 yeares, and expence of more then 100000. pesoes of Gold, discovered the royall provinces of *Guiana* and *Dorado:* Of the which he tooke possession to governe the same, but through want of his peoples health, and necessary munition, he issued out at the Iland of *Maguarita,* and from thence peopled the *Trinidado.* But now they had sent me to learne out and discover the waies most easy to enter, and to people the said provinces, and where the Campes and Armies may best enter the same. By reason whereof I intend so to doe in the name of his Majesty, and the said governour *Antho: de Berreo,* and in token thereof I require you *Fran. Carillo,* that you aide me to advance this crosse that lieth heere on the ground, which they set on end towards the east, and the said Master of the Campe, the Captains and soldiers kneeled down, and did due reverence unto the said crosse, and thereupon the Master of the Campe tooke a bole of water and dranke it of, and tooke more and threw abroad on the ground: he also drew out his sword and cut the grasse of the ground, and the boughs of the trees saying, I take this possession in the name of the king *Don Phillip* our master, and of his Governour *Antho: de Berreo:* and because some make question of this possession, to them I answere that in these our actions was present the *Casique* or principall *Don Antho:* otherwise called *Morequito,* whose land this was, who yeelded consent to the said possession, was glad thereof, and gave his obedience to our Lord the King, & in his name to the said governor *Antho: de Berreo.* And the said Master of the Campe kneeled downe being in his liberty, and all the

[107]

Captaines and soldiers saide that the possession was well taken, and that they would defend it with their lives, upon whosoever would say the contrary. And the said Master of the Campe having his sword drawne in his hand, said unto me, register that art heere present, give me an instrument or testimoniall to confirme me in this possession, which I have taken of this land, for the governor *Antho: de Berreo,* and if it be needfull I will take it anewe. And I require you all that are present to witnes the same, and do further declare that I will goe on, taking the possession of all these landes wheresoever I shall enter. Signed thus.

Domingo de vera *and underneath, Before me* Rodrigo de Caranca, *Register of the Army.*

AND in prosecution of the said possession, and discoverie of the way and provinces, the 27. of April of the said yeare, the Master of the Campe entred by little and little with all the Campe and men of warre, more then two leagues into the Inland, and came to a towne of a principall, and conferring with him did let him understand by meanes of *Antho: Bisante* the Interpretor that his Majesty & *Antho: de Berreo* had sent him to take the said possession. And the said fryer *Francis Carillo* by the Interpretor, delivered him certaine thinges of our holy Catholique faith, to all which he answered, that they understood him well and would become Christians, and that with a very good will they should advance the crosse, in what part or place of the towne it pleased them, for he was for the Governor *Antho: de Berreo,* who was his Master. Thereupon the said Master of the Campe tooke a great crosse, and set it on ende toward the east, and requested the whole Campe to witnesse it and *Domingo de vera* firmed it thus.

It is well and firmely done, and underneath, before me Rodrigo Caranca, *Register of the Army.*

[108]

THE first of May they prosecuted the said possession and discovery to the towne of *Carapana.* From thence the said Master of the Campe passed to the towne of *Toroco,* whose principall is called *Topiawary* beeing five leagues farther within the land then the first nation, & wel inhabited. And to this principal by meane of the interpretor they gave to understand that his Majesty and the said *Corrigidor* commaunded them to take the possession of that land, and that they should yeeld their obedience to his Majesty, and to his Corrigidor, and to the Master of the Campe in his name, and that in token thereof he would place a crosse in the middle of his towne. Wherunto the said *Cassique* answered they should advance it with a very good will, and that he remained, in the obedience of our Lorde the King, and of the said Governour *Antho: de Berreo* whose vassall he would be.

The fourth of May[125] we came to a province above five leagues thence, of all sides inhabited with much people, the principall of this people came and mette us in peaceable manner: and hee is called *Renato,* he brought us to a very large house where he entertained us wel, & gave us much Gold, and the interpretor asking him from whence that Gold was, he answered from a province not passing a daies journey of, where there are so many Indians as would shadow the sunne, and so much Gold as all yonder plaine will not containe it. In which Countrey (when they enter into the *Borachera)* they take of the said Gold in dust and anoynt themselves all over therewith to make the braver shewe, and to the end the Gold may cover them, they an-

[125] It is at this point that Ralegh's translation diverges in content from the Spanish version; see Chapter 1 (iv).

noynt their bodies with stamped herbes of a glewenous substance: and they have warre with those Indians. They promised us that if we would goe unto them they would ayde us, but they were such infinite number as no doubt they woulde kill us. And being asked how they gat that same Gold, they told us they went to a certaine downe or playne and pulled or digged up the grasse by the roote, which done, they tooke of the

[109]

earth, puting in great buckets which they caried to wash at the river, & that which came in powder they kept for their *Boracheras* and that which was in peeces, they wrought into Eagles.

The eight of May we went from thence, and marched about five leagues: at the foote of a hill we founde a principall called *Arataco,* with 3000 Indians, men & women all in peace and with much victual, as hens and venison in great abundance, and many sortes of wine. Hee intreated us to goe to his house and to rest that night in his towne being of 500. houses. The interpretor asked whence he had those hens, he said they were brought from a mountaine not passing a quarter of a league thence, where were many Indians, yea so many as grasse on the ground, and that these men had the points of their shoulders higher then the Crownes of their heades, and had so many hens as was wonderfull, and if we would have any we shoulde send them Jewes harpes, for they woulde give for every one two hens, we tooke an Indian and gave him 500. harpes, the hens were so many that he brought us, as were not to be numbred: Wee said we woulde goe thither, they told us they were now in their *Borrachera* and would kill us, we asked the Indian, that brought the hens if it were true, he said it was most true: We asked him how they made their *Borrachera,* he saide they had many Eagles of Gold hanging on their breasts, & pearls in their eares, and that they daunced being all covered with Gold. The Indian said unto us, if we would see them, we should give him some hatchets, and he would bring us of those Eagles. The Master of the Campe gave him one hatchet (he would give him no more because they should not understand we went to seeke Gold) he brought us an Eagle which wayed 27 pounds of good Gold. The Master of the Campe tooke it, and shewed to the soldiers, and then threwe it from him, making shew not to regard it. About midnight came an Indian and said unto him, give me a pickaxe and I will tell thee what the Indians with the high shoulders meane to doe, the Interpretor told the Master of the Campe who commaunded one to be given him, he

[110]

then told us those Indians were comming to kill us for our marchandize. Heereupon the Master of the Campe caused his company to be set in order, and beganne to march. The 11. day of May, we went about 7 leagues from thence to a province, where we found a great company of Indians apparrelled, they tould us that if we came to fight, they woulde fill up those plaines with Indians to fight with us, but if we came in peace, we should enter and be well entertained of them, because they had a great desire to see Christians, and there they told us of all the riches that was. I doe not heere set it downe, because there is no place for it, but it shall appeare by the information that goes to his Majesty, for if it should heere be set downe, fower leaves of paper would not containe it.

The letter of George Burien Britton, *from the saide* Canaries *unto his cosen a french man, dwelling in* S. Lucas, *concerning the* Dorado.

SIR, and my very good cosen, there came of late certaine letters from a new discovered countrey not farre from *Trinidado*, which they write, hath Gold in greate abundance, the newes seemeth to be very certaine, because it passeth for good amongst the best of this City. Part of the information of the discovery that went to his Majesty, goeth inclosed in *Alonsos* letters, it is a thing worth the seeing.

The report of Domingo Martines *of* Jamica, *concerning the* Dorado.

HE saith that in 93 being at *Carthagena* there was a general reporte of a late discovery called *Nuevo Dorado,* and that a little before his comming thither, there came a *Frigot* from the said *Dorado,* bringing in it the portrature of a Giant all of Golde, of weight 47 kintals, which the Indians there helde for their Idoll. But nowe admitting of Christianitie

[11 *sic*/111]

and obedience to the King of Spayne, sent their said Idoll unto him in token they were become Christians, an[d] helde him for their King. The company comming in the said *Frigott* reported Golde to be there in most abundance, Diamondes of inestimable value, with greate store of pearle.

The report of a french man called Boutillier *of* Sherbrouke, *concerning the* Trinidado *and the* Dorado.

HE saith that being at *Trinedado* in 91. he had of an Indian there a peece of Golde of a quarter of a pounde in exchaunge of knife, the said Indian tolde him he had it at the head of that river which commeth to *Paracoa* the *Trenidado,* but said within the river of *Orenoque,* it was in great abundance. Also in 93 being taken by the Spanyards, and brought prisoner into the

Iland of *Madera* (the place for his prison) there came in this meane time a barke of 40 tunnes from a newe discovery, with two millions of Gold, the company whereof reported Gold in that place to be in great abundance and called it the *Nuevo Dorado.* This french man passed from Spayne in the barke, and having a cabben neere a gentleman, one of the discoverers that came from that place in the said barke, had divers times conference with him, and amongst other thinges, of the great abundance of Golde in the said *Dorado* being as they said within the river of *Orenoque.*

Reports of Certaine Marchantes of Rio de Hacha, *concerning the Nuevo* Dorado.

THey said (advancing the kings great treasure in the *Indies)* that *Nuevo Reyno* yeelded very many Gold mines, & wonderful rich, but lately was discovered a certain province so rich in

[112]

Gold as the report thereof may seeme incredible, it is there in such abundance, and is called the *Nuevo Dorado: Anthonio de Berreo* made the said discovery.

The Report of a Spanyard, Captaine with Berreo in *the discoverie of* Nuevo Dorado.

THat the information sent to the K. was in every point truely said, that the river *Orenoque* hath seaven mouths, or outlets into the sea, called *Las Siete bocas de drago,* that the said river runneth farre into the land, in many places very broad, and that *Antho: de Berreo* lay at *Trinedado* making head to goe to conquere and people the said *Dorado.*

Glossary

accompanie	consort with
artificiall	cleverly made
bables	currents
boies	servants, persons of low status
booteles	pointless, unprofitable
boyed and bekonned	marked with a buoy
brute	report, news
budgets	leather bags or pouches
champaine	flat and open
cheape	with little trouble, likely
Civil	Seville
composition	arrangement
factors	merchants, shopkeepers
foot(e)man	runner, walker; infantry (pl.)
forsloe(w)	be slow about
fouling peeces	bird guns
galiota, gallego	galley, small sailing vessel with steering oars and/or lacking a keel
handfasted	seized and tied up
harquebush	arquebus, matchlock gun
Ho:	Honours
knew	had sex with
Lo.	Lordships
mare caspium	Caspian Sea
marishes, marish	marshes, marshy
offred	threatened
Opus laboris, . . .	laborious work but not clever or ingenious to do
pioners	sappers, miners
pipe	105 gallon measure = 4 barrels = 2 hogsheads
provant	basic subsistence, allowance of food for soldiers
senciblie	perceptibly, appreciably

shold	shoal, sand-bar
sithence	since
slent	gust, breeze
spoiled	laid waste
watched	blue, blueish

Select bibliography

Abbreviations used in citation of manuscript materials

AGI	Archivo General de Indias, Sevilla
AN	Archive Nationale, Paris
AR	Algemeen Rijksarchief, Den Haag
BL	British Library, London
Bodleian	Bodleian Library, Oxford

Anderson A. and D. Posey (1989) Management of a tropical scrub savanna by the Gorotire Kayapó of Brazil. In D. Posey and W. Balée (eds), *Resource Management in Amazonia: Indigenous and Folk Strategies,* pp. 159–73. Advances in Economic Botany 7. New York: New York Botanical Garden.

Arens, W. (1979) *The Man-Eating Myth: Anthropology and Anthropophagy.* New York: Oxford University Press.

Arvelo-Jimenez, N. and H. Biord (1994) The impact of conquest on contemporary indigenous peoples of the Guiana Shield: the system of Orinoco interdependence. In A. C. Roosevelt (ed.), *Amazonian Indians: From Prehistory to the Present,* pp. 55–78. Tucson: University of Arizona Press.

Asad, T. (ed.) (1973) *Anthropology & the Colonial Encounter.* Atlantic Highlands: Humanities Press.

Bancroft, E. (1769) *An Essay on the Natural History of Guiana in South America.* London: T. Becket and P. A. DeHondt.

Bennett, J. (1989) An Arawak–English dictionary. *Archaeology and Anthropology* 6 (1, 2).

Bourdieu, P. (1977) *Outline of a Theory of Practice.* Cambridge: Cambridge University Press.

Bray, W. (1972) Ancient American metal-smiths. *Proceedings of the Royal Anthropological Institute* 6: 25–43.

Brown, J. and E. Vibert (eds) (1996) *Reading Beyond Words: Contexts for Native History.* Ontario: Broadview Press.

Brown, M. and J. Fernandez (1991) *War of Shadows: The Struggle for Utopia in the Peruvian Amazon.* Berkeley: University of California Press.

Bry, Theodor de, (1599) *Historia Americae sive novi orbis . . .*, vol. VIII. Frankfurt: De Bry.

Buchan, John (1935) *Sir Walter Raleigh.* London: T. Nelson and Sons, Ltd.

Campbell, Mary B.(1988) *The Witness and the Other World: Exotic European Travel Writing, 400–1600.* Ithaca: Cornell University Press.

Carvajal, G. de (1934) *The Discovery of the Amazon.* J. T Medina (ed.), B. T. Lee (trans.). New York: New York Geographical Society.

Clastres, H. (1995) *The Land-Without-Evil: Tupí–Guaraní Prophetism.* Urbana and Chicago: University of Illinois Press.

Clendinnen, I. (1987) *Ambivalent Conquests: Maya and Spaniard in Yucatan, 1517–1570.* Cambridge: Cambridge University Press.

Clifford, J. (1988) Reply to Sangren. *Current Anthropology* 29 (3): 297.

Colleción (1884) *Colleción de documentos inéditos VI: America y Oceania.* Madrid.

Colson, A. (1956) Ritual blowing: 'Taling' – a causation and cure of illness among the Akawaio. Man 48: 48–55.

Combès, I. (1992) *La Tragédie cannibale chez les anciens Tupi–Guarani.* Paris: PUF.

Corti, Count (1931) *A History of Smoking.* London: Harrap.

Denevan, W. (1992) The pristine myth: the landscape of the Americas in 1492. *Annals of Association of American Geographers* 82 (3): 369–85.

Dirks, N. (ed.) (1992) *Colonialism and Culture.* Ann Arbor: Michigan University Press.

Douglas, D. (1969) *The Norman Achievement.* London: Eyre & Spottiswoode.

Dudley, R. (1899) A voyage of the honourable Gentleman M. Robert Duddeley, now Knight [. . .]. In G. F. Warner (ed.) . . . *The Voyage of Robert Dudley [. . .] to the West Indies, 1594–1595.* London: Hakluyt Society.

Edmundson, G. (1906) Early relations of the Manoas with the Dutch. *English Historical Review* 21: 229–53.

Fabian, J. (1995) Ethnographic misunderstanding and the perils of context. *American Anthropologist* 97 (1): 41–50.

Feeney, D. 1993 Towards an account of the ancient world's concept of fictive belief. In C. Gill and T. Wiseman (eds), *Lies and Fiction in the Ancient World*, pp. 230–44. Exeter: University of Exeter Press.

Ferguson, R. B. and N. L. Whitehead (eds) (1992) *War in the Tribal Zone: Expanding States and Indigenous Warfare.* Santa Fe: SAR Press/University of Washington Press.

Foucault, M. (1969) *L'Archéologie du savoir.* Paris: Éditions Gallimard.

Fox, J. W. (1987) *Maya Postclassic State Formation.* Cambridge: Cambridge University Press.

Friedman, J. B. (1981) *The Monstrous Races in Medieval Art and Thought.* Cambridge (Mass.): Harvard University Press.

Fuller, M. C. (1993) Ralegh's fugitive gold: reference and deferral in *The Discoverie of Guiana.* In S. Greenblatt (ed.), *New World Encounters,* pp. 218–40. Berkeley: University of California Press.

Galloway, P. (1992) The unexamined habitus: direct historic analogy and the archaeology of text. In J.-C. Claudin and C. Peebles, *Representations in Archaeology,* pp. 179–92. Bloomington: Indiana University Press.

Geertz, C. (1988) *Works and Lives: The Anthropologist as Author.* Stanford: Stanford University Press.

Gil, J. (1989) *Mitos y utopias del descubrimiento, 3. El Dorado.* Madrid: Alianza Editorial.

Goeje, C. H. de (1931) Oudheden uit Suriname: op zoek naar de Amazonen. *West-Indische Gids* 13: 449–82, 497–530.

—(1939) Nouvel examen des langues des Antilles. *Journal de la Société des Américanistes* 31:1–120.

van's Gravesande, S. (1911) *The Rise of British Guiana – Compiled from his Despatches.* C. A. Harris and J. A. J. Villiers (eds). London: Hakluyt Society.

Greenblatt, S. J. (1973) *Sir Walter Ralegh: The Renaissance Man and his Roles.* New Haven: Yale University Press.

—(1991) *Marvelous Possessions: The Wonder of the New World.* Oxford: Clarendon Press.

Greenwood, L. B. (1986) *Sherlock Holmes and the Case of the Raleigh Legacy.* New York: Athenaeum.

Guapindaia, V. (1993) *Fontes históricas e arqueológicas sobre os tapajó.* Master's Thesis, University of Recife.

Hakluyt, R. (1927–8) *The Principal Navigations, Voyages, Traffiques, and Discoveries of the English Nation.* 10 vols. London: J. M. Dent & Sons Ltd.

Harlow, V. T. (ed.) (1928) *The Discoverie of Guiana, by Sir Walter Ralegh.* London: Argonaut Press.

—(1932) *Ralegh's Last Voyage.* London: Argonaut Press.

Harcourt, R. (1613) *A Relation of a Voyage to Guiana.* London: John Beale.

Hemming, J. (1978) *The Search for El Dorado.* London: Joseph.

Herodotus (1942) *The Greek Historians: The Complete and Unabridged Historical Works of Herodotus.* G. Rawlinson (trans.), F. Godolphin (ed.). New York: Random House.

Hulme, P. and N. L. Whitehead (eds) (1992) *Wild Majesty: Encounters with Caribs from Columbus to the Present Day. An Anthology.* Oxford: Clarendon Press.

Humboldt, A. von (1907) *Personal Narrative of Travels to the Equinoctial Regions of America During the Years 1799–1804.* 3 vols. T. Ross (ed. and trans.). London: George Routledge & Sons Ltd.

Hymes, D. (ed.) (1969) *Reinventing Anthropology.* New York: Vintage Books.

Jones, H. G. (1987) *Raleigh and Quinn: The Explorer and his Boswell.* Chapel Hill: North Caroliniana Society, Inc. and the North Carolina Collection.

de Jonge, J. K. J. (ed.) (1862) *De opkomst van het Nederlandsch gezag in Oost-Indië.* 13 vols. Den Haag.

Kappler, C. (1980) *Monstres, démons et merveilles à la fin du Moyen Age.* Paris: Payot.

Keymis, L. (1596) *A Relation of the Second Voyage to Guiana.* London: Thomas Dawson.

Lacey, R. (1973) *Sir Walter Ralegh.* London: Weidenfeld & Nicolson.

Langebaek, C. H. (1987) *Mercados, poblamiento e integracíon etnica entre los muiscas, siglo XVI.* Bogotá: Banco de la Republica.

—(1990) Buscando sacerdotes y encontrado Chuques: de la organizacíon religiosa Muisca. *Revista Antropologica y Arqueologica* 7: 81–103.

Latham, A. M. C. (1951) *The Poems of Sir Walter Ralegh.* Cambridge (Mass.): Harvard University Press.

Lefranc, P. D. (1968) *Sir Walter Ralegh, ecrivain, l'oeuvre et les idées.* Paris: A. Colin.

Lemmo, A. (1970) *Etnografía y fuentes históricas.* Caracas: Escuela de Historia.

—(1986) *Notas acerca de la historiografia inglesa sobre Venezuela: siglos XVI, XVII, XVIII.* Caracas: Universidad Central de Venezuela.

Lévi-Strauss, C. (1968) *Structural Anthropology.* Harmondsworth: Penguin Books.

Lorimer, J. (1979) The English tobacco trade in Trinidad and Guiana, 1590–1617. In K. R. Andrews, N. P. Canny and P. E. H. Hair (eds), *The Westward Enterprise: English Activities in Ireland, the Atlantic, and America, 1480–1650*, pp. 124–50. Detroit: Wayne State University Press.

—(1982) The location of Ralegh's Guiana gold mine. *Terrae Incognitae* 14: 77–95.

—(1989) *English and Irish Settlement on the River Amazon, 1550–1646.* London: Hakluyt Society.

Markham, C. R. (ed.) (1861) *The Expedition of Pedro de Ursua and Lope de Aguirre in search of El Dorado and Omagua in 15560–1: Translated from*

Fray Pedro Simon's Sixth Historical Notice of the Conquest of Tierra Firme by William Bollaert. London: Hakluyt Society.

Mártir, P. de Anghiera (1555) *De Orbe Novo.* Alcalá de Henares: Miguel de Eguía.

Mason, P. (1990) *Deconstructing America: Representations of the Other.* London: Routledge.

Metraux, A. (1948) The Tupinambá. In J. H. Steward (ed.), *Handbook of South American Indians* 3: 687–712. Washington: Smithsonian Institution.

Mocquet, J. (1696) *Travels and Voyages [. . .] performed by Mr. John Mocquet. Book II, West Indies. Translated by Nathaniel Pullen, Gent.* London: William Newton.

Montrose, L. (1993) The work of gender in the discourse of discovery. In S. Greenblatt (ed.), *New World Encounters,* pp. 177–217. Berkeley: University of California Press.

Naipaul, V. S. (1969) *The Loss of El Dorado: A History.* London: André Deutsch.

—(1994) *A Way in the World.* New York: Alfred Knopf.

Nagy, A. S. (1982) Las rutas del comercio prehispanico de los metales. *Cuadernos Prehispanicos* 10: 5–132.

Needham, R. (1972) *Belief, Language and Experience.* Oxford: Basil Blackwell.

Nicholl, C. (1995) *The Creature in the Map: A Journey to Eldorado.* New York: Jonathan Cape.

Nye, R. (1982) *The Voyage of the Destiny.* London: Hamish Hamilton.

Obeyesekere, G. (1992) *The Apotheosis of Captain Cook: European Myth-making in the Pacific.* Princeton: Princeton University Press.

Ojer, P. (1966) *La formacion del oriente venezolano.* Biblioteca de Estudios Universitarios I. Caracas: Universidad Catolica Andres Bello.

Oramas, L. R. (1947) *En pos del Dorado.* Caracas: Garrido.

de Oviedo y Valdes, F. (1959) *Historia general y natural de las Indias.* Madrid: Biblioteca de los Autores Españoles.

Pagden, A. (1982) *The Fall of Natural Man: The American Indian and the Origins of Comparative Ethnology.* Cambridge: Cambridge University Press.

—(1993) *European Encounters with the New World.* New Haven: Yale University Press.

Pané, R. (1987) *Relación acerca de las antigüedades de los Indios.* Coyocoan: Siglo Veintiuno.

Parry, J. H. (1966) *The Spanish Seaborne Empire.* London: Hutchinson.

Penard, F. P. and A. P. Penard (1907) *De menschetende aanbidders der zonnes-lang.* Paramaribo.

Pratt, M. L. (1992) *Imperial Eyes: Travel Writing and Transculturation.* London: Routledge.

Price, R. (1990) *Alabi's World.* Baltimore: Johns Hopkins University Press.

Purchas, S. (1905–7) *Hakluytus Posthumus or Purchas His Pilgrimes.* 20 vols. Glasgow: James MacLehose & Sons.

Quinn, D. B. (1947) *Raleigh and the British Empire.* London: Macmillan.

Rabasa, J. (1994) *Inventing America: Spanish Historiography and the Formation of Eurocentrism.* Norman: University of Oklahoma Press.

Ramos, A. (1995) *Sanumá Memories.* Madison: University of Wisconsin Press.

Ramos-Perez, D. (1973) *El mito del dorado: su genesis y proceso.* Caracas: Academia Nacional de la Historia.

Relaciónes (1964) *Relaciónes geograficas de Venezuela.* Biblioteca de la Academia Nacional de la Historia, vol. 70. Caracas: Academia Nacional de la Historia.

Ricoeur, P. (1971) The model of the text: meaningful action considered as a text. *Social Research* 38 (3).

Rivet, P. (1923) L'Orefèverie precolombienne des Antilles, des Guyanes et du Venezuela. *Journal de la Société des Américanistes* 15: 182–213.

Rivière, P. G. (1995) *Absent-minded Imperialism: Britain and the Expansion of Empire in Nineteenth-century Brazil.* London and New York: I. B. Tauris.

Roosevelt, A. C. (1989) Resource management in the Amazon Basin before the European conquest. In D. Posey and W. Balée (eds), *Resource Management in Amazonia: Indigenous and Folk Strategies,* pp. 30–62. Advances in Economic Botany 7. New York: New York Botanical Garden.

—(1991) *Moundbuilders of the Amazon: Geophysical Archaeology on Marajo Island.* New York: Academic Press.

—(1994) Amazonian anthropology: strategy for a new synthesis. In A. C. Roosevelt (ed.), *Amazonian Indians: From Prehistory to the Present,* pp. 1–32. Tucson: University of Arizona Press.

—(1996) Paleoindian cave dwellers in the Amazon: the peopling of the Americas. *Science* 259: 1383–9.

Roosevelt, A. C., Imazio, M., Maranca, S. and Johnson, R. (1991) Eighth millennium pottery from a prehistoric shell midden in the Brazilian Amazon. *Science* 254: 1621–4.

Roth, W. E. (1915) *The Animism and Folklore of the Guiana Indians.* 13th Annual Report of the Bureau of American Ethnology. Washington: Smithsonian Institution.

—(1924) *An Introductory Study of the Arts, Crafts, and Customs of the Guiana Indians.* 38th Annual Report of the Bureau of American Ethnology. Washington: Smithsonian Institution.

—(1929) *Additional studies of the Arts, Crafts, and Customs of the Guiana Indians.* Bulletin of the Bureau of American Ethnology 91. Washington: Smithsonian Institution.

Rowse, A. L. (1966) Ralegh's voyage. In *The Discoverie of Guiana by Sir Walter Ralegh, 1596 and The Discoveries of the World by Antonio Galvão, 1601.* Cleveland: World Publishing Company.

Sahlins, M. (1985) *Islands of History.* Chicago: University of Chicago Press.

—(1995) *How Natives Think: About Captain Cook For Example.* Chicago: University of Chicago Press.

Schomburgk, R. (1848) Editor's Introduction. In *The Discoverie of the Large, Rich and Bewtiful Empyre of Guiana . . .* London: Hakluyt Society.

Schwartz, S. (ed.) (1994) *Implicit Understandings: Observing, Reporting and Reflecting on the Encounters between Europeans and Other Peoples in the Early Modern Era.* Cambridge: Cambridge University Press.

Seed, P. (1995) *Ceremonies of Possession in Europe's Conquest of the New World: 1492–1640.* Cambridge: Cambridge University Press.

Sider, G. (1987) When parrots learn to talk, and why they can't: domination, deception, and self-deception in Indian–White relations. *Comparative Studies in Society and History* 29 (1): 3–23.

Siegel, P. and K. Severin (1993) 'The first documented prehistoric gold–copper alloy artefact from the West Indies. *Journal of Archaeological Science* 20: 67–79.

Skelton, R. A. (1963) Ralegh as geographer. *The Virginia Magazine of History and Biography* 71: 131–49

Staehelin, F. (1913–19) *Die Mission der Brudergemeine in Suriname und Berbice im achtzehnten Jahrhundert.* Paramaribo-Hernhutt.

Stagl, J. (1995) *A History of Curiosity: The Theory of Travel 1550–1800.* Chur: Harwood Academic.

Steele, C. (1975) *English Interpreters of the Iberian New World from Purchas to Stevens (1603–1726).* Oxford: Dolphin.

Strabo (1917–33) *The Geography of Strabo: With an English Translation.* H. Jones (ed.). London: W. Heinemann.

Sued-Badillo, J. (1978) *Los Indios Caribes: realidad o fabula?.* Rio Pedras: Editorial Antillana.

—(1979) *La mujer indigena y su sociedad.* Rio Pedras: Editorial Antillana.

—(1995) The Island Caribs: new approaches to the question of ethnicity in the early colonial Caribbean. In N. L. Whitehead (ed.), *Wolves from the Sea: Readings in the Archaeology and Anthropology of the Island Carib,* pp.91–112. Leiden: KITLV Press.

Taussig, M. (1987) *Shamanism, Colonialism, and the Wild Man: A Study in Terror and Healing.* Chicago: Chicago University Press.

—(1993) *Mimesis and Alterity: A Particular History of the Senses.* New York: Routledge.

Thomas, N. (1991) *Entangled Objects: Exchange, Material Culture and Colonialism in the Pacific.* Cambridge (Mass): Harvard University Press.

Todorov, T. (1982) *La Conquête de l'Amérique: la question de l'autre.* Paris: Editions de Seuil.

Vega, B. (1980) Metals and the aborigines of Hispaniola. *Proceedings of the Eighth International Congress for the Study of the Pre-Columbian Cultures of the Lesser Antilles,* pp. 488–97. Tucson: Arizona State University.

Vidal, S. (1993) *Reconstruccion de los procesos de etnogenesis y de reproduccion social entre los Bare de Rio Negro (Siglos XVI–XVIII).* Ph.D. thesis. Caracas: IVIC.

Viveiros de Castro, E. (1992) *From the Enemy's Point of View: Humanity and Divinity in an Amazonian Society.* Chicago: University of Chicago Press.

Warner, George F. (ed.) (1899) *The Voyage of Robert Dudley [. . .] to the West Indies, 1594–1595.* London: Hakluyt Society.

Whitehead, N. L. (1988) *Lords of the Tiger-Spirit: A History of the Caribs in Colonial Venezuela and Guyana, 1498–1820.* Dordrecht and Providence: Foris Publications.

—(1989) *The Ancient Amerindian Polities of the Lower Orinoco, Amazon and Guayana Coast.* Paper prepared for the Wenner-Gren International Symposium 109.

—(1990a) The Mazaruni pectoral: a golden artefact discovered in Guyana and the historical sources concerning native metallurgy in the Caribbean, Orinoco and Amazonia. *Archaeology and Anthropology* 7: 19–38.

—(1990b) Carib ethnic soldiering in Venezuela, the Guianas and Antilles: 1492–1820. *Ethnohistory* 37 (4):357–85.

—(1992) Tribes make states and states make tribes: warfare and the creation of colonial tribe and state in northeastern South America. In R. B. Ferguson and N. L. Whitehead (eds), *War in the Tribal Zone Expanding States and Indigenous Warfare* pp. 127–50. Santa Fe: SAR Press/Seattle: University of Washington Press.

—(1993) Ethnic transformation and historical discontinuity in native Amazonia and Guayana, 1500–1900. *L'Homme* 33: 289–309.

—(1994) The ancient Amerindian polities of the Amazon, the Orinoco and the Atlantic coast: a preliminary analysis of their passage from antiquity to extinction. In A. C. Roosevelt (ed.), *Amazonian Indians: From Prehistory to the Present,* pp. 20–35. Tucson: University of Arizona Press.

—(1995a) The Island Carib as anthropological icon. In N. L. Whitehead (ed.), *Wolves from the Sea: Readings in the Archaeology and Anthropology of the Island Carib,* pp. 9–22. Leiden: KITLV Press.

—(1995b) Ethnic plurality and cultural continuity in the native Caribbean: remarks and uncertainties as to data and theory. In N. L. Whitehead (ed.), *Wolves from the Sea: Readings in the Archaeology and Anthropology of the Island Carib*, pp. 113–38. Leiden: KITLV Press.

—(1995c) The historical anthropology of text: the interpretation of Ralegh's *Discoverie*. *Current Anthropology* 36: 53–74.

—(1996a) Monstrosity and marvel: symbolic convergence and mimetic elaboration in trans-cultural representation. An anthropological reading of Ralegh's 'Discoverie'. *Studies in Travel Writing I(1): 72–95.*

—(1996b) Searching for paradise? Recent research in Amazonian archaeology. *Journal of Archaeological Research 4 (3): 241–64.*

—(1996c) Ethnogenesis and ethnocide in the settlement of Surinam. In J. Hill (ed.), *History, Power, Identity Ethnogenesis in the Americas,* pp. 20–35. Iowa City: University of Iowa Press.

—(1996d) The Patoma of Paramakatoi and the Yawong valley. *An Oral History. (*Register) Publication of the Walter Roth Museum. Georgetown: Harborough.

—(*1997*) *Native South American* cartography. In D. Woodward (ed.), *The History of Cartography*, Vol. III. Chicago: University of Chicago Press.

Wilbert, J. (1987) *Tobacco and Shamanism in South America.* New Haven: Yale University Press.

—(1993) *Mystic Endowment: Religious Ethnography of the Warao Indians.* Cambridge (Mass.): Harvard University Press.

Williams, D. (1981) Three sites of the Taruma phase in southeast and east Guyana. *Archaeology and Anthropology* 4 (1/2): 81–103.

—(1985) Petroglyphs in the prehistory of Northern Amazonia and the Antilles. *Advances in World Archaeology* 4: 335–87. New York: Academic Press.

Index

Where relevant, entries follow the orthography in the *Discoverie*; because that orthography varies entries are made as they appear on their *first* usage in the text. Modern versions of the toponyms and personal names occurring in the *Discoverie* are indicated in **boldface** if the equivalence is not obvious from Ralegh's text.

Native terms are given an English gloss in **boldface**. The names of ships appear in *italics.*

Page numbers in *italics* indicate an illustration.

The names of native leaders are indicated by †.